To Dr Margaret [illegible] [illegible]
from the autho[r] [illegible]
for reading the proofs.

SOVIET LABOUR AND INDUSTRY

Books by L. E. Hubbard

SOVIET MONEY AND FINANCE
SOVIET TRADE AND DISTRIBUTION
THE ECONOMICS OF SOVIET AGRICULTURE

SOVIET LABOUR
AND
INDUSTRY

BY

LEONARD E. HUBBARD

MACMILLAN AND CO., LIMITED
ST. MARTIN'S STREET, LONDON
1942

COPYRIGHT

AUTHOR'S PREFACE

THIS book was written before Nazi Germany attacked Soviet Russia. War is the great test of a nation's strength and power of survival ; in peace-time the Soviet régime seemed to suffer from not a few rather important defects and weaknesses that boded ill for Russia's ability to withstand the furious assaults of the greatest military power that an unscrupulous and despotic ruler has ever created to fulfil his designs.

It was believed by many foreign observers that a considerable minority of the Soviet citizens, particularly those not of Russian race, was discontented and at heart antagonistic to the Bolshevik régime. It was also widely held that the purges of 1936 to 1938 had deprived the military forces of vigorous and efficient leadership. The Finnish campaign, or rather the earlier phases, seemed to indicate a lack of expert organisation and fighting spirit, and did little to enhance the reputation of Soviet munitions and armaments. The latter stages of the campaign afforded a better indication of the real qualities of the Red Army, but did not sufficiently counteract the poor impressions created by the set-backs suffered in the initial stages. Moreover, the Russians as the wanton aggressors of a small and gallant people earned a general opprobrium, and public opinion in Britain was only too ready to believe in the legend of Russian inefficiency and muddle.

When they became the victims of Nazi aggression the Russians became our allies and, though their cause was also ours, many people expected their early collapse, basing their opinion on what they had heard and read of Russia under the Soviets. However, after nearly three months of what is the greatest battle waged by the greatest armed forces of all time, the Soviet forces are not only not defeated but are fighting back with undiminished vigour and spirit. They have proved themselves the equal of the Germans in tenacity and courage, their technical equipment is not inferior either in quality or design, and their commanders have certainly not proved incompetent. What is perhaps most worthy of note is the fact that the army transport and supply organisation is working smoothly and efficiently, for it was in this that a breakdown was most to be expected; though, since the Red Army has been on the defensive all the time, the Higher Command has not had an opportunity to show what it could do were the initiative to pass to the Russians.

The Germans confidently expected an early breakdown in the morale of the Russian people. Even Germans, through long residence thoroughly acquainted with the country and the people, had failed to understand the Russian mentality and were convinced that the mass of the people would be indifferent to the fate of Bolshevism. In fact the notion was fairly widely held in Germany that large sections of the Russian people, and particularly the collectivised peasants, would not be averse to " liberation ". But instead of bringing to the surface any anti-Bolshevik movement, if such existed underground before, the war seems to have united the people, not only of Russia proper but of the non-Slav regions, in a common determination to defend their land. On the other hand, the Russians have not yet been thoroughly tested. The war has not yet been brought home to the masses behind the fighting line. Air raids on Moscow have done negligible damage compared with that inflicted on London and other English towns, and there is no shortage of food or other essentials. In fact, life proceeds almost normally. Only global casualty figures are published and these mean nothing to the ordinary man.

It was perhaps excusable to imagine that the stress of war would bring to light latent antagonisms among the races inhabiting Soviet Russia, for certain nationalist and separatist tendencies undoubtedly did exist among the Caucasian and Central Asian peoples and even in the Ukraine, which even now perhaps are not completely allayed. Though there is a danger of over-stressing minority movements, which were mainly manifested among a small number of the intellectual class and scarcely touched the masses. The war has, however, united the younger Soviet generation because it presents them with a tangible and external enemy whom they can understand, instead of the vague and changing class-enemy always altering his appearance and colour. Also, another bond that creates a common feeling is a sense of a common heritage in the land which belongs to the people and which they have collectively developed for just a generation.

After years of toil and abstention the people were at last beginning to enjoy the fruits of their labour. It is true that the standard of living was still low by our standards, but, compared with the first decade of the Soviet régime, life in the last two or three years was easier and fuller, and those who had toiled could take stock of what they had accomplished. The worst was over and it was possible to look forward with some confidence to a steady improvement and a future of reasonable prosperity. The war now thrust on Russia must postpone for years the better life that was just dawning, and this, no less than the sense of outrage at the hands of a treacherous enemy, has aroused a bitter feeling of hate and loathing against Nazi Germany.

Under the stimulus of the war, factories are working with greater precision and efficiency than ever before. Absenteeism and loafing are practically unheard of and, so far as can be gathered, the quality of the equipment and munitions turned out by Soviet industries shows no signs of the deterioration which is apt to result from strained efforts to increase output. But again, it must be remembered that the novelty of war has not had time to wear off. It cannot be denied that the workers are displaying an admirable spirit of determination and self-sacrifice. How far this is synthetic, attributable to the initial excitement and the propaganda which is issuing in an enormous flood from the Kremlin, or is intrinsically strong enough to withstand a long strain and heavy shocks, remains to be seen.

That the war, whichever way it goes, will have a permanent effect on the present régime goes without saying. But it is not too much to hope that the sense of unity it has created between Soviet Russia and her democratic allies will result in breaking down the isolation in which the Russian people have existed for the past twenty years and inaugurate a better understanding and replace suspicion with a genuine effort towards social and economic collaboration.

L. E. H.

Moscow,
6th September 1941.

CONTENTS

INTRODUCTION

Contents

CHAPTER XI

CHAPTER XII

CHAPTER XIII

Contents

CHAPTER XIV

CHAPTER XV

abolished — Planning is not in every respect a good Substitute
for Economic Competition — And has its own particular Problems — The Soviet Financial System — Planned Prices are
apt to stifle Initiative — Supply and Demand determine Retail
Prices — Soviet Currency; a true Money or merely a Caricature?
— A Medium of Exchange or a Unit of Account — The Bolshevik Version of Soviet Currency — Soviet View of Gold — The
Difference between Wages and *Kolhozniki's* Earnings — Two
Sorts of Money — The Lessons of Soviet Planned Economy.

CHAPTER XVI

Equality of the Sexes — Women performing hard Manual
Labour — The Emancipation of Women — Why Women enter
Industrial Employment — Economic Necessity the Chief Factor
— Careers of Upper-class Women — Wives and Husbands
pursue Independent Careers — Soviet Society Ladies — Women
as Sailors — Women in the Building Trade — Women Police —
Women in Coal Mines — Employment of Women in really heavy
Industrial Work will probably not be a Permanent Thing —
Women's prominent Part in the Professions — Russian Women
are often better " Business Men " than the Men — *Intourist*
guides and Interpreters — facility in Foreign Languages.

CHAPTER XVII

The traditional Conflict between Industrial and Agricultural
Interests — The Land Reforms of 1906–16 — Commercialisation
of Farming — Bolsheviks industrialise Agriculture — Market
Exchange of Food for Industrial Goods breaks down — Reasons
for Collectivisation — Why Agricultural Wages are on a lower
Level than Industrial Wages — Cheap Peasant Labour hinders
Mechanisation — Decline of Peasant Handicrafts — The
Peasants are becoming industrialised and proletarianised.

CHAPTER XVIII

The Jews' Part in the Revolution — Persecution of the Jews in
Tsarist Russia — Economic Activities of the Jews before the
Revolution — Many Jews among the Revolutionary Terrorists —
Jews suffered in the Red Terror equally with Christians — The
Effect of the Repudiation of Religion — Many Jews liquidated
in Stalin's Purge — Great Numbers of Jews in the Soviet
Bureaucracy — Anti-semitism Past and Present — The De-

Contents

INTRODUCTION

CAUSES AND EFFECTS

BROADLY speaking, two schools of thought on the genesis of Soviet Communism may be detected ; one holds that the Bolshevik régime was established by a body of gangsters, who achieved power by deception and trickery and succeeded in imposing their dictatorship on an ignorant and credulous population ; the other would make out that the Soviet régime was the spontaneous creation of the masses goaded to revolution by the tyranny and injustice of the Russian autocracy. A very small amount of historical research will show that the revolution, or rather the form it took, was the result of two distinct reactions. The revolt of the workers and peasants was essentially an economic movement for the improvement of their standard of living and working conditions, and the conviction that by supporting the Bolsheviks they would bring the war to an end. The political malcontents were intellectuals, whose grievance against the form of government was more acute than against the actions of the Government. In 1917 the peasants and industrial proletariate were ready to follow any leaders who promised them better conditions of life. The Bolsheviks secured their support because they were well organised and were ready to promise anything that appealed to the masses, regardless of its practicability. The results of the revolution have been very different from what the peasants and workers originally expected, but it would be wrong to believe that the Russian people is held down by force and that disaffection is rampant. That is not saying that there may not be a good deal of disappointment among certain sections of the population who expected some sort of millennium.

It is a mere truism to say that the course of any national movement, however initiated, must ultimately be determined more by the national character than by any outside

1   B

influence. The form of the Bolshevik revolution owed much to Karl Marx, but the influence of Marx on its subsequent development is less than the twists given to the Marxian philosophy by the Russian temperament. The Russian character contains certain Asiatic ingredients which differentiate the Russians from Western Europeans and which caused the revolution to follow its own peculiar and distinctive course. Probably the Marxian theory suffered most from the Russian lack of political sense. It was not an empty justification for the old autocratic form of government, that the Russians were incapable of governing themselves. It will, of course, be objected that the Russians have always shown a genius for local self-government as exemplified by the *Zemstva*, the village *Mir* and the merchant guilds. But there it stopped. In wider national matters the Russians have never shown the necessary capacity for taking the broad view and subordinating local or class interests to the common good. The early *Dumas* in the last years of the Imperial régime were good examples of the inability to compose differences and reconcile conflicting opinions. The last two *Dumas* showed far more constructive capacity and less factious obstruction than their predecessors, but that was the result of the electoral law amendments which arbitrarily and unconstitutionally ensured a large majority of deputies representing the gentry and bourgeois classes, whose interests did not conflict and whose political ideas were based on similar conservative views. The Russian is prone to defend abstract principles with more vigour and obstinacy than his moral reputation or material belongings, and to maintain his opinions without taking much account of their practicability. This tendency was illustrated in the conflict between Stalin and the Old Guard Bolsheviks, whom he exterminated. For whatever the proximate cause of their trials and condemnations, the root of the trouble was in their inability to modify their principles and betray their communist faith, though events had shown that a number of academic communist theories were unrealisable.

Another significant side of the Russian character was

brought out during the great purge of four years ago. I
happened to be in Moscow when Yagoda, the G.P.U. chief,
was arrested ; and what impressed me was the detached
way in which the ordinary citizen regarded the fates of the
victims. I do not think that the people really believed
that these had committed the crimes attributed to them,
nor did the injustice of the proceedings move popular sentiment. For centuries people had been arrested, exiled or
executed for no reason except that they were inconvenient
to the ruling powers. Not even the cruelties of Ivan IV
nor the callousness of Peter I caused any concerted protest
much less anything in the nature of rebellion ; as a matter
of fact Peter's ecclesiastical reforms and his contempt for
Russian social traditions and national prejudices regarding
beards, dress and the position of women were much more
fruitful causes of discontent than, for example, his liquida-
tion of the *Streltsy*. Possibly it is an inheritance from the
Tartar Domination, when the Russian princelings found the
best way of looking after themselves was to betray their
neighbours. Moscow was able to swallow up her neighbouring principalities in the fifteenth century because the
Grand Duke Vasili I adopted a policy of submission to the
Khan of the Golden Horde, and Vasili II so successfully
followed this lead that Moscow became the general tax-
collector for the Tartars. When princes were not loyal to
their own race and religion it could not be expected that
lesser folk should be loyal to their own kin in more or less
parallel circumstances. The more so when loyalty was not
evoked against an alien suzerain, but against their own
native rulers. So in later times the Russian Government
could persecute a section of the population without risking
a sympathetic movement from the rest.

This lack of tradition and spirit of loyalty was the cause
during the great purge of innumerable instances of de-
nunciation, sometimes to pay off old scores, sometimes to
clear the way for promotion, perhaps most often simply to
curry favour with the Party bosses. Thousands of innocent persons were expelled from the Party and dismissed
from their posts on the unsupported allegations of their

denouncers. Eventually the scandal became so open that courts to revise sentences had to be set up and many false accusers found themselves accused. The Bolsheviks certainly encourage informers, just as the Nazis do, but they cannot be held entirely responsible for this objectionable trait in the Russian character. In Tsarist times the police relied mainly on informers and *agents provocateurs* to discover revolutionary plots. In the World War there were many cases of Russians betraying their country to the enemy. Another manifestation of the same sort of moral obliquity was the corruption in public life, ranging from petty blackmail by the humble policeman to bribery of ministers disposing of contracts and concessions. The difference being that the policeman called regularly for his Easter and Christmas tribute, in return for which he refrained from troubling the householder about icicles overhanging the pavement and other small matters that the municipal by-laws required to be removed or attended to ; while the bribery of an important civil servant was a matter of tact and finesse. In the first place it was necessary to find out indirectly and unobtrusively what figure would overcome the important man's scruples. The second problem was to transfer the sum safely and yet so tactfully that the recipient could ignore the insult. A long time ago an English merchant in St. Petersburg desired a timber concession, for which the goodwill of the Minister of Commerce was priced at R.10,000. It was advisable to transfer the money direct, for to employ an intermediary almost certainly meant that a large percentage would be detached *en route* ; but to call on the Minister and leave a bundle of notes on his desk would be a breach of etiquette. Fortunately he was a kind-hearted man and hated the idea of embarrassing his benefactor ; so, having heard that the Englishman possessed some pictures of rather more than ordinary merit, he discovered a mutual appreciation of art and craved permission to view the collection. The rest was easy. The Minister arrived in a top-hat, which with the greatest consideration he projected behind his back instead of the more usual attitude of supplicants for alms. But the invitation

4

was none the less unmistakable. The corruption in public life in nineteenth-century Russia was entirely comparable to that in eighteenth-century England.

Quite a number of Tsarist ministers and high state officials were honest and incorruptible. But public opinion did not account it so much a righteousness as a mere personal idiosyncrasy; for the Russians were the most tolerant people in the world, being so conscious of their own frailties that they were always ready to condone the faults of others. Even the far more rigid discipline of the Communist Party has not changed these aspects of the national character. Bribery in its crudest form has, I think, been practically eradicated, mainly because few Soviet citizens have the means to pay. But the principle reappears in the system of *blat*, which covers all sorts of private transactions between heads of state enterprises for their mutual advantage. Private and unplanned traffic has to be transacted verbally and this accounts for quite an appreciable part of the railway congestion that always astonishes foreign tourists. But, in fact, it is not a purely Soviet phenomenon; in pre-revolutionary times personal interviews were preferred to written communications, even on the most straightforward routine matters, because letters usually remained unanswered, at least for a long time; and because Russians have a constitutional inability to give a straightforward and concise answer to a simple question. This peculiarity comes out even in the Soviet Government's foreign relations; having negotiated some agreement almost to a conclusion, the Bolsheviks at the last moment will interject a new condition that means starting all over again from the beginning.

One would scarcely ascribe tolerance to Bolsheviks. Nevertheless Government spokesmen and the newspapers are constantly complaining of local courts and factory managers who take a too " liberal ", *i.e.* lenient, view of breaches of factory discipline, illegal procedure by collective farm presidents and so on. After the introduction of the eight-hour day in June 1940, when it was also made a punishable offence for a workman to quit his job without special permission, it was found necessary to pass a law that heads of enterprises who neglected to hand offending workers to the courts were themselves to be charged with neglect of duty. Later it was decreed that the people's courts which tried such workmen were to sit without the usual lay assessors (ordinary citizens co-opted to sit with the professional magistrates), presumably because these were apt to be too indulgent.

In Soviet Russia crime comes under two heads, against the community and against the individual. Because the State owns practically the whole commerce and industry of the country, embezzlement is a crime against the State. Even the office clerk who makes a mistake in his books commits a crime against the State and will probably receive a harsher sentence than a man who feloniously robs a fellow citizen. Speculation, that is buying goods to resell at a profit, is a crime against the community because it is an exploitation of the needs of the people. Speculation thrives when controlled prices get out of alignment with supply and demand. The Government, understandably, always postpones increasing retail prices until the intensification of demand creates an indisputable shortage. This gives the speculator his chance, and whenever newspapers contain more than usually numerous reports of trials for speculation one may be sure that it marks a more than usually acute shortage of goods. For particularly flagrant cases speculators may be shot ; few escape with less than eight to ten years' imprisonment.

Imprisonment for mistakes, innocent of any suggestion of deliberate misdoing, in factory or office can befall anyone. Sometimes a person sent to prison for some error of judgment or careless mistake is offered another job before he comes out, quite likely at a higher salary than he was getting in his old job. The chief penalty to the culprit is not the few weeks in prison, but having to leave his home, that is if he worked in one of the chief cities. For nobody is allowed to live in Moscow, Leningrad, Kiev, etc., unless he holds some recognised post, and conviction automatically means dismissal. The clerical and technical staffs of enterprises in

Siberia and Central Asia are to a very large extent manned by people who have lost jobs in the metropolis. A system which prescribes imprisonment for unintentional errors and banishes the culprit to remote parts seems inconsistent with the proclaimed freedom and democracy of the U.S.S.R. Actually, like so many other manifestations of Bolshevism, it is a legacy from the former régime. True, under the Tsarist Government people were not imprisoned nor exiled for commercial mistakes ; but offences against the Government, even the suspicion of revolutionary inclinations, were punished by exile, the place and term depending on the seriousness of the offence. Exile did not preclude the exercise of a profession, consequently the doctors, lawyers, engineers and other representatives of the professions, particularly teachers and writers, in out-of-the-way spots in North Russia, Siberia, the Caucasus and Central Asia were as likely as not political exiles.

To appreciate the anti-religious policy of the Bolsheviks one must see it against the background of old Russia, when it appears in its true perspective. In the seventeenth century, primarily as a result of the policy and energy of the Patriarch Nikon, a close union between Church and State was forged. In fact Russia was ruled by a Diarchy of Tsar and Patriarch. Peter cancelled the Church's temporal power, and as autocratic monarch became the political head of the Church. In such circumstances it became a recognised principle that a loyal subject of the Tsar must belong to the Orthodox Church, reservations being made in favour of his Mohammedan subjects and the Lutheran inhabitants of the Baltic provinces. The Roman Catholics of Poland were tolerated ; but all schismatics from the Orthodox Church were persecuted, many being exiled to regions such as Karelia and the Kola peninsula. The Government was not satisfied with mere nominal conformity ; all persons in public employment had to communicate at least twice a year and produce a certificate that they had performed this duty. Persons in state employment belonging to alien Churches were expected to do the same. These were partly foreigners in posts such as teachers of languages in

7

universities and state high schools, or descendants of foreign parents, who in the second generation born in Russia automatically became Russian nationals, though they could remain members of their ancestral religious community provided that no ancestor had been a member of the Orthodox Church. For, like the Roman Church, the Russian Church insisted that the children of parents of whom one was Orthodox must be brought up in the Orthodox faith, even though through the father they had alien nationality. Curiously enough many descendants of English parentage in the second or third generation born in Russia and therefore Russian nationals, pathetically clung to membership of the Anglican community, though often enough they hardly spoke a word of English. At Easter and Christmas, particularly, they attended celebration at the English churches partly as a gesture of membership and partly for the more practical object of obtaining a certificate, lacking which they ran the risk of being officially classed as churchless, than which for official purposes there was scarcely a more damaging label. However, many chaplains, rather naturally, refused to issue certificates in these circumstances.

Communism should be regarded as a state religion and the immediate successor to the Orthodox Church. In its intolerance of schism and insistence that all servants of the State must be active participators in its rites it is only following the example of the Orthodox Church, and it requires no great stretch of imagination to see in the Party leaders the political commissars in the Army and Navy, the " activists " and " agitators " in civil life, a parallel with the former ecclesiastical hierarchy. The regimental political commissars, who no longer have the authority to interfere in the administration and military training of their units, exercise *mutatis mutandis* the same functions as the regimental chaplain. They are responsible for the religious instruction of the soldiers ; that is, they expound the gospel of Marx — Engels — Lenin — Stalin instead of the Holy Scriptures ; they are supposed to take an interest in, if not actually supervise, the secular education of the men, and advise them on matters of conduct and ethics and, of course,

8

constantly preach loyalty to the Socialist Fatherland personified in Comrade Stalin, in whom the offices of secular and religious head of the State are curiously combined. Stalin has avoided the mistake of arrogating the titular headship of the nation, which would be an anomaly in a communist State. The oath of loyalty taken by all members of the defence forces runs as follows : " I swear . . . until my last breath to dedicate myself to my nation, to my Soviet Fatherland and to the Worker and Peasant Government ". In this I find a significant exemplification of the difference between Bolshevism and Nazism, for the latter enjoins loyalty to the person of the Führer, to whom by name the German soldier consecrates himself. While Hitler has become apotheosised as the regenerator of Germany and the founder of a cult, if not a new religion, which owes nothing to any antecedent witness, Stalin poses as the repository of the true Marxian gospel and the sole ordained interpreter of communist doctrine, and as such to be infallible. He is, as it were, the Primate in a hierocracy : his authority is extrinsic, while that of Hitler is intrinsic.

It is difficult for a foreigner to appraise the position Stalin holds in the affections of the Russian peoples. In personal contact with Russians I cannot recall any spontaneous and obviously sincere expression of genuine veneration or devotion to Stalin. He does not appeal to the imagination of the Russians in the same way as Hitler to the imagination of a very large part of the German nation. Party and government spokesmen scarcely make a speech without dragging in some mention of Stalin's wisdom and genius, and in private interviews high officials are apt to do the same. But these tributes are perfunctory and seldom, if ever, carry conviction. Whether Russians are conscious of Stalin's alien origin I cannot say, but my impression is that the fact of his Georgian parentage and membership of a former subject minority does not irk the ordinary Russian. I do not think that the significance of this is sufficiently realised. It is almost as if the British people tolerated an Indian as Prime Minister or the Americans a President of Mexican origin. The Russians have never possessed a racial consciousness in the same way as the Anglo-Saxon and Teutonic races. In fact the Russian peasant a generation ago had but the vaguest conception of the Russian nation ; he would have described himself as *pravoslavny*, that is, a member of the Orthodox Church, never as *Russky*, a word he would have used almost exclusively to define his language. I imagine this lack of a sense of racial homogeneity was the product of the illimitable extent of the country and to the extraordinary number of different races inhabiting it ; for the minorities were not concentrated only on the outskirts of the Empire, such as the Caucasus and Central Asiatic provinces, but Tartars and all sorts of odd tribes such as Chuvashes and Mordvins, not to mention innumerable German settlements, were scattered about among the Slav inhabitants of European Russia. Thus it was natural for the genuine Russians to differentiate themselves from their non-Slav neighbours by their common religion rather than ethnological origin ; for by nationality in the political sense they were all Russians.

Russian nationalism is a quite recent development, brought about by a reaction from the internationalism of Lenin, which proved illusory and sterile. But the Bolsheviks' attempts to imbue the citizens of the U.S.S.R. with a sense of national pride seem to have met with scant success so far. That is to say, one seldom finds a Russian who is proud of being a Russian or believes in the superiority of Russians over other races. In former days the Russian habit of self-depreciation was almost nauseating until one realised that it was not hypocritical or sycophantic, but a genuine sense, often quite unwarranted, of inferiority. The Russian peasant, conscious of his ignorance, described himself as dark ; even the educated townsman unreservedly admired foreign technique and efficiency, for which no doubt there was a sound reason seeing how much Russian industry was indebted to foreign inventions and foreign technical managers. But what used to impress me even more than the Russian admiration of foreign technical superiority was the ordinary Russian's respect for the British character, or rather his apprehension of it. Russians being naturally impulsive, subject to sudden moods of enthusiasm alternating with pessimistic listlessness and conscious of a certain instability of character, admired, perhaps too indiscriminately, the British reputation for resolution, thoroughness and imperturbability. The young Russian of to-day still admires foreign industrial efficiency and technique, which he is constantly being exhorted to copy and eventually to surpass ; but he has lost any sense of intellectual and moral inferiority. In fact as a Communist he is taught to despise and ridicule what is presented to him as the capitalist mentality. But this is merely the old attitude of the Orthodox Church towards other religions translated to a wider secular field. The Orthodox Russian was convinced of the absolute superiority of his Church. In fact the peasants regarded non-Orthodox Christians as little better than benighted heathen. Servants in protestant houses would wonder and, if fresh from the village, might be a trifle shocked when the family did not observe the Orthodox fasts. But the Russian Church did not proselytise ; serene in its impregnable sanctity and antiquity, it had no urge to convert. It is, of course, true that conversions to Orthodoxy, pre-eminently of Jews, were encouraged by the State. But this belonged to the political side of religion. I think I am right in saying that the Russian Church carried on no missionary activities either among the non-Christian subjects of the Tsar or abroad.

Like the Orthodox Church, Communism despises all other forms of social structure, holding that to those who have seen the light the truth is self-illuminated and needs no reasoned evidence. In Tsarist times the censorship banned all foreign religious books equally with political and social works. In the same way the Bolsheviks protect Communism from heresy and criticism by a rigid censorship, which excludes almost every form of foreign literature except scientific and carefully selected examples of imaginative fiction. The Orthodox Church became formalised and inert because it shut itself up in a vacuum impervious to changes of thought and outside influences. Communism is still young and vigorous and pursues its missionary activities with

11

energy. But are there not signs that it too is in danger of becoming stereotyped and inert. Through constant vain repetitions of slogans and threadbare phrases the average Soviet citizen is becoming apathetic and unresponsive to propaganda. I recall a sort of variety entertainment I attended at Rostov-on-Don in 1937 ; a Caucasian dancer, some vocalists, a scene from a Chekhov play and a long and turgid recital of a poem about Soviet passports, which to-day are regarded with suspicion and distaste at every capitalist frontier but in due time will be respected and honoured. It was this last that received the minimum of applause, and that merely a few perfunctory claps. Communist propagandists to-day are intellectually far inferior to those who in the early days roused the masses with their oratory. Addresses at political meetings and broadcast propaganda talks are seldom inspiring and often reveal the speaker's profound ignorance of conditions abroad with which he compares the lot of the Soviet citizen. I have often, in my more recent visits to the U.S.S.R., been struck by the questions asked by ordinary Russians about conditions and life abroad, showing that they do not by any means accept as infallible the alleged facts served up to them by the Bolshevik propaganda machine. The Russian may in some ways be rather credulous, but he is usually intelligent enough to refuse to accept extravagant *ex parte* statements at their face value. My experience has been that the most fanatical Communists are apt to be the least intelligent and the least susceptible to reasoned argument, which, of course, is only what one would expect. Abroad, propaganda as dictated by the Comintern is to-day peculiarly maladroit and singularly ineffective. This is partly due to the expulsion of so many of the more intelligent and capable members of foreign communist societies, because their intellectual honesty forbade them slavishly following every twist and turn in Bolshevik policy ; and partly, I think, because those who direct foreign propaganda from Moscow are no longer men of wide knowledge and experience of foreign peoples and their problems and outlook, like the Old Bolsheviks who founded the Comintern, but inexperienced and parochially minded new model Communists. Their error is a belief that Communism on Russian lines is applicable everywhere and that it can and should be forced on people with totally different standards and viewpoints. More than one promising revolutionary movement has been wrecked when the Russian Bolsheviks intervened with support ; partly because they tried to force it into their own mould and refused to adopt their methods and principles to local conditions.

Whether the Bolshevik revolution is the herald of changes in the social and economic structure of other countries in the world, or whether Bolshevism (by which I mean that particular form of state socialism established in Russia) is fated to run its course in Russia alone, only time will reveal. When we regard the revolution, which to some contemporary observers seems to have opened a new era, in the perspective of Russian history we cannot help noticing that it has closely followed the lines of former eruptions in the life of the nation. For the course of the history of the Russian people has more than most been marked by recurring episodes of intense intellectual and emotional stress, usually accompanied by abnormal physical activity. Every such period has had permanent as well as transient effects on the social and political structure, but the fundamental character of the Russian people and their institutions has not been modified so much as externals.

The course of the revolution in the twentieth century has certain points in common with the evolutionary changes in the seventeenth century that transformed Russia from a secluded semi-Asiatic state into a European power. During the fifteenth and sixteenth centuries a greater Russia had gradually become united and unified around Moscow as the seat of government and the bulwark of the Orthodox East. The system and methods of government that had served the original Principality of Muscovy proved incompetent to administer a large and ever-growing Kingdom, and in the seventeenth century the breakdown of the existing order led to a belief that the nation's creative forces had become exhausted and that antiquity offered no guide for the future.

In fact the Russians lost faith in themselves and turned to the West for instruction and guidance in administrative, economic and military technique. This period culminated in the reign of Peter I, who completed rather than initiated the Westernisation of Russia. It was, needless to say, the ill-success of the Russian military organisation in conflict with Western neighbours that was mainly responsible for the sense of inferiority and frustration. Though cultural influences from the West had already gained a strong influence and the Russian Army had been remodelled largely on Western principles before the time of Peter, it was he who introduced the revolutionary tempo into Russian life in his endeavour industrially to " overtake and surpass " Europe. In actual fact, when the reign ended Russia was industrially among the leading countries of Europe, a position she had never held before and was not to hold again for two centuries.

The Japanese war of 1904–5 and the World War of 1914–1918 discovered Russia as a country in many ways as backward compared with Western Europe as before the accession of Peter I. The circumstances antecedent to his revolution bore many resemblances to those immediately preceding the Bolshevik revolution. The two revolutions had other points in common besides an intense industrial development based on foreign technique and assistance. Both demolished and trampled on tradition and customs, not only those that were outworn and obstacles to progress. Peter, it is true, considered himself a Christian autocrat, which did not prevent many of his subjects regarding him as anti-Christ. But he subdued the Church to the State, transformed the Holy Synod into a Government Department and made it serve his own ends. The Bolsheviks introduced their own religion, but Stalin's treatment of Communism is comparable for cynicism with Peter's treatment of the Church. Communism serves Stalin's ends, and if the analogy between the Comintern and the Holy Synod is not too forced, it may be pointed out that the former, like the latter under Peter, has been subdued to the interests of the State. Like Peter, Stalin has also had trouble with Old Believers, who, regarding his distortions of the pure communist faith in much the same way as the conservative Orthodox regarded Peter's Western importations, might paraphrase them in asking, "Has this culture no peril for the (Orthodox) communist faith and for right living and for the lasting stability of the (national) communal life ? "

Between the reorganising of the Russian Army in the second quarter of the seventeenth century and the industrial reorganisation just three hundred years later, there is a strange, though fortuitous, coincidence. The Thirty Years War resulted in Europe being full of wandering soldiers of fortune with swords to hire to any country having employment for them, and many found a field for their activities in Russia. In 1930 the world depression threw immense numbers of engineers and skilled industrial workers out of work, thousands of whom found temporary employment under the Soviet Government. In both cases the foreign experts cost Russia a great deal of money, while the presence of large numbers of foreigners with different cultural traditions and religious beliefs eventually aroused fears of the corruption of Christian Orthodoxy in the seventeenth century and of the communist Orthodoxy in the twentieth.

It would be idle to deny that the Bolshevik revolution has not had repercussions outside Russia : it has stimulated modern thought on social, economic and political problems and aroused controversy to an extent never before achieved by the domestic affairs of Russia. But that it can be compared with Christianity as an influence on the spiritual and ethical concepts of mankind, as certain of its most fervent admirers would pretend, is absurd. History, I think, will rank the Bolshevik revolution as an episode in the life of the Russian people, not as an epoch-making world phenomenon. The intense interest, apprehensive or hopeful, aroused throughout the civilised world in the early years has sensibly declined. Bolshevism has not proved inventive, it has adapted capitalist methods and instruments rather than discovered new ones, and in its relations to the outside world it has been more influenced by than it has itself influenced international events.

If, as I have suggested, the Bolshevik revolution has a good deal in common with the Petrine revolution, it is possible that the end and consequences of the latter may have some bearing on the future course of Bolshevism. This is a matter more appropriate to a concluding than an introductory chapter.

CHAPTER I

CONDITIONS UNDER THE TSARS

CAPITALIST industry in Russia dates back only to the first half of the seventeenth century, when increasing contact with the Poles, chiefly it is true of a hostile nature, caused the Muscovite rulers to realise that in the military field it was time to adopt Western methods. Foreign engineers were engaged to establish iron foundries for the manufacture of weapons and some landowners began the production of woollen cloth on factory lines. It was, however, Peter I who provided the first real impulse to industry. Mainly because of his need of armaments and munitions, his reign saw an industrial revolution in Russia comparable only with the industrial expansion in Soviet Russia. Russian society was divided into three main categories : the nobility, the serfs and the non-noble citizen. The nobility alone had the right of owning land and serfs ; the citizen category included a multiplicity of sections from the free labourer and artisan to the rich merchant. Peter's demands for arms, munitions and military supplies of all sorts could not be satisfied by the existing small and generally primitive enterprises run by noble landowners with the labour of their own serfs. Since private enterprise was quite inadequate, Peter created large state enterprises, to manage which he imported foreign engineers and experts ; the labour problem was solved by the employment of state serfs. However, state enterprise did not prove entirely satisfactory. Costs of production were high and the administration of state industry was a big strain on the Government, which disposed of very few officials capable of running any sort of business. Also, in the best Russian tradition, the whole civil service was riddled with graft. Peter therefore decided to transfer most of his state undertakings to private concessionaires, with the result that he was able to buy their products

17   C

for less than it had cost to manufacture them in state factories.

Among the concessionaires were many merchants, for when he wanted something done Peter was careless whom he employed so long as he was well served. Exclusive rights and privileges of the nobility were abrogated wholesale, including that of serf-owning. The new industrialists working on government contracts were permitted to hold serfs for factory labour, though not for cultivating agricultural estates, which remained a noble monopoly. In most cases when a concessionaire took over a government factory as a going concern he took over the serfs already attached to it. But a number of new factories were built by merchant industrialists with their own capital or with state grants, and these were permitted to hire or buy—the distinction is unimportant—serfs from noble serf-owners. Since Peter, with the object of putting all available labour to the best use for his own purposes, reduced to serfdom a large part of the previously free labour, it will be seen that practically all industrial workers at that time were serfs, or bonded labourers.

When the word factory is used in connection with industrial enterprises in Peter I's reign, it should not call up the picture of a large building full of machinery and a tall chimney belching smoke from a power-house. All processes were carried out by hand, and what machinery there was, such as weaving looms, was hand-operated. In such conditions the industrialists' prosperity depended on plenty of cheap labour, and since bonded labour was cheaper than free labour it was more economical. It was bad economy to starve the labourer and thereby reduce his physical efficiency, but it was extravagant to provide him with more than the bare necessities of life. Circumstances dictated the maintenance of bonded labour ; some factory owners paid money wages with which their workers had to buy their food and necessities, some issued rations in kind and some combined rations with a money wage. These conditions usually prevailed when the factory was situated in an urban area. Many factories, however, especially those belonging

18

to the landed nobility, lay near the villages which supplied
their labour. In such cases the serf-owner simply transferred a part of his serf labour from his fields to his factory.
Merchant industrialists, having bought the labour of a
village from the serf-owner, sometimes set part of the serfs
to grow food for the others employed in the factory. And
when the factory was engaged in working up local raw
material, such as flax, part of the labour might be set to
producing the raw materials for the rest to manufacture.
In country factories manufacturing was often a seasonal
activity, the peasants working in the fields during the
agricultural seasons and in the factory during the winter.
In the absence of valuable capital equipment this did not
involve any serious loss through capital lying idle.

A fairly important part of the industrial labour until
the emancipation of the serfs was supplied by serfs on
Obrok. These were serfs who, in consideration of the payment of annual sums to their owners, obtained a licence to
leave their village and work for wages under another employer, with whom their relations were similar to those of
free men. In districts where the population was relatively
dense and surplus to agricultural requirements, and where
local industry was not highly developed, landowners with
large numbers of serfs received the principal part of their
incomes from this source.

The system lacked every shadow of justification. Broadly
speaking, the principle originally underlying serfdom was,
that as the *Boyar* (feudal baron) held his land on condition
of rendering service to the Grand Duke for the time being
(the title Tsar was first adopted by Ivan IV), the peasants
owed an analogous feudal duty towards the holders of the
land they cultivated. Serfdom was first introduced in a
comparatively mild form to prevent the peasant population
deserting one *Boyar* for another or migrating beyond the
borders of feudal Russia. A *Boyar* was clearly of small use
to his overlord if he was destitute and unable to provide
his quota of arms and men, and unless he had a proper
complement of serfs to exploit his estate, the land alone
was useless. Originally the *Pomestie* (an estate held on

19

condition of service) was not hereditable property, but reverted to the State on the death of the *Pomestchik*. Gradually, however, the principle of hereditary ownership gained recognition and with it the hereditary ownership of the serfs ; correspondingly the conditions of hereditary bondedness was imposed on the serfs so that the descendants of serfs were born the serfs of the owner of their parents. Thus, from conditions that might be described as a sort of compulsory share-cropping the peasants, in course of about a couple of centuries, were reduced to something not much removed from slavery. In fact after the reign of Peter I, in which the wholesale employment of serf labour in industry was introduced, the serf-owners assumed, more or less arbitrarily, the right of selling the persons of their serfs apart from the land. At about the same time, the second half of the eighteenth century, that serfdom approximated most nearly to outright slavery, the nobility was released by Peter III from all service and personal obligations to the State.

Slave labour is more economic than free labour only in conditions of minimum capital equipment. When power-driven machinery began to find its way into Russian factories, the employment of serf labour began to decline in favour of the employment of free workers or serfs on *Obrok*. Still, conditions of employment were extremely bad and the standard of living of wage-earning industrial labour not a noteworthy improvement on that of the bonded labour. In such circumstances it was scarcely surprising that the industrial workers continued to show a good deal of the old serf mentality ; few were able to grasp the fact that, by improving their skill and qualifications, they could better themselves materially. In fact it is only since the Soviet industrial revolution that the notion of raising earning capacity by improving qualifications has become a guiding principle among Russian industrial workers. It has always been a debatable question whether the Russian character is the result of centuries of serfdom or whether serfdom was successfully imposed on the Russians because of certain qualities of the Russian character. But whether the typical

20

Russian character was the cause or effect of serfdom, it is certainly a fact that, up to the Bolshevik revolution, the Russian was less prone to great exertion in order to acquire material wealth than the Westerner, less ready to accept responsibility and less tolerant of the monotony of industrial labour. Naturally these characteristics gave rise abroad to the popular belief that Russians were congenitally lazy. Actually, while the Russian possesses a truly Oriental capacity for doing nothing, he can be subject to fits of extreme enthusiasm coupled with periods of acute activity, to which he is aroused more often than not by a subjective idea rather than by the prospect of material gain. These qualities are apt to prove a drawback in the industrial worker and are scarcely appropriate to those in command ; therefore the higher ranks in industrial administration, particularly in the technical branches, were largely filled by foreigners, who arrived in the country with a poor opinion of the Russian worker and seldom saw reason to revise this estimate. Other factors that militated against advancement were the want of educational facilities and the peculiar conditions that kept the factory worker still a peasant. For until quite the latter end of the nineteenth century the great majority of Russian industrial workers were still legally peasants with responsibilities towards their home village. This was the effect of that part of the Emancipation Law which made every peasant personally responsible for a share in the land indemnity payments due from his commune. The 'Mutual Guarantee' meant that every peasant had to obtain permission from his commune to accept employment elsewhere and had to remit part of his earnings to pay his communal dues, including the land indemnity, and for the maintenance of his dependants, if any. At the same time the absent peasant retained his right to a share of the communal land, which was usually farmed by the members of his family staying at home. As a rule he tried to return to the village to help with the harvest. In fact so great was the flow of industrial workers back to the land at harvest time, that many factories had to shut down for July and August and almost all found it impossible to maintain normal output during those months.

By 1861 the employment of serf labour, not of course of serfs on *Obrok*, in industrial factories had almost ceased and the Emancipation had little immediate effect on industry. In the more densely populated parts of the country, generally speaking the central and south-western provinces, the peasant population was surplus to the needs of agriculture ; in the northern provinces, though the population was much less dense than in the traditional grain lands of the central and " black earth " regions, farming was handicapped by the climate and the relative infertility of the soil and was practically limited to growing food for purely local consumption. For this reason industry had made much more progress in the north than in the centre and south, where it paid the landowners to employ labour to grow grain for the market. The distribution of land to the emancipated peasants resulted on the whole in their receiving about 15 per cent less than they had cultivated for their own needs as serfs. In the fertile central and southern grain zones the landowners, naturally, endeavoured to retain as much of their estates as possible, with the result that the proportion of land allotted to the peasant communes was less than the average for the whole country and the area available for each individual peasant homestead was ridiculously small. In such circumstances there would have been a strong flow of rural population towards urban industry had it not been deliberately checked by the Government, which for political reasons was anxious to prevent the rapid creation of a large urban proletariate. This end was served by the mutual guarantee and restrictions on the alienation of peasant land, which made it extremely difficult for the peasants to divest themselves of their land and migrate permanently to the towns. This, of course, did not prevent large numbers of peasants taking employment in industrial enterprises, but by keeping them legally attached to their villages it hindered and delayed the creation of a genuine urban industrial proletariate.

With the development of railway transport and a high protective customs wall, industry received a great impetus in the latter half of the nineteenth century. Large sums of foreign capital were invested in textile factories, engineering and metallurgical enterprises, coal mining, etc., and with the increasing complexity and cost of industrial machinery the employers became less tolerant of unskilled peasant labour with the annoying custom of returning to the villages in the summer months, leaving factories to carry on as best they could. In spite of the difficulties created by the government policy, industrial undertakings began to muster scores of skilled workers in their permanent employ, and these, by the close of the nineteenth century, already formed a very small but genuine industrial proletariate. In the last decade of the century the industrial workers showed unmistakable signs of class consciousness ; in 1896 and 1897 labour strikes occurred in St. Petersburg, being about the first manifestations of a genuine and organised labour movement. Labour discontent continued to smoulder threateningly until the disastrous war with Japan gave the working classes the opportunity to flare up in open revolt. As a result of the " first revolution " of 1904–5, which all but succeeded in overthrowing the existing régime, a series of political and economic reforms were granted by the Tsar. Among the most important, economically, were the abrogation of the mutual guarantee in 1905 and the land reforms initiated by P. A. Stolypin in 1906. The gist of these was to enable peasants to dispose of their land and sever all pre-existing ties with their villages. At the same time the conditions of the industrial workers were sensibly improved by new factory legislation.

The first legislation for protecting the interests of the workers was passed in the 1880's. About the middle of the decade discontent with bad living conditions came to a head and resulted in serious labour troubles, especially in the textile industry. Strikes as well as trade unions were illegal, consequently there was no organised movement to cease work in a whole industry. Nevertheless the workers in a number of large enterprises spontaneously came out on strike, and it was clear that even more serious troubles could be averted only by legislation to improve the lot of the workers. At the same time, opinion among the more liberal sections of the educated classes was beginning to realise that on humanitarian grounds an improvement in the condition of the workers was overdue. During the years 1885–7 various factory laws were adopted prohibiting night work of women and minors, and laying down rules for hiring labour and paying wages to prevent victimisation by employers. These measures were, however, far from adequate and the remuneration of industrial labour still afforded little more than a bare subsistence, while hours of work were long. In 1887 N. K. Bunge, the liberally inclined Minister of Finance to whose influence these early attempts to alleviate the lot of the workers was due, was dismissed by Alexander III. Reactionary policies gained the ascendant and for the next ten years nothing further was done for the workers. In 1897, after another series of labour troubles, a law was adopted fixing $11\frac{1}{2}$ hours as the maximum working day in factories. Perhaps greater advances were made in legislation governing the internal organisation of factories than for securing the workers reasonable working hours and fair wages. Factory hygiene and safety precautions as imposed by law were by no means backward, and government factory inspectors were employed to see that the regulations were observed and to supervise labour contracts. It must also be noted that probably a majority of the really big enterprises, particularly those owned and managed by foreigners, did much more for the welfare of their workers than they were compelled by law to do. In one or two of the very largest enterprises the workers were housed in model garden settlements complete with schools, recreation rooms, etc., on the most modern lines. Such employers were, perhaps naturally, even more subject to the vindictiveness of the professional revolutionaries than the bad employers, because the last thing these revolutionaries desired to see was a contented working class. Nevertheless in the rioting and destruction that accompanied the revolutionary troubles in 1904–5 the property of good employers suffered indiscriminately with that of bad employers, in just the same way as in the countryside insurgent peasants made no distinction between benevolent landowners and exploiters, but enthusiastically and impartially burned and looted all the country houses in their vicinity.

The reforms granted as a direct consequence of the first revolution made it legal for industrial workers to strike in furtherance of economic, but not political, aims and legalised trade unions. And in 1912 a scheme for social insurance of workers was introduced. Although the Government, reactionary to the last, tried to sabotage every concession wrung from it, the period between 1905 and the outbreak of the War was one of important advances in both the political and economic sphere. The Bolsheviks, understandably, invariably ignore or minimise the progress achieved by Imperial Russia between the grant of a constitution and the outbreak of the World War. The following affords some comparisons between economic developments in Tsarist Russia and in Soviet Russia during the First and Second Five-Year Plans :

	1905	1913	% Increase	% Increase 1928–34
Railways :				
Mileage in operation	36,808	43,378	18	8
Goods transported (in millions of tons) .	189·4	253·8	34	103
Industry :	1906			
Output of pig iron (in millions of tons) .	2·7	4·6	70	150
Output of coal .	21·7	36·3	67	135
Output of sugar (000 tons) . .	837 (1904–5 average)	1532 (1913–14 average)	83	− 8

In contradistinction to the Soviet policy of developing heavy industry at the expense of the light industry, prewar industrial development increased the production of consumers' goods to a greater degree than that of producers' goods. Thus between 1900 and 1912 the cotton textile industry about doubled its capacity, while the production of cotton material in 1934 was actually slightly less than in 1928 and only some 22 per cent more than in 1913.

Figures of the production of consumers' goods in Soviet Russia compared with Tsarist Russia, designed to show the greater supply per head of population and the consequent improvement in the standard of living, are misleading since they take no account of the output of the *kustarny* (or cottage handicraft) industry under the old régime. Factory production of many goods in pre-war Russia was actually less than the *kustarny* production.

While the condition of the industrial workers was materially improved during the last decade of the Imperial régime, wages remained inadequate, the average earnings being no more than R.25 a month, about £2 : 10s. at parity of exchange. The income of skilled factory operatives was higher, but unskilled labour in industries such as mining, employing large numbers of purely manual labourers, received considerably less. In such enterprises it paid better to employ a large quantity of cheap unskilled labour than to install expensive labour-saving machinery. According to our ideas a weekly income of about 12s. a week is sheer starvation. In pre-war Russia, however, the prices of necessities consumed by the working classes were low. For instance black bread, the main constituent of the workers' diet, cost the equivalent of less than one penny a pound ; potatoes, about a halfpenny a pound ; poor quality meat for soup, threepence or fourpence a pound. After feeding himself and buying the irreducible minimum of clothing, etc., the Russian worker had a few kopeks to spend on *makhorka* (a peculiarly villainous sort of tobacco) and *vodka* for festivals, but nothing for amusement, recreation or any form of cultural amenity. The Bolsheviks, of course, make out that the pre-revolutionary worker was unconscionably exploited by his employer. In point of fact the average rate of profit earned by industrial enterprise was not extraordinarily high considering the intensity of the demand for investment capital and the extremely high protection given to industry. On the other hand, costs were heavy and labour, if cheap, was inefficient. First of all, the industrialist had to import practically all his machinery at considerable expense ; then all large-scale factories employed a number of foreign technical experts at much higher salaries than they would receive at home ; the enormous area of the country meant high transport costs for fuel or raw material and in the distribution of finished goods. The Russian worker, nominally working ten or more hours a day, spent up to two hours over meals and standing easy to drink tea and smoke cigarettes : Church festivals, apart from Sundays, counting as holidays occurred on an average at least once a week, so that few factories worked more than some 250 days in the year. And when he was working the Russian was much less productive than the worker performing a similar task in the West. In textile mills, for example, the Russian weaver tended about half the number of looms tended by a Lancashire weaver. If the Russian factory operative's wages bore no comparison with wages paid for similar work in the West, there was no question of his being worth the same remuneration.

Prior to the beginning of the twentieth century the efforts of the different intellectual revolutionary movements (the *Narodniki*, who flourished in the 1870's and whose aim was to educate and improve the condition of the peasants, and the social revolutionaries and social democrats, who came on the scene somewhat later, devoting themselves primarily to the industrial workers) to arouse political consciousness among the peasants and workers had always been frustrated by the ignorance and inertia of the masses. It was a tribute to the more liberal attitude of the Government towards education in the early years of the twentieth century that by the outbreak of the World War the urban proletariate had become receptive to the ideas propagated by the revolutionary intellectuals and had become politically conscious. And it was mainly because the majority of industrial workers were only one degree removed from peasants and still retained connections with their former village homes, that revolutionary propaganda succeeded in spreading to the countryside.

At the outbreak of the War some four million industrial

workers formed a relatively small but genuine class-conscious proletariate even more revolutionarily inclined than the old-established proletariates in Western industrial countries. The social structure of Russia had developed in a different way from Western countries. It has been said by historians that there were no social classes in Russia, only different categories. This is another way of saying that everybody in Russia belonged to a fixed legal category, *noblesse*, peasant, townsman or clergy ; and his label being indelibly inscribed in his passport, nobody could pretend to be other than he was. The hard-and-fast lines dividing these categories, or castes, prevented the growth of a sense of common nationality and common interests. In truth it had always been the settled policy of the autocratic Tsars to keep the people in watertight compartments, discouraging any feeling of unity except in common allegiance to the throne. In accordance with this policy the Government not only refrained from giving education to the masses, but consciously hampered the efforts in this direction of the *Zemstva* and local governing authorities. When at the beginning of the twentieth century the Government was compelled by public opinion to adopt a more liberal policy it was too late. From the early days of Russian history the peasants, and latterly the working classes of peasant origin, had accepted their inferior status without question ; and when Western culture began to dominate the aristocracy in the eighteenth century it merely widened the gap between the *élite* and the masses. To the peasant or ordinary worker the upper classes were just as remote and incomprehensible as foreigners. Such circumstances were anything but calculated to arouse a feeling of mutual respect and understanding between employers of labour and their workers. Also the merchant industrialist class, that to a great extent controlled the country's industry and commerce in the latter half of the nineteenth century, was new and crude and without tradition. It consisted largely of Jews, Balts and other non-Russians, who were naturally devoid of any sense of *noblesse oblige* and responsibility towards their workers, and through exploiting them added fuel to the revolutionary fires.

28

Conditions under the Tsars

In 1917 the success of the Bolshevik revolution was largely due to the lack of any other leadership among the peasants and workers. Apart from the fact that the new trade-union movement was expressly excluded from engaging in political activities, the concession so unwillingly granted had been neutralised by the insinuation of police agents into administrative posts. Therefore when the Bolsheviks bid for the support of the workers by promises they never intended to keep, nor could have kept had they wished to, there was no reputable opposition to expose the fallacies. Possibly a few of the more intelligent and level-headed workers entertained doubts about the advertised millennium, but undoubtedly the mass of industrial workers believed that when they owned and controlled the means of production with which they laboured they would not only be freed from their servitude, but live a life of comparative ease and comfort.

Whether the Russian worker has benefited from the revolution is still a subject of keen and often acrimonious controversy. That it is disputable shows that incontrovertible proof, one way or the other, is lacking. And when those who believe that Bolshevism is justified in its results, base their faith on comparisons between present and pre-revolutionary conditions, they should be reminded that the true comparison should be between present conditions and conditions that would obtain to-day had the revolution not intervened. For if the conditions of the working classes improved during the last ten years of the Tsarist régime, as they certainly did, it is only fair to assume that this improvement would have continued had the Tsarist régime persisted.

CHAPTER II

THE EXPERIMENTAL PERIOD

ALMOST immediately after the revolution industrial enterprises were nationalised. On the 27th November 1917 the Central Executive Committee of the Party issued a decree establishing control by the workers of all the activities of industrial enterprises. This control was in practice to be exercised by councils of members elected by the workers and employees, whose duties included procuring raw material and stores, supplies of food and other necessities for the workers and the disposal of finished output. On the 11th November a decree had been issued instituting an eight-hour day for all industrial workers, prohibiting night work for women and all persons under sixteen and underground work in mines for women and youths under eighteen. On the 14th November a workers' insurance scheme was published. This provided (1) for the extension of insurance to all workers and employees in town and country; (2) for the extension of insurance to cover all loss of earning power from whatever cause and unemployment; (3) for the payment of the full contributions by the employing enterprises; (4) for the payment of full wages in cases of disablement; (5) for complete self-administration of all insurance organisations by the insured persons. Another decree of the 31st December amplified the scheme of sick insurance, the funds for which were formed by the payment by employers of a sum equal to 10 per cent of their total wages bill. The relief accorded to sick workers and to women for eight weeks before and eight weeks after confinement was the full amount of their normal earnings.

On the 31st January 1918 the Government abolished private employment bureaus and instituted labour mobilisation offices under the management of the Trade Unions. In May a labour inspectorate was organised with very wide powers, the inspectors being elected by workers' conferences or appointed by the Trade Unions. On the 14th June the right to two weeks' holiday was granted to all workers and up to one month for workers in dangerous trades.

On the 2nd July a law of collective contract, to fix rates of wages and conditions of labour, was passed. Prior to this wage scales as recommended by the Trade Unions had been confirmed by the People's Commissariat of Labour.

The above are the principal labour laws adopted by the Government during the first year of the revolution and afterwards codified in December 1918. In actual fact they represented little more than the pious intentions of the Bolsheviks ; none of them was put into effect nor were the living and working conditions of the workers thereby improved. This is no reflection on the sincerity of the new leaders' intentions to alleviate the lot of the workers : in the conditions then prevailing it was a sheer impossibility to reform the conditions of industrial labour. As a result of the war and the revolution, industrial production had fallen to about one-seventh of 1913, and the number of workers employed had fallen by half and the average real wage by rather more than half. To what extent the workers really assumed control of enterprises is hard to say ; workers' factory committees certainly did exercise a large measure of control over the domestic policy of their factories, but how far these committees genuinely represented the workers is another question. In any case the workers exercised sufficient control to show that their ideas of management were limited in practice to exploiting their new property for their own benefit exclusively. It may be imagined that if the workers had really exercised full control the state of industry would have been even more chaotic than it was.

In January 1918 the Trade Unions held their first congress under the new régime. Some conflict of opinion developed between the Bolshevik and Menshevik wings regarding the proper functions of Trade Unions in the Soviet State. The Mensheviks' conception of Trade Unions was organisations to represent and protect the workers' interests and politically neutral. The Bolsheviks stigmatised this point of view as bourgeois and eventually carried a resolution to the effect that the main task of the Trade Unions was in the field of economic organisation of production and labour. They thus formulated the principles that have ever since been the foundation of Soviet Trade Unions. The congress also recommended that all important industrial undertakings should be formed into trusts, thus bringing to a close the short period of direct workers' control, which had demonstrated to even the most idealistic of the Marxists that the workers were incapable of management. On the 28th June 1918 a decree of general nationalisation was issued : the original owners had, of course, been expropriated long before this. The decree meant that industrial enterprises now became the property of the State, and were no longer, even nominally, the property of the workers. The obvious corollary was that the workers became the employees of the State.

In 1918 the Bolsheviks became engaged in a life-and-death struggle with the anti-Bolshevik " white armies " aided by the intervention of the Allies. Owing to the lack of food and general disorganisation in the towns a large proportion of the workers who still retained their connection with the country returned to their villages ; also a very large number of industrial workers were recruited into the Red Army, with the result that the factories, on which alone the Bolsheviks relied for munitions and military supplies, were short of labour. It was the necessity of mobilising labour and material for their military needs that, more than anything else, caused the Government to introduce " War Communism ". At the end of 1918 skilled workers were conscripted, and in the following January the Government passed a law introducing compulsory labour for the whole population. The Third Red Army was converted into the First Labour Army and set to work on the railways and coal mines and in the forests of the Perm, Ekaterinburg and Ufa governments. Later the Second Army was despatched to the Donetz mining and industrial region and the Seventh Army was employed in the Petrograd region.

In pursuance of the communist theory that a communist state can exist without money, the Bolsheviks had already begun to discredit currency by printing unlimited quantities of notes. Though money never entirely disappeared (actually the quantity of paper roubles in circulation reached astronomical proportions) it became practically valueless, which was precisely what the Bolsheviks intended. Thus the remuneration of the workers in kind was not only in accordance with communist principles, but an absolute necessity. In addition to rations the workers received money wages, said to be equivalent to about 20 per cent of their total wages, to enable them to buy things not included in their rations. The shortage of foodstuffs and the complete lack of most other commodities reduced everyone to the same level. The theoretical principle that the worker should receive according to his needs irrespective of his productive capacity came as near realisation as at any period in the history of the Soviet State. The consequence was that the workers' individual productivity was reduced to the same low level, about 70 per cent below pre-war. In addition to lack of incentive to excel, factory machinery had become worn out, supplies of fuel and raw material were short and irregular, and the workers themselves were under-nourished ; a large proportion of the best workers had gone into the Army and the more intelligent and ambitious had become Party and government officials, managers and directors of state institutions and enterprises or anything else that raised them above the ordinary manual labouring class. Factory discipline deteriorated alarmingly. The capitalist discipline of the stick had been abolished, but the workers did not cherish the socialist attitude to labour as expounded by Lenin, who declared that "communist labour in the narrower and stricter sense of the word is unrewarded toil for the common good, toil not to discharge a fixed duty, nor to earn a claim to certain goods, nor according to previously fixed standards, but voluntary toil without a fixed task, given without calculation or condition of remuneration, toil performed through the habit of toiling for the common good and the consciousness that toil is necessary for the common good,— in other words, toil must be regarded as a vital necessity of the healthy organism ". As Lenin deplored, too many of

D

the workers failed to realise that labour in the new State was not simply the means of earning a selfish livelihood but an end in itself. Lenin himself confessed that this ideal was unrealisable, at least for a long time, because he unequivocably subscribed to the principle that the differences between the skill and capacity of different workers should be recognised by differences in remuneration. As, however, the State was unable to pay any worker a living wage, the factory hands spent part of their time in making things for private sale or barter, such as petrol lighters, out of any material they could appropriate, while others did odd jobs outside for private hire.

In spite of the decay of industry, which in 1920 gave employment to about half the number of hands as in 1913, unemployment practically ceased. In 1918 about 800,000 unemployed workers were registered at the labour exchanges ; by 1920 there were 167·8 vacancies for every 100 applicants although the number of employed was much less. This phenomenon was nothing new : unemployment always tended to rise in Russia when industry flourished, and sank when industry slumped. A rise in wages and increasing demand for industrial labour attracted the floating surplus agricultural labour to the towns in larger numbers than could be absorbed, while an industrial slump not only checked the influx from the country, but caused the unemployed and many of the partially employed to flow back to the land, where at least they could earn enough to eat. The fact that the period of War Communism was characterised by the disappearance of industrial unemployment seems to show that conditions in the towns were even worse than in the country, in spite of the wholesale requisitioning of the peasants' crops.

When industrial enterprises were transferred from the workers' control to the State, committees of management consisting of workers were created with the view of training workers for management in actual practice. However, it soon became evident that this system was anything but efficient ; the lack of individual responsibility and initiative resulted in urgent decisions being indefinitely postponed and inordinate waste of time in discussions which resulted in no concrete action. A controversy ensued among the Party leaders, Lenin, in his realistic manner, stating his conviction that efficient management could be achieved only by adopting the principle of single and responsible heads ; the more doctrinaire of his followers professed the tenet that to abandon the collegiate system of management was to surrender the principle of workers' control. Lenin expounded his convictions as follows :

(1) The domination of a class is determined by the extent of its ownership of the means of production. Having expropriated the expropriators, the working class becomes the ruling class.

(2) Every new class learns from its predecessor and preserves representatives of the Government of the old class. When feudalism gave place to capitalism the bourgeoisie was compelled to employ survivors of the feudal class in administrative positions. In order successfully to establish socialism the working class must adapt to its own use not only the technique and science of the capitalist class, but also employ bourgeois specialists.

(3) The working class must produce and train administrators and economic directors from its own class.

An important milestone in the history of Soviet labour policy was the ninth Party Congress held in March 1920. This congress declared in favour of the compulsory mobilisation of labour ; laid down the principle that the Trade Unions were state organisations and not independent ; and recommended that single responsible managers replace the committees of management in state enterprises. When possible a member of the Party was appointed manager, but since the supply of Communists with the necessary experience and qualifications was very small, the former managers and technical specialists often had to be reinstated in association with a Party colleague to prevent anti-Bolshevik activities and to see that communist principles were not violated.

War Communism ended in March 1921 when, at the tenth Party Congress, Lenin announced his " New Economic Policy ". Nowadays the Bolsheviks pretend that War Communism was introduced out of necessity to enable the Government to mobilise all its resources for prosecuting the civil war and was never intended to be permanent. As a matter of fact the proceedings at the contemporary Party conventions and All Union congresses of Soviets do not show that any of the basic principles expounded and adopted were meant to be merely a temporary expedient. There is no doubt, for instance, that the idea of abolishing money in favour of a direct distribution of goods to the workers and a direct exchange of manufactured commodities for the foodstuffs of the peasants was intended to be a permanent feature of the new order. The reason for abandoning War Communism was not, as now alleged, the defeat of the White Armies and the foreign interventions allowing the country to start to develop socialism in peace, but the utter failure of War Communism to find acceptance among the masses. The workers, as Lenin complained, had not grasped the benefits conferred on them by the revolution, but persisted in regarding Soviet enterprises in much the same light as they had regarded their former capitalist employers, and in addition expected all sorts of indulgences and privileges from their Bolshevik rulers. In other words they were no more disposed to work for nothing under the "Dictatorship of the Proletariate " than they had been under the autocracy of the Tsar. Lenin's decision to end War Communism boiled down to this ; that as the workers and peasants were too short-sighted and self-seeking to co-operate with their Bolshevik leaders in creating the communist order, but still hankered for the flesh-pots of the late capitalist order and quite unreasonably protested against the privations they were asked to bear for the sake of the revolution, the only thing to do was to restore the old order within certain limits. It also seems probable that in his academic days, when engaged in constructing Communism on paper, Lenin genuinely believed that the organisation and administration of production and distribution did not require special experience and training. His ideas of management were summed up in the following aphorism : " The book-keeping and the control necessary for it have been simplified by capitalism to the utmost, till they have become the extraordinarily simple operation of watching, recording and issuing receipts within the reach of everyone who can read and write and who knows the first four rules of arithmetic ". When faced with the realities of economic administration Lenin's lieutenants proved incompetent and he realised that there was a lot more in it than he had imagined ; and being wise enough to recognise his mistakes, he confessed that he had been too sanguine in attempting to introduce Communism overnight.

The main features of the New Economic Policy were : the restoration of money as the recognised legal medium of exchange, which naturally connoted the restoration of a market in place of barter ; permission to private enterprise to engage in industry and commerce within limits and to hire workers and employees ; the right of labour to take and leave employment without hindrance ; and for the peasants the right to sell their produce on the open market and pay their taxes to the State in money. Thus many forms of capitalist economy were reinstated, but without undermining the socialist principles already in force. Lenin explained the nature of the change as follows : " The New Economic Policy does not modify the essential principle of the Workers' State ; it does, however, substantially alter the methods and forms of socialist construction, in that it permits economic competition between the builders of socialism and those aspiring to restore capitalism on the foundation of a market for supplying the needs of the multitudinous peasantry ". In order to paralyse all attempts of private enterprise to compete dangerously with the State, banking, transport and foreign trade were made state monopolies, nor was private enterprise permitted to regain control of large-scale industrial enterprises.

The change imported material alterations in the status and functions of the Trade Unions. During War Communism membership of a Trade Union had been compulsory for every industrial worker, and the Unions themselves had exercised considerable influence in the administration of industry, but above all their relations to the workers were rather those of a monitor than an ally. They had, in fact, more disciplinary power over the workers than the enterprises which employed them. The New Economic Policy meant that a large part of the workers became the employees of private enterprise (in 1925–6 something like 20 per cent of all workers, or nearly two million persons, were working for private employers, including foreign concessionaires). The Trade Unions therefore had a large field for the exercise of their traditional functions of protecting their members from capitalist exploitation. At the same time their position in regard to the Government as the chief employer of labour became somewhat ambiguous. State enterprises were decentralised to a large degree and were managed on commercial lines by managers and managing boards enjoying considerable autonomy and initiative. The Trade Unions thus had a duty towards their members and did press for increased wages and improved conditions from state enterprises. Arbitration commissions were created and the right of workers to strike was formally recognised. At the same time the Trade Unions continued to collaborate with the Government in enforcing factory discipline, the introduction of piece-work, etc. In fact it was difficult to say whether the Trade Unions most served government interests or labour interests. They were, at least, no longer part of the government machine, because to allow them even a small share in formulating policy would have diluted the Government, which at the time could not afford to lose its character as a select body.

While private enterprise was permitted during the few years of the New Economic Policy, the workers in the larger private enterprises, those employing twenty or more, were somewhat better off as regards wages and conditions than workers in state enterprises. The Trade Unions saw to that. Labour inspectors with the active co-operation of the workers brought hundreds of private employers before the courts. Probably most of the charges were trumped-up or

38

trivial. For instance, wages had to be paid in the employer's time, and if for any reason at all a worker did not receive his pay till a minute or two after knocking-off time it would serve as the basis of a charge against the employer. State enterprises were, naturally, immune from such vexations. Nevertheless, the existence of private enterprise did something towards keeping state enterprise up to the mark, for theoretically the same wage rates and labour regulations applied to both, and the workers in state enterprises, seeing how their Trade Unions bullied private employers, naturally expected them to take measures against their own state employer when guilty of the same faults. The fact that private enterprise in spite of persecution and discrimination was able to compete successfully with state enterprise affords an idea of the general inefficiency of the latter. The Trade Unions as Party organisations were supposed to be schools of Communism, and one of the things they had to teach was that the worker's remuneration depended on his own output. The workers were bluntly informed that if wages were to increase they must be earned by increased output. The Trade Unions had to work out rates of wages and normal tasks in accordance with this principle.

Communist theory proclaimed the ideal of collective effort and collective remuneration, but the workers were not sufficiently converted to the communist way of life to sink their bourgeois preferences for individual careers. Therefore, while their leaders preached collectivism, in practice it was found necessary to use the stimulus of differential wages to get the best out of the workers. The twelfth Party congress in April 1923 recommended that wages be regulated in accordance with individual performance, with special attention to increasing wages in heavy industry and transport, and to removing the differences between the wages of workers with equal qualifications in different branches of industry.

In spite of all the resolutions and recommendations affirming the principle of wages increases depending on increased production, the plenary session of the Central Committee of the Party in August 1924 reported that during the period from October 1922 to January 1924 wages in fourteen of the principal branches of industry had increased relatively faster than the productivity of labour. In 1923 prices of agricultural produce fell and prices of industrial goods rose, resulting in what was called the " scissors " crisis. Bank credits to industry expanded largely, because manufacturing enterprises could not sell their products at a remunerative price and preferred holding large stocks to selling at a loss. The truth of the matter was that production costs, owing to unwarranted increases in wages and general inefficiency and waste, rendered the prices of goods too high for the peasants to afford. Eventually the Government ordered the banks to restrict credit and call in their loans to enterprises holding large stocks of goods. As a result large quantities of goods were thrown on the market ; prices fell and the banks were left with large amounts of frozen or doubtful assets.

In 1918 the principle had been adopted of placing industrial workers in a number of wage categories according to their skill and the nature of their work. At the beginning five main categories were fixed, the highest category receiving 210 per cent of the lowest wage. In January 1919 the number of categories was reduced to four with wages ranging in the proportion of 1 : 1·75. In the following year it was decided to increase the difference between the minimum and maximum rates. The number of categories was increased to eight and the difference between the lowest and highest rates to the ratio 1 : 2 ; in some industries twelve categories were created with a ratio of 1 : 2·8. With the coming of the New Economic Policy with payment of wages entirely in money and the restoration of commercial principles it was found necessary greatly to increase the difference between the wages of ordinary unskilled labour and skilled labour and to increase the number of categories to seventeen. The highest rate was eight times the lowest, but for some reason or other the differences between successive categories were not uniform. Thus for instance the third category received 25 per cent more than the second, the eighth 10·7 per cent more than the seventh, the tenth 20 per cent more than the ninth, the sixteenth 7·5 per cent more than the fifteenth.

By 1925 industrial wages were claimed to have reached pre-war level. It may have been true that the prices of the most essential necessities of life bore about the same relation to the average wage as in 1913, but that does not mean that the standard of living was equal to pre-war. The total agricultural and industrial output of the country was still considerably smaller than the immediate pre-war average and the population slightly larger, therefore average per head consumption must have been less than pre-war. The industrial workers were preferred to all other sections of the community and suffered no intolerable privations, but their conditions of life were certainly harder than in 1913. In their attempts to prove that the revolution had already benefited the workers, the Bolsheviks laid much emphasis on the social services rendered gratis, such as free education, medical attention, invalid pensions, etc., which were valued at a third of the money wage, the implication being that to arrive at the real remuneration of the worker his money wage should be increased by a third. But social services were not unknown in Imperial Russia. At the end of 1914 there were about 123,000 primary and secondary schools with about 8·4 million pupils, excluding commercial and technical schools, military schools and church schools. In 1924–5 the number of schools was 93,000 with 9·14 million pupils. In Tsarist Russia, too, quite important medical services were maintained by the *Zemstva*, mainly for the peasants, which also provided valuable assistance to agriculture in the form of instruction by travelling experts, loans to purchase seed and machinery, etc. Even if the free social services provided by the Soviet Government for the urban industrial population were somewhat more comprehensive than those provided by the late Tsarist Government the peasants were left much worse off because no substitutes were provided for the services rendered by the *Zemstva*.

In the autumn of 1922 a new code of labour laws was issued. This differed from the previous codes in being formulated to meet the requirements of a society in which labour, instead of being conscripted, was free to conclude collective contracts with employers ; and the new laws were

41

intended to be fulfilled instead of being mere pious declarations. The general provisions of the new laws were practically the same as before, such as the eight-hour day, two weeks' holiday on full pay, protection of women and young people in industry, and social insurance, the contributions to which were payable wholly by the employer. The insurance scheme embraced all wage and salary earners irrespective of position and earnings, which was just as well, since unemployment was most intense among the intellectual workers. From the beginning of 1922 unemployment increased very rapidly, due partly to the return of workers from the country and partly to the " scissors " crisis already mentioned. On the 1st January 1922 there were only 160,000 unemployed registered at the labour exchanges ; by the middle of 1924 this number had increased to 1,344,300, of whom 354,900 were skilled workers, 412,700 intellectual workers and 379,100 unskilled manual workers. In the course of 1924 and 1925 the organisation of labour exchanges was revived, employers having to engage workers exclusively through the exchanges.

The period of the New Economic Policy was divided into two phases, which merged into each other gradually in 1925–6 without any of the violent changes that marked the end of War Communism or the inauguration of the First Five-Year Plan. The first phase was a period of restoration in which the Bolsheviks were occupied in clearing up the mess resulting from the war and the revolution and setting industry on its feet again. Communist principles that had proved impracticable were dropped or indefinitely deferred ; capitalist practice, adjusted to socialist need, was revived. And nowhere was this more clearly shown than in the treatment and circumstances of the industrial workers. In effect they reverted to what they had been before, namely wage-earners ; the only difference being that while formerly they had been employed by private capital now they were employed by state enterprises, which competed on the labour market in the same way as private employers. In deference to the new ideology, the workers were allowed the fiction of a voice in management through their factory committees and the right to participate in factory conferences. To some extent this enabled them to feel that they had a real share in their enterprises and were no longer mere hirelings. To give a certain verisimilitude to this conception the workers should have enjoyed almost complete security of tenure, but in practice superfluous employees were dismissed as readily as in the capitalist world. The high degree of unemployment among clerical and intellectual workers in 1924 was largely due to the retrenchment of excessive staffs. The most unquestionable benefit conferred on the workers was the improvement in social status. At a bound they had become the country's aristocracy and were flattered and acclaimed by the Bolshevik leaders, not many of whom were of genuine proletarian origin themselves. The feeling that they were now the privileged and ruling class may have compensated the workers in some manner for the failure of the revolution immediately to raise their material standard of living. And that the workers were becoming more contented was indicated by the improvement in factory discipline shown by a great fall in the number of days' work lost through *progoul*, a term covering absence from duty for any unjustifiable cause. In 1921 the average number of days' work lost per worker without reasonable excuse was 20·6 and in 1925 only 7·4 ; while the number of days lost for unavoidable reasons fell from 22·3 to 3·8.

In 1926 the question had to be decided, whether to allow the existing system to continue, involving the surrender of many of the ideals of the revolution, or to take up more energetically the task of completing the socialisation of the country. A major problem was whether the new bourgeoisie, the so-called " Nepmen ", who were thriving on private enterprise, the *kulaks* who were becoming comparatively prosperous farmers, and all the other anti-social elements who were flourishing under the liberal toleration of the New Economic Policy, should be allowed to continue or be liquidated. A bitter controversy raged in the Party, the opposition led by Trotsky attacking the Government with the charge of neglecting the interests of the industrial proletariate and fostering individual enterprise in agriculture.

43

The conflict was embittered by the rivalry between Stalin and Trotsky for the leadership of the Party, the weapons used being the proper interpretation of the gospels of Marx and Lenin. Eventually Trotsky was defeated not by oratory nor logic, but because Stalin was politically more adroit and had gained control of the Party machine. Politics apart, the situation was by no means satisfactory from the Party standpoint. The revolution had been mainly supported by or was ostensibly in the interests of the industrial proletariate, a very small section of the population. The revolution could be fulfilled only with the support of a large and more or less satisfied proletariate, but the number of workers in large-scale state industry had increased by only 67 per cent between 1922 and 1926 and was still considerably below the pre-war level. The urban population as a whole was only slightly larger than in 1914 and was actually a smaller proportion of the total population. In the country the *kulaks* were increasing their holdings, hiring the labour of the poor and landless peasants and rapidly consolidating their position as small capitalist farmers. Lenin had expounded and believed in the *smychka*, or union, between town and country, industry and agriculture, but experience had shown that the traditional conflict between industry and agriculture had not only persisted but become more acute, and that reconciliation of their divergent interest was as distant as ever. The accusation made by the Trotsky opposition, that the Government had become lax and liberal and was failing both the communist cause and the proletariate, was not without foundation. And as soon as Trotsky had been disposed of Stalin began, tentatively at first, to initiate a drive towards socialism that culminated in the Five-Year Plan.

CHAPTER II

THE PLANNING PERIOD

THE fifteenth Party congress in December 1927 marked the close of the period of liberalism in economic policy. A formal resolution was adopted that the country was to advance rapidly and unequivocally towards Socialism, the first manifestation being a much more vigorous persecution of private enterprise and the *kulaks*. It was also decided that, as industry had nearly regained its pre-war standard, the time was ripe to begin the programme of industrialisation, which was to fit the country for Socialism and eventually Communism. The Bolsheviks believe implicitly and uncritically in every word Marx wrote, though it was rather a surprise that the social revolution had its first and unique success in a country industrially backward and with an insignificant proletariate. In any case they guessed, probably quite correctly, that they must hurry up and create a proletariate if they were to save the revolution. Therefore industry must be rapidly expanded. They were also inspired by the idea of showing the capitalist world how much more progressive and efficient was a socialist economy in which production was not undertaken for profit, but for the benefit of the whole community. Events had shown that the proletariate of the world was not prepared to take Bolshevism at its own valuation, but demanded concrete proof that the Russian revolution had really brought about a substantial improvement in the lot of the industrial worker. A further motive for the industrialisation of Russia was the desire for independence and self-sufficiency. So long as the country was dependent on the capitalist world for many industrial products it would continue to be at the mercy of foreign capital. It was therefore desirable to equip the socialist State with the means of producing its own requirements, more particularly arms and munitions of war. Three main

45

tasks were affirmed : to re-equip industry with modern machinery and apparatus ; increase the productivity of labour by raising the standard of skill of the workers and tightening up factory discipline ; and accumulate capital for reinvestment, the prospects of obtaining investment loans from abroad being imperceptible. Stalin delivered his opinion that the machine was everything ; what was wanted was more and better machines—a few years later he had to confess that machines required skilled hands and he came out with the slogan that Soviet industry needed more skilled and better skilled workers. Some members of the Party expressed doubts on the wisdom of extreme mechanisation, quoting from capitalist experience that machines deprived workers of employment. The Government retorted that it is not the increased use of machinery that reduces employment of labour, but the private ownership of machinery.

Various devices were adopted in 1928 and 1929 to increase the productivity of labour ; a number of large enterprises introduced " social competitions " between departments and workshops with the idea of stimulating the workers to greater effort. It resulted in some speeding-up of processes, often at the expense of quality of output and abnormal wear and tear of machines. To stimulate individual workers the so-called " shock-worker " was invented.

An *oudarnik* is a worker who puts more skill and energy into his job than his fellows and thus sets an example as well as producing a higher output. To become an *oudarnik* a worker had to exceed the daily standard task by a certain margin over a fixed period. With the official rank of *oudarnik* went the right of buying larger rations at cheap ration prices, free or reduced price tickets for theatres, holidays at sanatoria in the Crimea and Caucasus, and some other privileges. An *oudarnik* was also in duty bound supposed to be a political agitator, losing no opportunity of impressing on his co-workers the advantages of socialism. *Subbotniki* (from *Subbota* Saturday) were persons who " volunteered " to work for love, generally at an unaccustomed job, on their free day, when clerks and typists used to carry bricks for builders, load and unload railway trucks

46

and river barges and make themselves generally useful. The manual worker was not expected to perform more manual work on his rest day, especially if his normal job was hard, and he would have been ill-fitted to do an odd day's clerical work in an office. *Oudarniki* and *subbotniki* were manifestations of what was described as the new type of socialist labour, that is labour performed cheerfully without reward from a sense of duty to the community and the socialist State.

In the autumn of 1929 the continuous week was introduced. All enterprises and institutions worked continuously without a general rest day, but the workers had every fifth day off, that is to say one-fifth of the workers in a factory were always absent and four-fifths always on duty. In factories the scheme had certain advantages, because the machines were running continuously, but in administrative offices, banks, schools, etc., it caused chaos. In fact heads of enterprises and higher officials often found it impossible to take their regular day off, for if they had done so, no board, committee nor conference could ever have met with all members present. Another drawback was that families seldom enjoyed the same rest day for all. On the whole the scheme was not a success.

In 1930 the standard day was reduced from eight to seven hours. In industries where work was particularly heavy or dangerous a six-hour day was the rule. The shorter working day was not to lower production nor wages, for the worker was supposed to labour more intensively and the machines to be used to fuller capacity. The workers were not, however, allowed to waste the extra hour of free time ; if they were not studying to improve their knowledge and qualifications they should attend political meetings or lectures on Marx and Communism. In practice a great deal of the workers' free time was spent in queues to buy the necessities of life, for rationing had been adopted in 1929 and was to continue to 1935.

The First Five-Year Plan officially opened on the 1st October 1928. Industrially it meant a great increase in the construction of all sorts of economic enterprises, particularly in heavy industry. Existing works were modernised and enlarged and new ones built, such as the Dnieprostroi hydro-electric power station, the Kuznetsk iron and steel works in Siberia and the tractor factory at Stalingrad, to mention only three of the largest. Whereas the number of workers in large-scale industry increased by about one and a quarter million between 1924 and 1928, and in the latter year was only about 200,000 above 1913, between 1928 and 1932 it expanded by nearly 3·4 millions and more than doubled itself. Of this increase nearly three-quarters were engaged in capital construction or in producing capital goods and only one-quarter in producing consumers' goods. The natural result was an enormous increase in the aggregate wage income of the urban population and a very moderate increase in the quantity of consumers' goods produced by state industry. In fact the production of some of the most basic essentials of life such as textiles and sugar was actually smaller in 1932 than in 1928. In addition to this an enormous number of private enterprises and handicraft workers, who had formerly supplied a very appreciable part of the retail market, had been liquidated. There is little doubt that the total quantity of the ordinary necessities of life available for the consuming population was actually smaller in 1930 than in 1928. In consequence of the great increase in the purchasing power of the population (total wages paid out by the State and state enterprises rose from R.8159 million to R.13,597 million between 1928 and 1930), demand far outran supply and prices would have risen to extraordinary heights had the Government not taken steps to control distribution.

Rationing began by the consumers' co-operative stores refusing to sell deficit goods to non-members ; from this they went on to limit the amounts purchasable by a member at a time. Finally when rationing was in full force, state shops sold only against ration cards and, since nearly everything was rationed, people without ration cards had to satisfy their needs as best they could in what remained of the open market or in the so-called " commercial " shops, where prices were up to ten times as much as in the " closed " shops. Persons not entitled to rations were private traders, anybody earning a living by independent enterprise, such as cab-drivers, artisans and handicraft workers, the clergy and all persons deprived of civic rights because of their bourgeois origin. Broadly speaking, ration cards were issued only to persons in some form of government employ and members of recognised producers' co-operative associations. In 1930 the total number of persons in possession of ration privileges, together with their dependants, was about 26 millions, or nearly the same as the urban population ; by 1935, just before rationing began to be discontinued, this had grown to over 40 millions, to which figure the urban population had also in the meantime increased. It should, however, not be assumed that practically the whole of the urban population was in receipt of rations, because state employees such as transport workers, school teachers, etc., living in villages and counting as rural residents were entitled to rations. But probably at least 80 per cent of the urban population had to a greater or less degree the right of purchasing rationed goods. The peasants were not rationed in the same way, but the supply of manufactured goods made available to the village consumers' co-operative shops depended on the quantity of agricultural produce delivered to the Government.

In 1931 the issue of ration cards was taken out of the hands of the consumers' co-operative organisation and entrusted to the town Soviets, or municipal councils. Previously the quantity of some foods obtainable by manual workers had been larger than the quantities allowed to non-manual workers ; but at this time several ration categories were established for different classes of the community. The highest category included heavy industrial factory work ; office workers and persons employed in distributive organisations received much less both in quantity and variety, while Party and government officials, directors and managers of large state enterprises and others included in the new bureaucratic aristocracy had the right of buying at special reserved shops, where both the quantity and quality of goods supplied were better than anywhere else. Thus rationing, at first adopted to ensure a more or less equitable distribution of available supplies to the workers and employees of the State, became the means of discriminating between different sections of the population and of stimulating the workers to greater efforts. For besides the extra rations allowed to *oudarniki*, anyone, as a reward for some special achievement, such as a mechanical invention, might be given the privilege of purchasing a given value of rationed goods in addition to his ordinary ration. The result of all this was that money was no longer a constant measure of value : a wage of, say, R.150 a month had a much higher purchasing power in the hands of an *oudarnik* in an engineering works than in those of a salesman in a retail shop, and might even be worth as much as a salary of R.500 paid to a qualified engineer in the same works, whose antecedents were bourgeois. The worker would be able to buy an overcoat or pair of boots at his factory co-operative shop at a reasonable price, while the engineer's rations would be limited to a few essential foodstuffs and he would have to buy clothing on the open market or in a " commercial shop " costing many times as much as the prices paid by the workman. The bourgeois engineer paid R.500 a month actually received more than double the salary of the Party director of the works, who as a member of the Party was debarred from receiving more than R.225 a month. But this vaunted ascetism was alleviated by the gratuitous privileges adhering to his position and Party membership, such as free or very cheap living quarters, the use of a motor-car and the right to buy provisions, clothing and luxuries at a special shop ; so that the Party director with his R.225 a month was intrinsically far better off than the engineer.

Although the industrial workers were the most privileged section of the community, even their standard of living was extremely low. The Soviet Government ceased publishing price and cost-of-living indices at the beginning of the First Five-Year Plan, therefore it is only possible to say that during the first part of the Plan the general standard of living deteriorated and that of the workers as a whole was certainly inferior to the last years of the old régime, that is as regards the consumption of food and other necessities of life. With regard to other things such as recreation and social services the balance on the whole was in favour of the Soviet régime. Certainly education in the broader sense to include public libraries, spare time technical training, physical culture, etc., was far more developed by the Soviet Government than it had been under the Tsarist Government. Still, it touched only the workers in a comparative few large centres : the great mass of unskilled or semi-skilled labour employed in mining, forestry, etc., reaped comparatively little benefit. The same applied to health services and as regards the much-advertised provision of sanatoria and rest-homes in country places and seaside resorts ; these were reserved for favoured factory workers, pre-eminently *oudarniki* and Party members. A holiday in the Crimea or the Caucasus was a reward for exceptional services both in the field of productive work and political activity : it was far from being the right of every worker.

A true estimate of the housing question is extremely difficult. At the beginning of the revolution the houses of the aristocracy and the flats of the professional and bourgeois classes were confiscated and made over to the workers, but whether this was a great improvement is questionable. On the one hand their new quarters were better built and more sanitary than the dismal log huts in the industrial suburbs and the basement dwellings in the centre of the town, formerly inhabited by the working classes : on the other hand, through the increase in urban population, the re-quisitioning of so many dwelling-houses for government offices and other social, political and economic organisations, the decay of many residential buildings owing to neglect, and the very small amount of new housing built since the revolution, overcrowding was terrible. By 1930 municipal councils and some of the largest state undertakings had built large blocks of workers' flats. These were a great im-provement on any existing workers' quarters, but the rooms were small and cooking and washing had to be done in com-munal kitchens, baths and laundries, though meals were usually taken in a communal restaurant. In such circum-stances the inmates enjoyed little privacy. The privilege of living in these surroundings was confined to the labour aristocracy. At the other extreme were the log barracks and *zemlyanki* (troglodyte dwellings consisting of a turf roof over a hole in the ground) in which the workers in new enterprises set down in the open *steppe* were compelled to live. Thus, only a comparatively small proportion of the industrial workers, consisting of the aristocracy of skilled labour in old-established industrial centres, can actually have enjoyed rather better housing conditions than formerly ; the mass of factory workers, miners and unskilled labour generally, lived under conditions probably no better than before the revolution, while conditions in the many new enterprises being constructed in the open country were worse than any large masses of labour had formerly been compelled to endure.

Owing to the complications introduced by rationing it is impossible to make any estimate of the purchasing power of wages during this period compared with the periods before and after rationing. The average money wage continued to increase year by year, more than doubling between 1928 (R.703 a year) and 1932 (R.1427 a year). To an appreciable extent this rise was neutralised by the increase in the proportion of the workman's wage deducted for various reasons. Between 1928 and 1932 the State's indebtedness to the population rose by R.8686 million, that is to say, the population during this period subscribed this sum out of wages to buy state loan bonds. Actually the value of bonds taken up by the public was R.12,128 million, the difference being the value of bonds redeemed ; the subscribers belonged almost exclusively to the wage and salary earning section of the population, because the peasants did not begin to subscribe any appreciable amount till some years later. The value of bonds issued in relation to the total sum of salaries and wages paid out during these years was

1928 .	.	. 4 per cent
1929 .	.	. 7 ,,
1930 .	.	. 9 ,,
1931 .	.	. 7 ,,
1932 .	.	. 9 ,,

The wage-earner had, therefore, to subscribe annually about one month's income. The pretence that subscriptions were voluntary is accepted only by those people who for their own intellectual comfort place implicit trust in Soviet protestations. The purchase of state loan bonds was not the only drain on the worker's income : union dues, cultural levies (in effect a special tax to provide funds for building schools, clubs, etc.), subscriptions to M.O.P.R. (International Class War Prisoners' Aid Society), to support strikes in capitalist countries, to build aeroplanes for the Soviet Air Force and in support of various other causes, probably absorbed up to 10 per cent of the average worker's income. In one way and another his wages were reduced by anything up to 20 per cent ; it is perhaps only fair to say that he paid no direct taxes, but indirect taxation on the goods he bought raised their retail price very materially. However, during the period of rationing the individual's money income was neither a true measure of his consuming power nor was it a true index of his condition in relation to his fellows. The State distributed nearly the whole of the available flow of consumers' goods among the population irrespective of the money wage paid out, the function of which was to act more or less as a voucher to simplify distribution, and so far as it exceeded the price of the worker's rations to enable him to buy certain non-rationed luxury or semi-luxury goods or augment his rations by purchases at the commercial shops. No worker received a smaller wage than was required to pay the price of the rationed goods he was entitled to, but only the better paid had a surplus large enough to buy any important additions. This view of money wages was, however, not held by the Government nor the Trade Unions, possibly for two reasons : firstly, rationing was a temporary expedient to cope with a temporary emergency ; secondly, the Bolsheviks refused to admit that the Soviet currency was an imperfect medium of exchange. In fact they boasted that the Soviet rouble was the most stable money in the world with the most assured purchasing power, because it was backed by all the capital wealth of the country in addition to the volume of consumption goods held by the Government. In actual fact the amount of money in circulation was far greater than was required to effect the exchange of consumption goods at ration prices, hence the enormously inflated prices ruling on the open market ; and, since the factories, railways and other capital assets of the State could in no conceivable circumstances be put up for sale, it was nonsense to pretend that they formed a backing for the currency.

A tendency to equality in wages accompanied the inauguration of the Five-Year Plan, partly because of the policy of increasing the wages of the lower paid categories of labour and partly because equalitarianism was considered to be in agreement with communist theory. Payment at piece rates was the rule wherever possible, but to prevent individual workers from unduly increasing their earnings by " speeding up ", their standard daily task was raised, or their piece rates lowered, if they persistently earned more than the standard norm. If workers in a particular process were found to be earning more than others performing other work requiring about equal effort and skill, the piece rate was cut. As a matter of fact this equalitarianism did not create as much discontent as might be supposed. The Five-Year Plan had been introduced with a terrific bally-hoo : the workers were told that after five years of hard work and simple living they would achieve a standard of living undreamt of in Tsarist Russia or in the capitalist countries. Appeal was also made to their socialist patriotism, for they were to show the world what socialism could perform, even in backward Russia, when private ownership was abolished and all worked for the good of the community. At that time the great majority of the workers were supporters of the Soviet régime, for they still believed in their leader's promises ; many of the younger people were distinctly enthusiastic and in some factories even went so far as to form workers' communes, living together and pooling their earnings. The collective idea was even carried into their employment, factory brigades being formed which always worked together and were paid a lump wage for the total work performed. An even more extreme instance of collectivism was found in schools, where students joined in brigades to study collectively and eventually pass out together on the basis of a collective test of their collective knowledge.

All this was part of the Bolsheviks' plan to fulfil socialist theory and gain the eventual support of the industrial proletariate, which was to be welded into a homogeneous collective whole with a collective will and collective ideas. To give the workers a sense of authority and partnership in the State, directors, managers and the higher officials of enterprises were subjected to indignities that effectively undermined their authority. Periodically all technical and administrative heads, being members or candidates of the Party, had to submit to an investigation by a " cleansing " commission. This process, known as the *chistka*, was intended to purge the Party of members of unsatisfactory origin or doubtful political orthodoxy. All workers in the enterprise were encouraged to attend the proceedings— indeed a worker absenting himself for no sufficient reason was suspected of political indifference—and were permitted to criticise and question the person under examination, though he be the head of the concern. At this period even an unusual fastidiousness in dress or manners might be construed as evidence of bourgeois leanings, so that on one score or another the workers could always find some theme on which to harass an unpopular official. As for the technical experts of bourgeois origin, they could be insulted and persecuted at any time with impunity and lived under the shadow of a charge of wrecking. For the beginning of the First Five-Year Plan was heralded by the first great sabotage trial, known to history as the Shachty trial, at which fifty-three Russian and German engineers employed in the Donetz coalfields were found guilty of wrecking the Plan. These stage-managed wrecking trials, which continued with varying intensity for the following ten years, were mainly to discover scapegoats for the failure of the Plan. At the same time it would be unsafe to assert that in no case was there any substance in the accusations, but the vast majority of charges were clearly fabricated. Against none of the accused in any of the numerous trials was conclusive evidence produced, and the " confessions ", on which the prisoners were mostly convicted, were worth just about as much as " confessions " extracted by torture in the days of the Inquisition.

Another form of " mass control " by the workers was the so-called " light cavalry " detachments of young Communists who paid surprise visits to enterprises and institutions to investigate the management and combat bureaucratic tendencies. These, as well as the regular workers' brigades organised for the purposes of visiting government departments, economic organs, villages, etc., to check up on administrative methods and take action when necessary, were supposed to instil into their members a sense of responsibility and afford them practical experience in organisation and administration. The principle was good, for in a democratic socialist State the workers should be afforded facilities for acquiring experience of government and economic administration. But these brigades and detachments of inspection were given considerable authority before they had acquired any experience to speak of. By all accounts their visits were more destructive than constructive, and no doubt they were actually the cause of much of the bureaucratism they set out to destroy ; for the head of an enterprise, knowing that his actions might at any moment come under the scrutiny of a deputation ignorant of his problems and very probably prejudiced against all managements on principle, would naturally endeavour to cover himself by sticking meticulously to rules and instructions and declining to take any decision on his own responsibility. A further defect in these organs of workers' control was that they were, naturally, composed mainly of politically conscious and orthodox workers of the type known as " activists ". These are apt to be loud-mouthed demagogues, full of slogans and clichés, unintelligent and fonder of exhorting their fellows than of performing hard work themselves ; definitely not the citizens painstakingly to carry out an investigation impartially and with knowledge. The chief indication that the measures adopted to introduce mass control in the early part of the First Five-Year Plan proved unsatisfactory, is their subsequent abandonment. Of course mass control was never intended, nor was it allowed, to interfere with the Government's own plans and policy. Its activities were strictly limited to supervision of the execution of the Government's designs.

In spite of the workers' control, or perhaps because of it, labour discipline became very lax. The labour turnover in industry as a whole was phenomenal, even when it is borne in mind that Russian labour had always been anything but constant and static ; in the economic years 1926–7 to 1929–1930 the turnover for industry as a whole expressed as a percentage of the average total number employed was :

	Labour Engaged	Labour Lost
1926–7	111·3	104·1
1927–8	101·4	96·1
1928–9	110·1	105·6
1929–30	172·3	150·6

Industries in which labour conditions were bad made infinitely worse showing ; for instance in 1930 the coal mining industry's turnover was about three times the total labour employed, that is to say, on the average each worker remained in his job only four months. Iron ore mining was nearly as bad, and in heavy industry as a whole the turnover was nearly twice the numbers employed. As another consequence of lax discipline the average number of days worked fell from 263 per worker in all industries in 1928 to 253 in 1930. Much of the dissatisfaction with conditions that was at the bottom of the fluidity of labour was due to the failure of the Trade Unions to look after the material welfare of their members and to maintain discipline. Complaints were made that the higher official circles were out of touch with the rank and file, that the administration was too bureaucratic, and that insufficient attention was paid to qualifying the workers for work of an administrative character. Tomsky, then President of the All-Union Central Council of Trade Unions, was one of the leaders of the " Right Opposition " (for which he was in 1936 degraded and arrested, and then anticipated the fate of his old colleagues, Zinoviev, Kamenev and others by committing suicide). His notions of trade-unionism were not irreconcilable with trade-unionism in capitalist countries, and it is worth noting that in retrospect he was later accused of precisely the same things that a certain type of diehard Tory loves to adduce against our own union leaders. Specifically his detractors allege that unemployment relief was distributed in such a way as to become in effect an inducement to the pseudo-unemployed to avoid working ; while sickness benefit, instead of promoting an improvement in labour productivity, encouraged malingering.

The First Five-Year Plan terminated at the end of 1932. It did not bring the promised improvement in the condition of the workers : in fact it entirely failed to result in any appreciable increase in the supply of the necessities, let alone the amenities, of life. It was officially claimed that the industrial production aimed at for the final year was about 95 per cent realised. This figure was arrived at on a basis of the total money value of industrial production, which depended on the value arbitrarly allotted to various commodities. In point of volume the output of the most important key industries fell much below the Plan ; for instance :

	Plan	Actual Output in 1932	Actual Output as per cent of the Plan
Coal, millions of tons .	75·0	64·4	86
Pig iron, millions of tons	10·0	6·2	62
Steel, millions of tons .	10·4	5·9	57
Crude petroleum, millions of tons . . .	21·7	22·3	103
Cotton textiles, millions of metres . .	4700·0	2719·0	58

CHAPTER IV

RESULTS OF THE FIRST FIVE-YEAR PLAN

EVEN before the First Five-Year Plan ran to its official close many of the communist principles and practices with which it began were scrapped or amended out of recognition. In June 1931 Stalin addressed a conference of Economic Administrators and found a very great deal to criticise in the conduct and organisation of industry. He then propounded six guiding conditions for the management of Soviet economic enterprises : the first problem was the supply of labour now that unemployment had been overcome and the flow of surplus agricultural labour to the towns no longer met the demands of industry. To meet the new conditions more labour-saving machinery must be installed and agreements made between employing enterprises and collective farms under which the surplus labour of the latter would be drafted into factories. Secondly, the wages system must be altered in order to bind a nucleus or cadre of skilled labour more firmly to the factory. In plain language, Stalin meant that the difference between the wages of the leading qualified workers and the wages of the ordinary unskilled and semi-skilled workers should be widened. By this means the unskilled workers would be encouraged to improve their qualifications and the qualified workers would be stimulated to put forth their best efforts. Thirdly, the organisation of labour required revising. A great fault in nearly all enterprises was the irresponsibility of the workers (*obezlichnost*, literally lack of individuality), resulting in neglect of machines and indifference to the quality of output. This was largely attributable to the five-day continuous week, which rendered it impossible to hold any individual or group of workers responsible for certain machines or a certain piece of work. The five-day continuous week was therefore to be cancelled and a six-day week substituted with every sixth day a common and universal day of rest. Fourthly, the rapidly increasing demand for engineers and technical experts made it necessary to increase the number of technical schools and to admit students of non-proletarian origin. Also the old suspicion of the bourgeois technical intelligentsia must be overcome. Though *saboteurs* still existed they were few and isolated ; the majority of the old bourgeois experts were ready to work loyally and they must be respected, given positions in accordance with their qualifications and a better standard of living. Fifthly, in order to accumulate the savings needed to make possible the enormous capital investments in progress, waste must be checked, production costs lowered and an efficient system of business accountancy (*khosraschot*) introduced. Finally, enterprises must be administered by single responsible heads. In trusts and combines controlling a number of factories there must be only one president and a few vice-presidents, the other members of the board or collegium being assigned posts as managers of individual enterprises.

The end of the First Five-Year Plan saw a remarkable change in the attitude of the Government towards the workers. At the beginning they were flattered, encouraged to imagine themselves the ruling class, given all sorts of privileges and allowed to indulge their new sense of equality by off-hand and casual manners to their factory superiors. I made my first visit to Soviet Russia in 1930, spending about eight weeks in an extended tour of the country. One of the greatest differences from Tsarist times was in the manners and behaviour of the working class. In the streets they walked about as though they owned the place. In offices and factories they addressed managers as equals, while the latter, unless they were themselves of good proletarian origin and Party members, seemed to issue orders rather apologetically. The former servility of subordinates was shown only by "white collar" workers of bourgeois origin, who always appeared terrified in the presence of the boss, especially when he was a Party man. In those days it was still not considered good form to dress better than one's neighbours, nor to show too obvious signs of refinement. In view of the dearth of goods it was in any case difficult enough to dress respectably without troubling about style, but the communist-bureaucracy, which in their special shops had the pick of available goods, ostentatiously affected simplicity, as often as not wearing Russian workman's blouses outside their trousers. The best seats in the theatres were full of workers, who paid less than the ordinary public and often nothing at all if they were shock workers, and attended in what might have been their working clothes. The few decent hotels, left over from the old days and still run on more or less international lines for the benefit of foreigners, sometimes produced a dance orchestra in the evenings as an accompaniment to an exiguous and exorbitant supper meal. The attendance was negligible, and what there was seemed to consist of young army or G.P.U. officers and their women and young people in black civilian garb, who were either G.P.U. agents or did not care if they did show a bourgeois hankering for night life. But, generally speaking, the night life which during the years of the New Economic Policy had attained quite a respectable degree of gaiety, under private enterprise of course, had been suppressed by the Five-Year Plan. The Russian worker was being educated to a sense of his responsibilities and mission, and had to put away the frivolity of the capitalist age.

Almost overnight the whole situation was changed ; after announcing that factory discipline must be tightened up, Stalin told his people to be gay and enjoy life. The first enthusiasm for the Plan had begun to wear off and the workers were beginning to wonder whether all the strain and stress was really worth while. This frame of mind was responsible for a marked increase in absenteeism : in 1929 the number of days lost by unauthorised absence was 4 per worker, in 1932 6 days, in the aggregate amounting to a loss of 27·8 million working days to industry or of R.864 million worth of output. A law of 15th November 1932 made the penalty for one day's unauthorised absence immediate dismissal ; also a worker thus dismissed lost his ration card and his room or flat if he were housed in a building belonging to his factory. In December internal passports were reintroduced in an even stricter form than in the pre-revolutionary era : no Soviet citizen might be absent from home for twenty-four hours without having his passport visaed. These measures were designed to check the liquidity of labour and tie the worker down to his job. At the same time, although unemployment had nominally been abolished in 1930, persons who had no official employment or means of subsistence in a number of the largest cities were compelled to leave. In practice the large population centres had zones of 100 or 50 kilometres radius within which residence was confined to persons whose passports were correspondingly endorsed. This rule meant that any worker who lost his job was liable to expulsion (they usually had to migrate to Siberia), and it also enabled the authorities to control the influx into the large towns of peasants and unskilled labour generally, who were irresistibly attracted to the big industrial centres. Unskilled labour was plentiful and the housing problem was becoming more and more acute. The urban population increased from 26·3 millions in 1926 to 40 millions by the end of 1932, and during the years 1929 to 1932, when industrial expansion under the First Five-Year Plan was intense, the average net increase through influx from the country was 2·8 millions. In 1933, owing to the new measures of control, it fell to 772,000.

By the close of the First Five-Year Plan piece-work had been introduced in practically all productive industrial work. Later it was also to be applied to clerical work, such as book-keeping. At the end of 1932 about 64 per cent of all industrial workers and employees were paid at piece rates. According to trade-union notions piece-work is a capitalist device for getting more out of the workers, and, where piece rates are in force, the unions take measures to prevent a few specially skilled and energetic workers from greatly exceeding the average and so giving the employers an excuse to cut rates for the many. An employer who cuts rates because a small minority of his workpeople were able to earn a lot of money would be very short-sighted and blind to his own long-term interests. Besides, piece-work in many kinds of work serves as an encouragement to the worker to speed up production at the expense of his machine and the quality of his output.

In Soviet industry other considerations are supposed to be valid. In the first place, the worker who through skill and energy is able to increase his own output above the average, is not making more profits for a private employer, the owner of the capital which his (the worker's) labour makes productive ; on the contrary he is adding to the wealth of the whole community of which he is a member. Clearly if the State be synonymous with the community in which everyone is a shareholder, it is ridiculous to speak of the State exploiting the workers. Secondly, piece rates are obviously the best way of putting into practice the principle that every member of the community shall be remunerated in accordance with his ability, or his individual contribution to the common good. A third, and perhaps the most potent reason though not one that is officially admitted, is that the workers had not yet come to realise, in Stalin's own words, that ". . . a fundamental change has been brought about in the people's conception of labour, for toil has been transformed from a dishonourable and heavy infliction, as it was formerly accounted, to an occupation of honour, glory, valour and heroism." Without the incentive of increased earnings it is to be feared that a majority of the workers would not have been inspired to put all they had into the job. And since foremen were generally inferior in quality, lacking in authority as well as being overburdened with returns, forms and other distraction, it was virtually impossible to keep lazy workers up to scratch. It is impossible to say whether piece rates gave a better return in output than time rates would have done. It is, however, incontestable that more workers were employed and more wages paid out during the First Five-Year Plan than had been allowed for, even though the Plan was nominally fulfilled as regards industrial output. The following shows the figures of the original Five-Year Plan, the later control figures for 1932, and the realised figures as given in the official Statistical Annual (*vide* page 64).

Piece rates are not so easily controlled as time rates. How many hours a week a man has worked, or more precisely

	Original Plan for the Year 1/10/32–30/9/33	Control Figures for 1932	Actual Results
Number of wage and salary earners, millions . .	15·8	21	22·9
Total sum of wages and salaries, R. million .	15,700	26,800	32,700
Value of total industrial output, R. million .	30,500	35,040	36,900

has spent in the workshop, can be accurately recorded. What his output has been is often liable to a margin of error, especially when it is more complex than the repetition of a single process ; the factor of quality must also be considered. Articles on wage calculations appearing over a long period in Soviet papers and technical journals indicate that the calculation of piece rates is often faulty, sometimes through carelessness or ignorance, sometimes because the factory administration deliberately increases earnings to attract better workers. It seems that the piece rate system may be largely responsible for the excess of the industrial wage bill over the annual wage estimates ; for in every year without exception the wage bill has surpassed the planned total, as the following figures show :

	R. millions			
	1934	1935	1936	1937
Planned wage bill . .	41,600	49,800	65,500	78,300
Actual wages paid out .	44,000	56,200	71,400	80,200

The relative position of different industries in order of wages changed between 1928 and 1935, since when the average wage in different industries has not been published. In 1928 coal mining came fourteenth in the list, the average wage being 10 per cent below the average for all industrial workers. In 1935 coal mining came fourth with an average wage 15 per cent above the general average. The petroleum industry, eighth in 1928, rose to first place in 1935, while the metal-working and engineering industry fell from first place to third and the printing industry from second to eighth. Theoretically there is no more a labour market in Soviet Russia than a commodity market, but one cannot avoid the impression that these changes in the order of industries according to wages was, partly at least, due to the reaction of supply and demand. Coal mining and petroleum are key industries. The demand for coal owing to the enormous expansion of heavy industry became very intense after the First Five-Year Plan had got well under way ; and the increasing production of tractors, motor vehicles and internal combustion engines for all sorts of purposes meant a rapidly increasing consumption of oil products. The increase in the total quantity of labour employed was not particularly great in comparison with other industries, but a much higher quality of labour came to be needed because of the increased use of machinery and the increasing complexity of the machinery in use. To attract workers with the necessary educational and technical qualifications much higher wages had to be paid than had formerly been earned by the unskilled and often illiterate peasants who were good enough when the work was mainly of the pick-and-shovel sort. The increasing quantity and complexity of machinery in industry generally prescribed greater differences between the earnings of skilled trained labour and unskilled labour. The official version, that every man should be remunerated according to his worth, was in fact inventing a principle to fit the facts ; for the Russian workman was no more inclined than any other to go to the trouble of attending technical schools or classes in his spare time unless he saw some material benefit at the end of it. As for the youngsters, the ambition to become an intellectual worker, which in spite of all communist theories about the equality of man and the dignity of manual labour does mean social elevation, was generally the chief motive for enrolling as students in universities and the higher technical schools.

One of the socially most significant developments at the close of the first and opening years of the Second Five-Year Plan was the improvement in the condition of the intellectual or white-collar workers. In 1928 the teaching and medical professions were among the worst-paid occupations, the average salary being only some 72 per cent of the average wage in industry and 90 per cent of the average wage for all workers, including agricultural labour. By 1935 the professional salary was about 95 per cent of the average industrial wage and slightly exceeded the average for all wages and salaries. Apart from the relatively large increase in their remuneration, members of the professions had gained a much higher social status in 1935 than in 1928, and this process has continued till to-day those at the head of their professions may be counted among the Soviet *élite*.

A phenomenon of the great industrialisation drive was a remarkable fall in the size of workers' families. In 1930 each worker on the average supported 2·05 dependants, in 1934 1·66. The first explanation is, of course, that life was so hard and supplies so short that a family was a burden instead of an asset and a delight. No doubt this had something to do with it, especially the housing shortage. But there was another reason that was much more important ; the total number of workers and employees, that is wage and salary earners, rose from 12·2 millions to 23·7 millions between 1929 and 1934, and of this increase a very large majority was young people having just completed their secondary or higher education or young peasants surplus to agricultural labour requirements. In 1933 the average age of all workers and employees in many big industrial enterprises was between twenty-five and twenty-eight, which of course meant that a large proportion was considerably younger. Another circumstance unfavourable to a natural increase was the increasing employment of women in industry. In 1929 3·3 million women were employed, in 1934 7·2 millions ; of these probably the great majority were married to male workers in industry. The women were earners mainly because few men earned sufficient to keep a wife merely as housekeeper, also because housekeeping in the exiguous quarters at their disposal was a long way from being a whole-time job. No doubt a few women worked because they liked to be independent and be on an equality with men, but it is doubtful whether the Bolshevik emancipation of women had as much to do with female employment as economic necessity. In any case a married couple both fully employed would obviously hesitate to burden themselves with children.

My second visit to Soviet Russia was in 1934. The First Five-Year Plan had been completed and the Second was in progress. The last year of the first period, 1932, had been one of almost intolerable stress because the Government was spurring on every industry and enterprise to make a final effort to fulfil the Plan. The compulsory collectivisation of peasant farms in 1930 and 1931 had completely disorganised agricultural production, which was further depressed by exceptionally dry years in 1931 and 1932. Consequently the food situation in 1932 was critical and, if the towns did not actually starve, some millions of the rural population succumbed to pure hunger and deficiency diseases. Naturally the Soviet Government concealed the situation as far as possible, but there is little doubt that the general standard of living in that year fell nearly to the low level reached in 1921 and far below the average for the last years of the Tsarist régime. The year 1933 saw some improvement in the situation ; the Government, realising the impossibility of maintaining the pace of 1932, reduced its demands and allowed the country a year of comparative rest : employment in industry actually sank and industrial production increased only 8 per cent compared with the preceding year, whereas the average annual rate of increase during the first two Five-Year Plans was about 20 per cent. The harvests of 1933 and 1934 were far better than 1931 and 1932, so that by the late summer of 1934 the food situation was fairly satisfactory. In my own experience of visiting Russia in 1930, 1934, 1937 and 1939, the 1934 visit was the only one when one could compare the hotel menus with Tsarist Russia. In 1930 outside the best hotels in the chief towns, such as Moscow, Leningrad, Kharkov and Kiev, the food was almost uneatable. Foreigners travelling about the country as my companion and I did, off the regular tourist routes, were likely to starve unless they carried supplies with them. We left Moscow with about a 50 lb. stock of tinned and preserved food against emergencies, and without it we should frequently have been seriously hungry. In almost every place we visited we heard complaints of food shortage : in Kazan a working man, for no apparent reason except that foreigners might be supposed to sympathise, accosted us in the street with a grievance about the prohibitive price of meat and the insignificant quantity one could obtain against ration cards. At a railway junction in the North Caucasus a porter excused his inability to handle our fairly modest baggage on the ground that he could not keep up his strength on mere bread and potatoes. At the same time, good and plentiful food was obtainable by the privileged. One of the places we visited was the new metallurgical works at Kuznetsk in Western Siberia. We were accommodated in a large new and well-appointed wooden house specially built for the American engineers supervising the work. They were supplied with white bread, real butter, eggs, unlimited meat and fish and fresh vegetables and fruit. But the Russian workers' rations were mainly black bread, potatoes and cabbage, with infinitesimal quantities of meat, tea and sugar ; butter was an unrealisable dream. Again at Stalingrad on the Lower Volga, where owing to the exertions of an *intourist* agent we were treated as honoured visitors and fed in the restaurant of the Park of Rest and Culture, we were served with white bread and butter, poultry and eggs, fresh fruit of all sorts, not only of good quality but in abundant quantity. The ordinary citizen had to be content with black bread and cabbage soup with infrequent bits of tough meat, and for a sweet a lump of some pallid gelatinous substance distantly related to blancmange, adorned with a speck of jam. Curiously enough the workers did not seem to resent this discrimination, at least not articulately. They were still hypnotised by the Five-Year Plan and the faith that it would lead to better times. As for foreigners, if they came to help they must be treated well, because they could not be expected to undergo hardships like the Russians themselves, or if they came as tourists prepared to spend foreign *valuta* they must be given the opportunity to spend it. The only time I saw any demonstration of discontent was in Leningrad, when a large party from a " Northern Capitals " cruise was banqueted at the Hôtel de l'Europe prior to a sightseeing tour in motor coaches. A small crowd, mainly of women, collected outside the hotel in a distinctly hostile mood until moved on by the militia.[1]

In 1934 the ordinary citizen had lost that hungry and tense look characteristic of the Russians in 1930. Clothing too had improved somewhat ; that is to say, one saw more leather boots and fewer canvas shoes on the streets, and suits to match were becoming quite a commonplace instead of a discordant selection of garments. The root of the matter was that money had again become a criterion of prosperity and had regained a very large part of its normal functions in the community. It is true that rationing was still in operation, but 25 per cent or more of the total retail trade was free, or " commercialised," and all the best-quality goods were obtainable only in the commercial shops. Since 1932 these shops had appeared in every largish town to sell both food-stuffs and manufactured goods without restriction, but at much higher prices than those charged for rationed goods. For example, the worker paid about R.2 a kilo for his sugar ration ; if he wanted more than the very small amount allowed on his ration card he could buy it at the commercial shop at R.10 a kilo. Similarly with clothing and footwear, the workman's allowance (he would be lucky to receive a permit to buy one suit and one pair of boots a year) was com-paratively cheap, but inadequate ; at the commercial shops it was possible to buy a suit or a pair of boots at prices two or three times more than those charged in the factory or co-operative shop. At the same time the goods sold commer-cially were always better quality, which was only natural.

The chief object of the commercial shops was to mop up the surplus money remaining in the pockets of the people after buying the quantities of goods they were entitled to as rations. Between the beginning of 1930 and the middle of 1933 the currency circulation expanded two and a half times, but the supply of goods on the retail market increased in a

---

[1] The word " police ", owing to its Tsarist connection, is never used in Soviet Russia. The guardians of law and order, regulators of traffic, etc., are known as *Militzia* or Militia. These have no connection with the uniformed troops of the G.P.U., or, as now styled, the Department of Internal Affairs.

much smaller ratio, as is shown by statistical returns according to which the output of consumers' goods during the same period increased by only some 36 per cent. In such conditions it would have been impossible to maintain a low and constant price level, even with the most drastic rationing, for the consuming public would have been left with large surplus sums of money which would have found an outlet on an illegal " black " market. As a matter of fact this was the case ; " speculation ", *i.e.* buying goods to resell at a high profit, became a popular if risky adventure, for the penalty was severe even to death, mainly undertaken by the remnants of the former small private traders, predominantly Jews. Speculation always flourishes when prices are kept artificially low, at a level that does not balance supply and demand. Then those goods whose price is too low disappear from the shops to reappear in the hands of speculators. Finally the authorities raise the price or increase the supply and so restore equilibrium. It took the Bolshevik economists some time to realise that it is impossible, even in a totalitarian socialist State, to fix retail prices without reference to the supply of goods and the amount of purchasing medium in the pockets of the consuming public.

The commercial shops, naturally, catered mainly for the higher income groups, the managers and senior officials of state enterprises, higher government officials, senior army officers and the like. These were prepared to pay the commercial prices, for one reason to avoid the time and trouble involved in buying at their closed factory or departmental shops, for another because the commercial shop offered them a better selection and better quality. The average working man could not afford the commercial prices as a rule ; if he badly wanted something that was unobtainable at his own ration shop, he saved up for weeks. The Bolsheviks and their foreign apologists, of course, tried to make out that the commercial shops were not a symptom of reviving class distinctions. Their object was, they said, to allow the public to supplement their rations and buy luxuries that were not included among the rationed necessities. Actually they were a perfectly logical consequence of the adoption of the principle of differential remuneration. Obviously the object of paying large wages or salaries to get the best men would be defeated if these could not get a more or less commensurate benefit from their higher money incomes : in Soviet Russia as in any capitalist State money is desirable only for what it will buy. And upon further examination the system conformed to one of the best dictates of socialism, namely, to soak the rich, for the commercial prices were really exorbitant compared with the normal or ration prices of the same goods.

People lucky enough to get hold of foreign currency or still in possession of gold, silver or jewellery could buy at *torgsin* shops. *Torgsin* is one of those Soviet portmanteau names derived from the initial syllables of two or more other words and means Foreign Trade. The peculiarity of these shops was that they sold for " gold " roubles instead of paper roubles and were under the Commissariat of External Trade instead of the Commissariat of Internal Trade. By "gold " rouble was meant the theoretical quantity of gold that was contained in the Tsarist rouble and the *Chervonetz* rouble of 1924, namely 0·775 gramme. It was possible to deliver " gold " roubles in the form of foreign bank-notes, in jewellery and plate, in silver coins including Tsarist silver roubles and, of course, gold coins. *Torgsin* sold all sorts of things, including groceries, clothing, medicines and household necessities, of much better quality and in better selection than even the commercial shops ; in fact it stocked quite a considerable quantity of imported foreign goods especially in the drug and medicine department ; and the prices were not very much higher than one would have paid for similar articles in any capitalist shop. The real object of the *torgsin* shops was to extract from concealment the last reserves of foreign currency and precious metals remaining in the possession of the people. How much *torgsin* added to the foreign purchasing power of the Soviet Government during its life of about five years was not a matter on which the Government has even given any information, but a figure of £20 million has been conjectured. It was certainly more successful than the earlier methods of the G.P.U., which imprisoned and tortured suspected owners of gold and foreign currency till they surrendered or succumbed. Some persons, it was said, even sacrificed gold teeth in order to buy something at *torgsin*. In my own experience a Russian woman, wanting some medicine or tonic for her child, which was to be got only at *torgsin*, was offering to buy a pound note for R.100, the official rate of exchange being then between R.7 and R.8. In fact *torgsin* was responsible for a flourishing black market in foreign currency, for the only way most Russians could buy was by first purchasing pound notes or dollars directly or indirectly from foreigners. And since foreigners had very little use for roubles except for tram fares and suchlike petty expenses, the demand outran supply.

Torgsin was liquidated at the beginning of 1936, when rationing was abolished and all retail trade reorganised on ordinary normal principles. Probably the remaining valuables still possessed by the people were insignificant and the remittances from abroad to friends and relations left behind in Russia were rapidly falling off. These had been the largest single source of *torgsin* receipts. In any case the Soviet Government's urgent need for foreign exchange had relaxed and so the main reason for its existence had disappeared.

CHAPTER V

THE END OF RATIONING AND THE RISE OF STAKHANOVISM

RATIONING came to an end in 1935. At the beginning of the year bread and most cereal foods were removed from the list and by the end of the year all consumers' goods were being sold without restriction. Rationing was introduced in order to distribute a seriously inadequate supply of food and manufactured goods, so that everyone working for the State should get at least the minimum quantity necessary to existence. It was ended when the supply of consumers' goods was sufficient to allow everyone his minimum requirements without the necessity of restricting the consumption of that section of the community wealthy enough to buy practically all it could reasonably consume. Still, the supply was not large enough to permit of the old normal, or ration prices, being maintained. The great majority of the people had been compelled by rationing and the high commercial prices to restrict their consumption to much less than they desired to consume, and for which they could have paid had they been allowed unlimited purchases at the low ration prices. Therefore had rationing restrictions been suddenly removed without the compensating restriction of a rise in prices, the result would have been such an intense demand that stocks would have been sold out in no time. Consequently the authorities had to fix new prices at a level that would restrict demand to supply. These prices, obviously, had to be somewhere between the former ration prices and commercial prices. A few examples will show how the new prices compared with the ration and commercial prices valid immediately before derationing.

The single prices were roughly just about twice the former ration prices, but only about 57 per cent of the former commercial prices. Whether this raised or lowered

Commodity	Ration Prices	Commercial Prices	Single Prices in Moscow after Derationing
Per Kilo	R.	R.	R.
Rye bread .	0·50	1·50	1·00 *
Wheat . .	0·60	3·00	2·00 *
Sugar . .	2·00	10·00	4·20 †
Butter . .	8·00	27·00	15·00 †

* Decree of 7th December 1934.
† Decree of 25th September 1935.

the cost of living to the ordinary working man depended on what proportion of his needs he formerly satisfied by buying rations. Clearly the lower income groups must have depended much more on their rations than the wealthier section of the community and therefore derationing was so much the more to their disadvantage. In fact derationing probably reduced the cost of living to the highly paid official aristocracy while raising it to the ordinary workers. This was recognised by the Government, which decreed wage increases of about 10 per cent to the lower paid workers in order partly to compensate them for the higher cost of bread. With their usual inconsistency and repudiation of facts, the Bolshevik leaders tried to make out that after derationing the retail price level was actually lowered. They compared the new single prices with the former commercial prices, ignoring ration prices on the ground that these were artificial and bore no relation to the true market price. Since, however, even in the last year before derationing, about 70 per cent of total consumers' goods distributed to the population was sold at ration prices, this argument was too specious to deceive anyone.

With the introduction of the single price system [1] it became

[1] This does not mean that goods were sold at the same price throughout the whole country. Actually a number of price zones, ranging from four to eight for different commodities, were established in which prices varied more or less in accordance with cost of distribution. For example the price of bread in the far eastern and extreme northern provinces was nearly twice that in the grain-growing districts of European Russia, to cover the cost of transport of the grain, etc. This was partly compensated by the higher wages paid in these remote regions on account of the higher cost of living.

possible to calculate the cost of living with some accuracy. The actual retail prices mean nothing when converted into £ s. d. at the official rate of exchange. The only way to get an idea of the cost of goods to the consumer is to compare prices with income. In 1935 the average wage and salary income of all persons employed by the State, that is the great majority of the non-agricultural population, was R.2269, or approximately R.44 a week. At the official rate of exchange at the time R.44 was equivalent to about £7 : 15s., but the real purchasing power of the rouble was better expressed by 3d, in which case the average weekly income was just 11s. If we convert the rouble prices of some of the stable consumption goods at the same rate we shall then get a good idea of what the average Russian consumer could buy with his weekly wage.

The undermentioned prices were those actually charged in Moscow shops on 1st October 1935 :

Commodity	Price	Equivalent per Lb. at 3d. to the Rouble		
Per Kilo	R.	£.	s.	d.
Black rye bread . .	0·85	0	0	1·16
White wheat bread .	1·70	0	0	2·32
Sugar . . .	4·50	0	0	6·14
Laundry soap . .	3·00	0	0	4·1
Beef (average cut) .	9·90	0	1	1½
Pork . . .	10·60	0	1	2½
Lard . . .	22·00	0	2	6
Butter (best) . .	23·00	0	2	7½
Milk . . .	1·60 (litre)	0	0	6½ (quart)
Potatoes . . .	0·35	0	0	0·48
Carrots . . .	0·40	0	0	0·55
Man's suit (woollen) .	650·00	8	2	6
Man's overcoat (woollen)	700·00	8	15	0
Man's shoes (leather) .	165·00	2	0	5
Man's shirt (cotton) .	40·00	0	12	0
Woman's shoes . .	167·00	2	1	9
Cigarettes (25 pieces) .	2·50	0	0	6 per 20

The above food prices worked out in our own familiar pounds, shillings and pence per pound do not at first glance appear exorbitant, though the prices of clothing are certainly rather

75

high. But the point to be remembered is, how would these prices be regarded by a person with an income of 11s. a week, out of which has to come rent, rates, taxes, etc., as well. Prices had to be high to restrict demand and consumption to the available supplies and were far above the level necessary to cover all production and distribution costs, including a reasonable profit to the manufacturing and distributing enterprises. The difference was collected in the form of a turnover or sales tax, the yield from which was, and is, the source of between 70 and 80 per cent of the Soviet Government's budget revenue. Some idea of the extent to which the tax increased retail prices may be gained from the following :

In the Moscow price zone the turnover tax on rye flour was R.111 per quintal (100 kilos), the wholesale price before the tax was paid being R.60 ; the tax on wheat flour was R.113 and the wholesale price R.66·70. In these two cases the tax was almost twice the net wholesale price. On most commodities, however, the tax was a percentage of the turnover. In other words the retail price included the following amounts of tax :

Beef . . .	69·5 per cent
Pork . . .	63·6 ,,
Sugar . .	85·0 ,,
Soap . . .	70·0 ,,
Boots .	15·0 ,,
Woollen cloth .	50·5 ,,

From these figures it may be concluded that on the whole retail prices were at least doubled by the turnover tax.

The year 1935 contained another milestone in Soviet Russia's economic progress. During the night-shift 30th-31st August a Donetz coal miner, Alexei Stakhanov, begat a movement that spread like wildfire throughout the country and wrought big changes in the whole condition of labour. Stakhanov, having some natural intelligence, observed that he and his fellow coal-hewers used their pneumatic picks for a part only of the shift, because when they had cut out a quantity of coal they had to clear it away from the working face and do other subsidiary and essential but not actually productive tasks. He came to the conclusion that if he worked his pick the whole time, while other men were exclusively employed clearing away the coal, timbering and so on, such a team would achieve better results than if each individual performed all the different jobs in turn. When he was allowed to put his theory into practice he had a gratifying success, hewing over one hundred tons of coal, about fourteen times the normal output per shift. Actually the result was not so astounding as the Soviet press made out by ignoring his assistants and comparing it with his average when working single-handed. But even after dividing the total among three, the quantity per man was much above the average.

An interesting question, to which no authoritative answer has, to my knowledge, been given is, why had this idea of rationalising production not already been conceived by the technical heads of the mine ? Plausible answers are (1) that the qualified mining engineers in charge were too apathetic or too ignorant and unenterprising ; (2) that they were afraid to introduce such a novelty, which would certainly be unpopular among the mass of miners ; (3) that it was not originally Stakhanov's own idea, but that he was chosen to demonstrate it and assume responsibility for it. In the social conditions of the Soviet State it is appropriate that a new movement should be initiated by a working man ; for this redounds to the credit of the working classes. Also there is no doubt that Comrade Stakhanov and his methods have not inspired unqualified approval among the masses of industrial workers, because the Soviet Government has used the performances of Stakhanovites in general as excuses to lower piece rates. Had Stakhanovism been the offspring of a qualified engineer, one of the technical intelligentsia, it would have aroused even more effective hostility among the workers. Therefore the suggestion that Stakhanov was selected as the eponymous hero for diplomatic reasons is not altogether far-fetched.

Stakhanov's own performance was comparatively elementary. The same principle applied to factories becomes more complex, taking account as it must of the repetition of muscular movements and cutting out every superfluous motion, the supply of material and tools at the most con-

venient place at the right intervals and in the right position.
As a matter of fact the subject of industrial efficiency and
workers' fatigue was being studied back in 1930, if not before,
because one of the places of interest we should have visited in
Moscow that year was the Institute of Labour, which carried
on laboratory experiments in those subjects. Unfortunately,
it happened to be vacation time. Stakhanov was not so
much a pioneer of discovery as the first to put into actual
practice scientific principles of rationalisation and the
economic application of labour. However, the chief interest
to us in Stakhanovism is from the social rather than the
technical or scientific point of view. It is quite definitely a
means of speeding up production, that is procuring an
increased output per worker in a given time.

Immediately after Stakhanov had performed his historic
shift a campaign of bally-hoo broke out all over the Soviet
Union. Newspapers published full reports ; every speaker at
every meeting to discuss every conceivable subject had to
drag Stakhanov into his address. The Trade Unions gave
him their unqualified approval and Stalin condescended to
preside at the first congress of Stakhanovites in November
1935. The unanimity and vigour with which the propaganda machinery of the Government and Party took the
matter up leads to the suspicion that the whole business had
been prepared beforehand. This is all the more probable
since previous attempts by individuals to increase their
output and earnings by a great margin over the average had,
if anything, been discouraged by the authorities, who did not
altogether like the idea of one individual earning a very great
deal more than his fellows. In this respect they seemed to
possess a relic of trade-union sentiment, but the unequivocal
acquiescence in the principle of speeding up, which is the
essence of Stakhanovism, showed what an abyss had by then
come to separate the socialist concept of the relations between
capital and labour in capitalist countries and the Bolshevik
notion of labour in the Soviet State.

The Stakhanov system has some points in common with
Taylorism, in that it aims at increasing the productivity of
labour by scientific methods or rationalisation. The im-

portant difference between the two lies in the fact that Taylorism is imposed from above while Stakhanovism is (officially at least) based on the inventive genius of the workman himself. The Bolshevik would point out that Stakhanovism is the product of an educated working class, trained to think for itself and consciously devoting its abilities to increasing output for the common good. This presentation is somewhat vitiated by the system of progressive premiums, which enable those workers who increase their output much in excess of the fixed norm to earn extremely large incomes. Every industry has its own system of premiums, but all are based on the principle that the worker who exceeds his norm is paid a premium or bonus on the whole of his output. As a concrete example, according to an instruction of the Commissariat of Light Industry of the 4th October 1935, cotton textile operatives exceeding their standard task by 5 per cent or less were paid a bonus of 10 per cent on the whole of their output, and a bonus of 15 per cent if their standard task was exceeded by anything over 5 per cent. In some industries the premiums were still higher, with the result that a Stakhanovite worker was able to earn two, three or even four times the standard wage without increasing his output to anything like the same degree. It appears probable that the chief inducement to becoming a Stakhanovite is the prospect of increasing one's personal prosperity. Other perquisites include the best flats in factory tenement houses, holidays at a fashionable watering-place, trips to Moscow, tours in the Caucasus, etc., and, infrequently, the right to buy and run a private motor-car.

Like so many movements initiated and directed by the Bolshevik leaders, Stakhanovism was exaggerated into a stunt. Factories vied with one another in producing record-breaking Stakhanovites, who were put into training like athletes and, when the day arrived, were given machines specially overhauled and tuned up, while all the resources of the workshop were mobilised to ensure that everything ran smoothly and that the supply of material was not interrupted for a moment. In such circumstances the worker performed prodigious feats which reacted to the glory and repute of his factory and its directors, but which were of no positive value since during the period of preparation and the trial itself the rest of the work in the shop was apt to be neglected. Eventually this sort of abuse had to be severely suppressed. Nevertheless, it would be a mistake to suppose that the Stakhanov movement has been entirely barren of results in improving industrial efficiency. The question may be asked, Is any worker who exceeds his norm a Stakhanovite; if not, what is the precise definition of a Stakhanovite? I am doubtful whether a satisfactory answer has been given officially. Of course it is open to any worker to exceed his norm and earn the relevant bonus, but this does not automatically make him a Stakhanovite, which is an official title given to those who have applied for permission to compete and have passed the required standard. The candidate must not only exceed the daily task by a certain margin over a certain period, but must reach a relatively high standard of quality in his work, keep his machines or tools in good order, avoid waste of material, etc. Thus a Stakhanovite is a worker who has been proved by practical test to be a better workman in all respect than his fellows. He then, in most industries at least, is given special facilities for maintaining a higher standard than the ordinary workers. To what extent, if any, the Stakhanovite is officially entitled to the best machines, the most efficient assistants and the pick of the raw material I cannot say; but there is little doubt that as a general rule he does obtain these advantages. For one reason, he is a person of importance and certainly commands more consideration from the management than the ordinary worker.

Any capitalist employer who attempted to create a minority of highly paid and specially privileged workers corresponding to Stakhanovites would very soon get into trouble with the Trade Unions. He would be accused of trying to undermine the solidarity of the workers and attaching to himself a nucleus of boss's men by bribery. Stakhanovism in a capitalist economy would inevitably split the Trade Unions from top to bottom. In Soviet Russia, it is argued, the circumstances are radically different, because, firstly, the Trade Unions do not exist to protect the workers' interests against the employers ; secondly, it is to the benefit of the whole community that workers should increase their individual productivity to their utmost capacity. The answer to this is, Does the Soviet State genuinely represent the real interests of the whole community, that is to say, are the people and their leaders an indivisible corporation in which no factional or sectional conflict of interests can exist ; or is the State, personified by the leaders of the Communist Party and the members of the Government, as the owner of practically all the national capital, to be regarded in the same light as the employer class in a capitalist system ? This problem, which is fundamental to the truth or falsity of Soviet Communism, must be dealt with in a later chapter. Meanwhile we may quote Trotsky himself, who says in *The Revolution Betrayed* (page 122), "The local ruling groups eagerly seize the chance to escape from their isolation by allowing the upper stratum of the workers to participate in their privileges". It is improbable that the ruling bureaucracy actually planned the Stakhanov movement with the deliberate intention of broadening the base of that section of the population or increasing the number of groups whose interests were bound up in the maintenance of the economic *status quo*. In Stakhanovism, I am sure, the rulers saw above all a means of gingering up the industrial workers and improving productive efficiency : but quite possibly they came to see that the movement could also serve to secure the unquestioning support of a large part of the most industrious, intelligent and influential workers. It is significant that all the industrial workers elected to the Council of the Union (House of Assembly in the Soviet Parliament) in December 1937 were Stakhanovites.[1] Thus the representation of the working classes was in the hands of Stakhanovites, who might confidently be relied upon to give the Government their unqualified support. That Stakhanovites are not on the whole popular with the mass of average workers is almost

[1] At the sitting of the Council on 14th January 1938 the Chairman of the Mandates Commission, A. S. Shcherbakov, reported that of 546 deputies, 247 were workers and that all of these workers actually engaged in production were Stakhanovites.

certainly the case. The evidence of anti-communist journalists and writers must be accepted with great caution. Personally I always hesitate to believe their reports unless I can find corroboration in Soviet sources. But in this case the foreigners' statements that the Stakhanovites are regarded by the ordinary workers as blacklegs and renegades, are not without foundation. The Soviet press itself has frequently printed accounts of Stakhanovites being waylaid and beaten up, of hindrances to their work in the factory such as sabotage to their machines. Many workers have been brought to trial, convicted and sentenced for such crimes and even for the murder of Stakhanovites. The official version, of course, invariably is that the perpetrators were anti-social elements, Trotskyist wreckers or agents of foreign governments. The same charges are made against all who show any symptoms of dissatisfaction and insubordination. The implication is that in the Soviet State every honest worker must *ex hypothesi* be happy and contented.

CHAPTER VI

THE SOVIET CONSTITUTION

BEFORE discussing current labour legislation and the conditions of the worker we should pay some attention to the Constitution of the U.S.S.R., commonly known as the Stalin Constitution, which was adopted at an extraordinary congress of Soviets on the 5th December 1936. The Bolsheviks say that it is the most democratic constitution in the world.

In Chapter I the Constitution declares that the U.S.S.R. is a Socialist State of Workers and Peasants and that all power belongs to the toilers as represented by their Soviet of Deputies. The principle of Socialism is summed up in two phrases, " He who does not work, neither shall he eat " and " From each according to his ability, to each according to the work performed ". . . . Thus all able-bodied citizens are under an obligation to work ; at the same time they have the right to work and earn wages. Rather curiously the right to work is said to be ensured by the socialist organisation of the country's economy and by the abolition of unemployment, but it is not specifically laid down that the Government is obliged to find work for everyone. In practice this means that in existing circumstances the demand for labour is great enough to absorb all the supply, but that the worker must find a job himself, since there are no longer any labour exchanges. With the right to work goes the right to rest and leisure, which is ensured by the seven-hour day for the great majority of workers (it may be noted here that on 26th June 1940 the seven-hour day was cancelled and replaced by an eight-hour day) and by the institution of annual holidays with pay and the provision of sanatoria, rest homes and clubs. When incapacitated by old age or sickness the worker has the right to maintenance.

Education is the right of every citizen and is ensured by universal and compulsory elementary education and by all education up to the highest being free of charge, while state bursaries are available for the overwhelming majority of students attending the universities and technical colleges. (From 1st September 1940 fees were instituted for students in the higher classes of secondary schools and in all universities and higher educational institutions. From 1st November state bursaries were abolished, except for grants or scholarships to students attaining a high standard in examinations.)

In Article 125 of the Constitution citizens have the legal right to freedom of speech, freedom of the press, freedom of assembly and of holding mass meetings and freedom of street processions and demonstrations. The notion that a citizen of the U.S.S.R. can say what he likes or print what he likes is absurd. It is equally absurd to think that any body of citizens can hold a public meeting or a street procession on their own initiative. Actually the article does not mean, nor is there any pretence that it means, what it apparently says. The argument is, more or less, that freedom of speech, etc., is to be applied collectively ; for instance the press reflects the views and policy of the whole nation, or community, whose voice is that of its leaders. I must confess that I do not fully grasp the whole train of reasoning, but so far as I understand it the principle is somewhat as follows : there are no classes in the U.S.S.R., hence no conflicting group interests ; from this it follows that the collective will of the people is not a majority decision, but the spontaneous and single intent of a homogeneous and united people expressed through their chosen leaders. Thus if we can imagine that the Soviet leaders are identical in some mystical way with the mind and intellect of the Russian people, it becomes more or less understandable that the citizens themselves enjoy the freedoms stated in the Constitution. It is difficult to imagine a political concept which merges the individual so completely in the mass that the distinction between the rights of the individual and the rights of the community is lost. But in a way we can, I think, begin to appreciate this doctrine if we consider the behaviour of the original Revolutionaries. So far as I know neither Lenin nor Trotsky nor any of the outstanding figures of those days ever expressed, in speech, writing or

84

deed, their sincere sympathy or commiseration with the individual victim of oppression. They were anything but philanthropists in the more specific and concrete sense ; they showed no feelings of common humanity, but were willing to sacrifice the well-being and happiness of millions in further-ance of their own ideas. Undoubtedly they were sincere in their indignation against what they called the capitalist exploitation and victimisation of the workers ; and were sincere in their intention to emancipate the working masses and improve their conditions of living. But they obviously regarded the masses, not as an agglomeration of individuals, but as an abstract whole. The leaders of to-day have been compelled by the course of Soviet history to recognise that the individual must be considered apart from the group ; for instance, the principle of treating the brigade as a unit in education, in examinations, in labour and in payment of wages had to be abandoned and attempts to induce the people to live in communes never had much success. Making a virtue of necessity, the Bolsheviks now stress family life in the private home as the ideal state, with which the private ownership of the means of living is naturally associated. But though the leaders have had to surrender their original designs for complete collective living, they adhere to their ideas of the collective spiritual life. Any member of the community who cannot conscientiously subscribe to the fundamental truths of Bolshevism is abnormal and possesses no legal right of nonconformity. Therefore the citizens of the Soviet Union are really the freest community in the world, because they have no desire to do anything which is for-bidden. Those who might abuse their freedom do not count, because the very fact of wanting to do that which is for-bidden is proof that they are not fit to enjoy Soviet freedom. One finds this concept running through the writings of Soviet proselytes such as the Webbs, who in their great work on Soviet Communism clearly indicate that in their opinion the prisoners in G.P.U. labour camps deserve their fate for refusing to accept the truths of Communism.

The Constitution instituted as the Highest Organ of State Power the Supreme Soviet of the U.S.S.R. (a sort of legislative assembly) consisting of two chambers, the Soviet of the Union and the Soviet of Nationalities. The first consists of deputies elected by the whole body of citizens in the proportion of one deputy for every 300,000 of population ; the second, of deputies elected by the citizens of each republic and autonomous national territory. Candidates for each chamber may be nominated by any public organisation or society of toilers such as Trade Unions, co-operative societies, party organisations and cultural societies, which includes sporting and athletic clubs. Originally it was intended, or at least allowed to be assumed, that any number of candidates might be nominated for a constituency according to the number of societies, clubs and organisations that were inspired to put forward a candidate ; and, as a natural consequence, that the candidates would hold election meetings at which to expound their views to the electors. But in practice the elections were conducted quite differently. In each constituency a meeting of electors was arranged by the local Party committee at which a single official candidate was announced. As a matter of form a few electors were put up to second the nomination with eulogies of the candidate, but no criticism much less an opposition candidate was tolerated. In fact all the deputies to both chambers were officially pre-selected Party candidates.

For some reason the farce of elections is carried through. The only reason why the candidates are not announced as returned unopposed seems to be the Government's notion that a 100 per cent vote in favour of its candidates in some way impresses foreign opinion with the solidarity of its popular support. Of course it has precisely the opposite result, because, it is argued, the Government fears to allow opposition candidates lest it should give the electors an opportunity of hinting at disagreement with government policy. A large proportion of deputies are government servants, Party officials and others having sound material reasons of self-interest for supporting the Government ; of the genuine workers the majority are Stakhanovites or " order-bearers " (*i.e.* persons decorated for service to the State) and therefore presumably politically reliable, for nobody under the slightest suspicion of heterodoxy would be allowed to become a Stakhanovite or receive a decoration.

The idea that the Supreme Council would initiate legislation or even be allowed to debate government measures soon proved baseless. At the sessions, which are held twice a year and last for the inside of a week, the Government presents for ratification the laws made since the last session and which have, of course, already been put into effect. This is a mere formality and is invariably unanimous. Changes in the list of People's Commissars and Military Commanders are announced and the appointments formally and unanimously confirmed. Now and then the Government presents a bill for a new law, apparently just to give the Assembly the verisimilitude of a consultative if not of a legislative body. A study of the press reports of the proceedings discloses that the speeches of members invariably consist of uncritical support for the Government's measure ; most speakers in practice confine themselves to explaining how much the measure will benefit their own particular district. When the labour Law of 28th December 1938 (which made insurance benefits dependent on the length of time the worker had been in the same job, reduced maternity grants to female workers and re-stated the rule of dismissal for one day's absence from work without excuse) came up for ratification at the next session of the Supreme Council, not one word of criticism was uttered, in spite of the fact that the measure undoubtedly infringed the liberty of honest and industrious workers, though primarily aimed at the lazy and unreliable.

The Constitution provides that no person may be placed under arrest except by decision of the court or with the sanction of a procurator ; that the homes of citizens and the secrecy of their correspondence are inviolable. So far as inviolability of the person is concerned, it is possible that the G.P.U. obtains a warrant from a procurator before effecting an arrest, but there is no doubt whatever that, after the Constitution was formally adopted and came into effect, people were arrested and disappeared just as before. Between nominations of candidates for the first Supreme Soviet and the elections in December 1937 some thirty or forty nominees

disappeared without explanation and were replaced by
others, without so far as could be ascertained any pretence
to explain their withdrawal to the electors or to submit
the new candidates to a nomination meeting. Among those
who thus disappeared were several prominent men such as
Kossior and Chubar, both members of the *Politbureau*. Of
course it is possible that the proper formalities leading to
their arrest were carried out in secret ; it is certain at least
that no proceedings anterior or subsequent to their arrest
were made public. But even if their arrests were not literally
illegal according to Article 127 of the Constitution, they
would seem to have infringed Article 52, which lays down
that no member of the Supreme Soviet may be arrested without the consent of the Supreme Soviet or of the Presidium of
the Supreme Soviet. Since the candidates were not opposed,
they certainly had the right to consider themselves returned
and to be to all intents and purposes already members of the
Supreme Soviet. But there is no record of the question of
their arrests having been mentioned *ex post facto* at any
meeting of the Supreme Soviet.

Article 103 provides that all court cases shall be tried with
the assistance of people's assessors, except in cases provided
for by law. Assessors, of whom two sit on the bench with
the full-time professional judge or magistrate, are laymen
combining the functions of a jury and advisers to the judge.
Verdicts are arrived at by a majority vote of the judge and
the two assessors. On 10th August 1940 a decree was issued
that, in cases of workers being tried for unauthorised absence
from work or illegally leaving their employment, the court
shall sit without assessors. That is, the accused workman is
tried and sentenced by the official judge alone. The reason of
this decree was not explained, but in all probability it was
found that the lay assessors, themselves no doubt workmen,
were apt to take too lenient a view of this sort of lapse. The
point to be noted, however, is that if a decree issued by the
Government without any sort of check or control can over-
ride principles specifically laid down by the Constitution, the
Constitution itself is not worth much. Thus, when Article
111 provides that all court cases are heard in public, unless

otherwise provided for by law, it would, apparently, suffice
for the Government to issue an *ad hoc* decree that a certain
trial shall be heard *in camera*, if for some reason this is
desired.

The right of the Government to issue decrees with the
force of law on its own authority is dubious. The Constitution provides for a Presidium, or permanent commission, of
the Supreme Council which has the right to interpret existing
laws and to promulgate decrees, while the Government, that
is the Council of People's Commissars, has the right to issue
orders which must, however, be approved by the Presidium.
There may be some uncertainty about the exact technical
distinction between an order of the Council of People's
Commissars and a law of the Soviet Union. But it would
surely seem that the measure of 28th December 1938, whose
full official title was " A Decree of the Council of People's
Commissars of the U.S.S.R., of the Central Committee of the
Communist Party and of the All-Union Council of Trade
Unions, concerning Measures for regulating Labour Discipline, for improving the Practice of State Social Insurance and
for combating Abuses in this Matter " was decidedly of the
nature of a law. It introduced an entirely new principle,
namely, that a workman's sickness benefit depended on the
length of time he had served in one employment. This
clearly revoked the worker's previous right to full benefit
irrespective of the number of times he had changed his job in a
given period. Yet the decree was issued with the full force of
law over the signatures of Molotov, as President of the
Council of People's Commissars ; Stalin, as Secretary of the
Central Committee of the Communist Party ; and Shvernik,
as Secretary of the All-Union Council of Trade Unions, whose
position as a legislative organ is, to say the least, extremely
ambiguous.[1] The publication of this decree in the official
bulletin of laws omitted all reference to the Presidium of the
Supreme Council, to which, presumably, the measure w

[1] The conjunction of the Soviet counterpart of the T.U.C. with the
Government and the Communist Party in legislation definitely curtailing
the rights of the workers might well be brought to the notice of certain
British Socialists who would like to see the Soviet organisation admitted
to the International Federation of Trades Unions.

not submitted. This is perhaps not so surprising when we discover that income tax rates may be drawn up by the Commissariat of Finance and published by it as a circular without, apparently, the Presidium, much less the Supreme Council itself, having the opportunity to discuss the matter.

In theory legislation may be initiated only by the President or a member of the Supreme Council, by any Commissariat or State Department in matters within its own sphere of activity, and by the Permanent Commissions of Legislative Proposals (*i.e.* general legislation), the Budget, and Foreign Affairs, each in its own sphere. These Commissions are principally drafting bureaus ; they examine, and if necessary amend, proposed laws and reports on them to the Supreme Soviet and, under instructions from the Supreme Soviet or the Presidium, draft bills. Though they have the technical right of initiating legislation on their own account, it may be presumed that they seldom if ever exercise the right. It is also extremely unlikely that an ordinary deputy to the Supreme Soviet would have the temerity to propose a private member's bill. In actual practice there is no doubt but that all legislation is directly or indirectly initiated by the Council of People's Commissars, which in turn takes its orders from the Central Committee of the Communist Party. And, so far as can be gathered, the decision whether a new measure is in the nature of a law requiring formal adoption by the Supreme Soviet, or may be treated as a government order or decree (*postanovlenie*) and therefore need only be promulgated, rests with the Central Committee or the still more paramount *Politbureau*.

CHAPTER VII

RECENT LABOUR LEGISLATION

IT is easy enough to criticise Soviet Democracy if we assume
that the Bolsheviks give the same sense to the word as we do.
But the Bolshevik notion of social freedom is quite different
from ours. It has always struck me as somewhat arbitrary
and as leading to false conclusions to try to pin the Russians
down to our conventional meaning of certain abstract terms
and then accuse them of failing to act up to their principles.
We ought, first of all, to try to find out exactly what the
Bolsheviks mean by these foreign words they have appropriated. As a case in point, a very favourite adjective applied
to Stalin is " genial " (Russian *genialny*). But when a
Bolshevik speaks of " our beloved and genial Leader " he
does not imply that Stalin is good company or a cheerful
companion, but that he is a man of genius.

When we speak of Democracy we mean government by
all classes for the benefit of all classes. But the interests of
all classes are not identical in all respects and compromises
have to be made. The Bolsheviks, not altogether without
reason, point out that in a society composed of classes some
classes will inevitably secure more influence than they are
entitled to by numerical proportions. For instance the
proprietor class, by reason of its wealth, can command the
material, labour and brains necessary for the production of
newspapers, books and journals, and thus possesses an
unfair advantage over the numerically superior working
classes in expounding its views and philosophy ; in other
words the employer class controls a far greater propaganda
power than the employee class. So, argue the Bolsheviks,
though all persons are legally and theoretically equal in so-
called democratic bourgeois States, in fact there exists a great
deal of inequality. In the Soviet Union classes have been
abolished, all are equal in fact as well as in theory because

wealth confers no privileges nor advantages. It is true that the citizens of the Soviet Union may be grouped as manual workers, peasants and brain workers, but between these groups there is no conflict of interest. From this it follows that the administration of the country cannot favour one class against another. Everyone is a toiler in his own sphere and it is the toilers that are in power. This postulates that the Government is truly popular and governs with the unanimous consent and approval of the people. In Soviet language democracy does not mean a political system in which everyone is entitled to his own opinion or to advocate his own particular views. What it does denote is a system in which all must conform to the rules laid down by the State, which is the incarnation of the collective will of the people. No law can be an undemocratic measure, even though it may restrict the liberty of individuals, because it has *ex hypothesi* been passed with the full consent and approval of the whole population for the common good.

If we denounce recent Soviet labour laws as harsh, arbitrary and undemocratic, we are judging them by our own standards, forgetting that they are really an act of self-discipline voluntarily and unanimously ordained by the very people they affect. That, of course, is the official Bolshevik exposition. We may point out that if the whole population were imbued with the true democratic spirit, in the Bolshevik sense, laws to enforce labour discipline would be unnecessary because everybody would conform to the rules laid down without compulsion. If therefore, it is necessary to compel people to observe the rules, it must be deduced that an appreciable minority is not democratically minded ; in other words, is in disagreement with the majority. Can it then be affirmed that laws are made with the complete and unanimous consent of the whole population ? The Bolsheviks' answer, the only answer that they can give, is that a minority of the people is still tainted with bourgeois ideas and must be compelled to fall into line with the majority. But this does not really invalidate their claim that Soviet laws are made for the people by the unanimous consent of the people, because it takes time to complete the transformation of a capitalist society into a socialist society, and during the interval there must inevitably be a regularly diminishing minority of dissentients.

By bourgeois ideas is meant the worker's predilection for obtaining the maximum remuneration for his toil, which leads him to leave one job for another if the second offers better pay and prospects. To this desire for the maximum return for his labour the Russian adds a natural inclination for change and movement, inherited from his nomadic ancestors. The liquidity of labour is mainly due to conditions of employment, which vary materially between district and district and between enterprise and enterprise, but also to the vagrant instincts of the Russian people. Certain of the more pronounced anti-socialist critics of the Soviet system have compared the Bolsheviks' treatment of the workers and peasants with the former serfdom. Without going so far as to suggest any similarity between the lot of the Soviet worker and the industrial serf of the eighteenth and early nineteenth centuries, I think there is an historic parallel between the restrictions on the free movement of the Soviet worker and the origin of serfdom. Serfdom was not the original state of the Russian peasant. It began in a comparatively mild way in the sixteenth century with regulations to hinder peasants from leaving the land they occupied under the *Boyars*. The peasant was not legally and permanently bound to the land ; he was rather in the position of a tenant who might change his landlord only at a certain time of year, after the harvest, and then only if he was free of debt to his then landlord. Since few peasants possessed any capital and were indebted to their landlords for seed, tools and possibly draught animals, this provision was a fairly effective restriction on peasant wanderings. During that period of Russian history the *Boyars* (roughly the equivalent of feudal barons) were bound to serve the ruling prince (after 1547 the Tsar), this service consisting chiefly of providing an armed force for war. In return the *Boyar* received a grant of land, or rather the right to tax the agricultural population occupying it. In practice the peasants had to surrender part of their produce to the landlord. If the peasants left the land, the landlord's revenue went too ; and if one landlord was particularly severe in his demands, his peasants would be inclined to leave him for another who was less rapacious. Later, after the Tartar power had been broken, dissatisfied peasants absconded to the frontiers of South and South-east Russia and formed free communities beyond the reach of landlords. These communities adopted the Tartar term *Kazak,* which signifies something like " free adventurer " and which we have corrupted into Cossack. As peasants became more and more addicted to running away, the laws to prevent it became stricter. Eventually, at the height of Russia's industrial development in the eighteenth century, serfdom became almost the same thing as slavery. The state of bondedness was inherited by the descendants of serfs, who were absolutely bound to the land and whose labour was completely at the disposal of their landlord. In the reign of Peter I whole villages of serfs were set to work in factories making munitions for that sovereign's wars. In fact the origin of diverting serf labour from agriculture to industry was the growing need for factory-produced arms and munitions as the science and appliances of warfare developed.

Thus serfdom started as a measure to ensure the efficiency of the country's military forces and developed, both in degree and magnitude, *pari passu* with the size of armies and their technical equipment. Of course, serf-owners did not stop at employing their serfs' labour directly or indirectly for maintaining the country's military strength. When their compulsory unpaid service to the State was dispensed with in 1762 the nobles did not free their serfs, on the contrary they began to exploit them even more ruthlessly for their own benefit and enrichment (see Chapter I).

Soviet legislation to keep the workers to their jobs and to tighten up factory discipline has shown a marked growth, both in volume and severity, as the prospects of the U.S.S.R. becoming involved in war have increased. When the First Five-Year Plan was inaugurated the Soviet leaders gave the defence of the country against the capitalist world as one of the chief reasons for the rapid development of industry. Whether or no they genuinely expected an early aggression against the Communist Fatherland is hard to say. But at least it was ostensibly the need to create the necessary heavy industries as the foundation of an armament industry, that inspired the factory laws of the early thirties. In fact these laws were not particularly drastic, compared with those of 1938 to 1940, or when they appeared severe, such as the law prescribing instant dismissal for one day's absence from work without excuse, they were more or less a dead letter. In 1938 war began to look imminent and in December the Soviet Government reintroduced labour books and issued the law reducing insurance benefits to workers who had changed their jobs within a certain period.

In May 1939 a Law was passed to limit the private enter-prise of *kolhozniki* to the legal maximum plots and number of animals (a very large number of collective farms had come to allow their members a great deal of latitude in regard to their private activities), making compulsory a certain minimum number of days' work per year on the collective farm (many *kolhozniki* had grown into the habit of devoting nearly all their time to their private affairs), and compelling *kolhozniki* living in outlying homesteads to dismantle their homes and concentrate them in village settlements.

A Law of 28th June 1940 extended the industrial working day from 7 hours to 8 hours, revoked the 6-day week and reinstated the 7-day week with Sundays as rest days. Workers were expressly forbidden to leave their employment without authority, the penalty being " correctional labour " for 6 months with a 25 per cent cut in wages.

A decree of 19th October conferred upon the People's Commissars at the head of industrial Commissariats the power to transfer workers and their families from one part of the Union to another. And a Law of 2nd October provided for the compulsory calling-up and training for industry of about a million boys a year between the ages of 14 and 17. When trained these boys will be at the complete disposal of the Government and will have to work for four years wherever sent. Another decree of the same date abolished free educa-tion in higher educational institutions.

All these laws restrict the citizens' freedom of activity

and movement and are to a greater or less extent due to the speed-up of industry in general and the armament industry in particular. Even the law concerning the private activities of *kolhozniki* was partly intended to increase the supply of foodstuffs and raw material at the disposal of the Government for supplying the needs of the ever-increasing industrial population.

The following are summaries of the main provisions of recent measures affecting the industrial workers.

Labour-Books. From 15th January 1939 all workers and employees in state and co-operative enterprises and institutions have had to possess labour-books. These contain the following particulars of the holder : name, age, educational standard, profession ; also particulars of his employment (grade, etc.), dates of changing employment and reasons for leaving or dismissal and pay and emoluments received.

Applicants for employment have to present their labour-books to the management of an enterprise as a prerequisite to engagement. After engagement the worker's labour-book is retained by the management and handed back with the appropriate endorsements only when the worker leaves.

It may be questioned whether these labour-books exerted much restraint on the worker who was seized by an impulse for a change. Even if the man just deserted without the formality of asking for the return of his labour-book, he would probably not find much difficulty in getting a job elsewhere ; but judging by press reports of prosecutions for indiscipline (published as a warning to others), it seems that the worker who wanted a change and had no acceptable excuse merely qualified for dismissal by omitting to turn up for work one day. This often resulted in the rather Gilbertian situation of the worker demanding dismissal as his right, while his manager did his best to overlook the lapse ! The endorsement in his labour-book did not worry the man. All he wanted was to get it back. No manager would refuse to take him on because of his dismissal, for he himself was losing hands in the same way and had to replace them somehow or other. In fact the circulation of workers from one job to another and not infrequently back to the old one after trying out several others became more or less an understood thing.

The Law of 28th December 1938. Factory managements and employers generally must rigidly observe the law prescribing prompt dismissal of any worker or employee missing a day's work without good cause. Penalties are incurred by those clocking in late, knocking off before time, spending too long over meals and idling during working hours. If such an offence is repeated three times in a month or four times in two months, the penalty is dismissal. These regulations played directly into the hands of restless workers, who just cannot stand the monotony of one job for long.

The main clauses of this law, however, concern the relation of insurance benefits with continuity in one job. In the majority of industries the worker, being a member of a Trade Union, is entitled to full relief for temporary incapacity only when he has been six years in his employment (further details will be found in Chapter XIII in the section devoted to Social Insurance).

The annual vacation cannot be taken before eleven months' employment in the same enterprise. Previously leave was granted after five and a half months' service, which, if a man took his holiday immediately he qualified for it and then quitted his job, enabled him to get two holidays in twelve months, or a little more. And the duration of maternity allowances to women workers was reduced.

This law seems to have had only a limited success in keeping workers to their jobs. The liquidity of labour was not very materially checked and, according to Soviet newspaper articles, one reason was that managers were too lenient or too lax in enforcing the regulations.

Oddly enough, but quite consistently with Soviet practice, the day before the above law was published the Government decreed three orders or distinctions for workers of great ability or industry. Of these the highest was the order of " Hero of Socialist Toil " which carried with it double pay or salary. The second was the order of " Prowess in Labour " which entitled the holder to a medal, R.10 a month and unlimited free tram rides throughout the U.S.S.R. The third was the order of " Excellence in Labour " with a medal, R.5 a month and tram rides.

The Law of 26th June 1940. By this law the 7-hour day was abrogated and an 8-hour day substituted. In industries in which, owing to the arduous nature of the work, the working day was 6 hours, a 7-hour day was decreed. At the same time the 6-day week, with rest days on the 6th, 12th, 18th, 24th and last day of the month, was abolished and the universal 7-day week with Sunday rest days was restored. In working hours these changes meant that the Soviet worker had in future to toil 6 days or 48 hours out of 7 days instead of 5 days or 35 hours out of 6 days. In a month of 30 days the hours of work under the new law amount to 200 or 208, according to whether the period includes 4 or 5 Sundays, compared with 175 hours under the old system. In 12 months the Soviet worker now works about 350 hours more than formerly. It should be noted that the new week does not include a Saturday half-holiday. A subsidiary decree laid down that wages should not be increased on account of the longer working day, while piece rates should be adjusted in order that the worker should not earn more by the extra hour worked. Briefly, the Soviet Government now gets about 7 weeks' work from every worker for nothing.

The 7-day week has other implications. For one thing it brings the Soviet Union back into line with the rest of the world and restores the meaning of the days of the week. Under the 6-day week nobody ever knew what day of the week it was ; appointments and engagements were always made for a certain date.

Now it again becomes possible to arrange that certain things, say wage payments, shall take place on a certain day in every week. Secondly, it brings the town back into line with the country, where the conservative peasantry persisted in sticking to the old order. This is a genuine gain because, for instance, the *kolhozniki* can now relate market day in the neighbouring town to a fixed day in their own calendar instead of having it fall on different days each week. Thirdly, it brings the church and secular week into line again. The Russian Church, which has survived to quite a considerable extent, refused to alter its calendar, with the result that those people who tried to keep up the observance of Sundays were faced with the difficulty that only once in seven weeks did Sunday coincide with a rest day.

The law also included more stringent provisions against job quitters. In fact it went to the limit and made quitting a job without special permission definitely illegal and punishable. Meanwhile to prevent employers releasing workers on trumped-up excuses, it was laid down that release from a job might be granted only if the worker became physically unfit to continue his existing work, if the worker had obtained admission to an educational institution for special study, or of course, if he were transferred to another enterprise by higher authority. The penalty for quitting a job was two to four months' imprisonment. The law requiring dismissal for absence from duty without due cause was revoked and a penalty of six months' correctional labour with a 25 per cent cut in wages was substituted. Managers refraining from reporting delinquent workers to the authorities or who engaged workers having quitted their previous employment without permission were made responsible before the courts ; and as a matter of record a series of prosecutions of managers actually ensued, as a result of which some were degraded and some sentenced to terms of imprisonment.

It was obvious from studying newspaper articles and reports of trials of both workers and managers that all previous laws for inculcating factory discipline had been treated very lightly. I think there were two main reasons for this : one certainly was the shortage of reliable and skilled labour which made every factory manager loth to dismiss any but his most troublesome, idle or useless hands ; the other was the relic of former days when the worker was allowed and even encouraged to consider himself a better man than his master. I have already mentioned the deterioration of discipline that followed the great purge. It must take some time to restore the authority and prestige of the manager class. Also, it must be remembered, a very large proportion of heads of enterprises are *vydvizhentsi*, that is men promoted from the ranks, or young men pitched into responsible posts immediately after completing their technical training and necessarily lacking in experience and self-confidence. Besides this, the heads of enterprises themselves have been placed in a rather equivocal position. They are under continual pressure to fulfil or over-fulfil their production plans. At the same time they are under the obligation to maintain strict factory discipline, and this means that, were they to dismiss every worker, or report them to the authorities for a technical breach of discipline according to the letter of the law, they would lose a lot of labour not easily replaced ; and it would certainly tend to cause a good deal of unrest and disorganisation in the works apart from the difficulty of replacing lost workmen and training new hands.

The new law provides that workers convicted of absenteeism shall undergo six months' correctional labour. I believe that this means that they are confined in barracks or something of the sort and marched to and from work under armed guard. When being shown over works I have seen gangs of workers being marched to work under guard, and an old factory foreman I once met in a Soviet train told me how refractory workers were put in the *isolator* and compelled to work more or less like prisoners. This was before the law under discussion was decreed, but the system of correctional labour is by no means new and I do not suppose the technique has been changed. But the point I wish to make is that, firstly, a man performing correctional labour with reduced wages (most of which is no doubt deducted for his keep in the *isolator*) is certainly not going to work as hard or as efficiently as he did when free, and, secondly, the presence of these prisoners working alongside the free workers is scarcely likely to improve the work of the latter. Thus the unfortunate manager has to strike a balance between running his factory as efficiently as possible and fulfilling his Plan, and maintaining discipline according to the strict letter of the law.

While on the subject of managers it may not be out of place to mention a decree of 10th July 1940, which provided that the production of poor quality, unfinished or

non-standard goods should be laid to the responsibility of
factory managers and chief engineers and dealt with as a
crime tantamount to wrecking. The penalty upon conviction is from five to eight years' imprisonment. It was
added that bad-quality production and low labour discipline
always went together and that " flyers " (*i.e.* workers continually going from job to job) were responsible for most of
the spoiled production. A number of trials were reported
in the press with sentences of five, six and eight years'
imprisonment, and undoubtedly a lot more went unreported.

Another trial to which managers are often subjected is
interference from local Party organisations. The eighteenth
Congress of the Communist Party in March 1939 conferred
upon primary Party organisations the right to supervise the
activities of the managers of productive enterprises. As a
consequence District Party Committees, consisting generally
of hard-boiled but seldom of very intelligent or technically
competent young Communists, began to interfere with the
activities of managers and in the internal affairs of their
enterprises. In some cases local Party committees even dismissed managers. To efficient and energetic heads such
interference was intolerable, and cases are on record of
managers applying to their Commissariat to be relieved of
their posts on account of the difficulties thus created. At
the Plenary Session of the Central Committee of the Party
in July 1940 it was agreed that local Party organs had
assumed powers it was never intended they should have and
that their functions should be confined to pointing out mistakes and helping to overcome difficulties. Since the type
of young Communist found in local Party committees enjoys
nothing so much as dictating to others and meddling in
matters of which he is ignorant, it is doubtful whether anything short of a legal circumscription of Party organs'
powers will have much effect.

State Labour Reserves. On 2nd October 1940 several
decrees were issued introducing conscription of labour. The
chief measures, after noting that an annual contingent of
800,000 to 1,000,000 recruits are needed in industry, laid
down rules for the annual conscription of about this number

of boys between the ages of 14 and 17 for training in industry and transport. Boys between 14 and 15 are drafted into technical schools for a two-years course and boys between 16 and 17 into training establishments giving a six-months course. I shall deal with the subject in detail in the chapter on education. At the moment the point to be made is that the required number of boys are to be obtained by a compulsory levy from the urban and rural population. Collective farms have to provide four boys for every hundred members of both sexes between the ages of 14 and 55, while the towns' contingent is to be fixed annually by the Council of People's Commissars. During their training the boys will be maintained at the expense of the State and afterwards ,they will be at the complete disposal of the Government for four years, having to work in the enterprise and at the job to which they are allotted. During this period they will receive the standard rate of wages for the work they perform. After the four years' service and after completing their military service they will be at liberty to choose their own career.

On the face of it this law imposes a very serious restriction on the liberty of the individual ; but it must be remembered that in the Soviet Union everybody must work to live, and it makes little difference to the young citizen whether he finds his own niche after leaving school or has it found for him by the State. In fact, if he is conscripted it will probably save him a good deal of trouble and possibly some disappointments. A lot depends, of course, on how the scheme is carried out, but there is no reason to imagine that it will impose any hardship. In practice it is quite likely that the number of volunteers will exceed the number of vacancies, for it looks as though boys taken for the labour reserve will have the best chances, if not the only chances, of setting their feet on the ladder of a sound industrial career. For the factory schools and training establishments formerly run by the heavy industry Commissariats are being taken over by the Government and will in future be available only to the boys selected for the scheme.

It is perhaps worth noting that the law applies only to boys. Formerly, when entry into factory schools, etc., was on a voluntary basis, the pupils consisted of girls as well as boys, and those who had not completed their courses when the schools were transferred to the Chief Administration of Labour Reserves were to be allowed to continue their studies. Apparently the intention was to confine the scheme exclusively to boys, but the Government subsequently changed its mind to the extent of permitting a certain number of girls to volunteer.

Law of 19th October 1940. This empowered Commissariats to compel the transfer of engineers, technicians, office employees and skilled workers to any enterprise or district where they are needed. It was stated that the success of socialist construction could no longer be secured on a voluntary basis and that the planned distribution of staffs on a basis of compulsion must be accepted in industrial life. This law was aimed chiefly at those technical workers who pull every string to get posts in the large towns, Moscow by preference, and show a strong preference for working in a comfortable office rather than in the actual mine, works or factory.

CHAPTER VIII

WAGES AND STANDARD TASKS

SOVIET wages are based upon a standard task or norm. In factories this will naturally be the production of so many units of output, but obviously this cannot apply to every kind of job. In retail trade, for example, the norm will be a sales turnover measured in money. Even clerks in offices have a norm to perform, upon the fulfilment of which their salaries depend. The fixing of these norms is the job of *normirovshchiki*, who perform much the same functions as rate-fixers in British works. For a description of their work I cannot do better than give a free translation of a passage in *Labour in the Socialist Community* :

In the Soviet Union the technique of determining standard tasks has nothing in common with the refined capitalist brutality.[1] In our enterprises norm-fixing is carried out not to the detriment of the worker, but in his interests. The Soviet rate-fixer relies on the experience of the foremost workers, whom he consults and whose opinions he heeds. The norm should be fixed at about midway between the performance of the foremost workers or Stakhanovites and that of the ordinary average worker. A revision of the norm should be undertaken whenever there is a change in the technical processes of production, or whenever the norm is rendered obsolete by the introduction of new methods of work, and should take place, as a rule, at least once a year.

[1] It is a cardinal article in the communist faith that in no circumstances can a capitalist employer ever behave otherwise than as a ruthless exploiter. If the workers in a capitalist State receive undeniably good wages and enjoy free social services, it is because (a) the workers themselves have extorted these concessions from unwilling and inimical employers, or (b) the employers have for their own ends improved the workers' conditions on the same principle that it pays to keep a beast of burden well fed and in good condition. Hence the extraordinary distortions of fact and misrepresentations of motive always found in Soviet references to conditions elsewhere.

The technique of norm-fixing consists of three stages :

(1) The rate-fixer must first carefully study various workers at their work and determine chronometrically (by stopwatch) the time taken to perform given operations :

(2) Next, having arrived at results by experiment and determined the actual capacity of the machinery, he should draw up a new and correct system of work, and fix the norm of output and the time to be taken in completing the task :

(3) Finally, he must inculcate the new arrangement of work by practical demonstration, instructing the workers in the correct methods, showing them which actions to perform and which movements are superfluous.

The above is a counsel of perfection which it is admitted is seldom realised. A rate-fixer must be a very skilled person with considerable scientific attainments. It would be difficult to find many persons in Soviet industry fully qualified to carry out these instructions. Theoretically the system ought to establish scientifically the capacity of the worker plus his machine. But, perhaps fortunately for the Soviet worker, norm-fixing in practice is usually much more rule-of-thumb. The rate-fixer simply studies workshop returns to find out how many articles are produced in a given time by a considerable number of workers and strikes an average, without worrying about the capacity of the machines or correct methods of work.

The performances of Stakhanovites during the last months of 1935 convinced the Soviet leaders that the average industrial worker's norm had hitherto been fixed much too low. They said that so many workers far exceeding their norms showed that the rate-fixers had not done their job properly. The plenary session of the Central Committee of the Party in December decided that in future factory engineers and technical personnel were to take part in norm-fixing under the immediate control of the director ; and that staff Stakhanovites were also to be drawn into the business, presumably to tender technical evidence. The Committee then resolved that the existing norms were to be replaced by new and higher ones, but that the scales on which progressive premiums were paid were to be maintained unaltered.

The Trade Unions, which, if they had retained the slightest vestige of their original trade-unionism, might have been expected to show a certain reserve concerning Stakhanovism, " fully and completely approved of the resolution of the December session of the Central Committee as a militant programme for developing the Stakhanovite movement ".[1] It was laid down that one of the chief duties of all trade-union organisations was to explain to the workers how it had become necessary to replace the out-of-date norms which had been confuted by Stakhanovism. In other words, the Trade Unions, instead of trying to prevent a cut in wages, had to break it to the workers that in future they would have to work harder for the same money, or get less money for the same amount of work. Quite possibly the average daily task in industry had become too easy in view of the improvement in machinery and the workers' qualifications, but that is not the point. The Central Committee of the Party decided on its own authority that norms must be raised and instructed the Trade Unions to help put the change into effect. Officially, of course, the workers, having realised that their daily tasks were not in accordance with their capacity, were only too glad to work harder for the glory of Communism and in defence of the Soviet Union. Those who could not see it in that way and who felt aggrieved, were guilty of *petit bourgeois* mentality and anti-social tendencies, so their opinions did not count. The Trade Unions were also instructed to see that the Stakhanovites were given the best dwelling quarters and that they had preference in the matter of holidays in rest homes and sanatoria and sending their children to crèches and kindergarten. The ordinary rank-and-file worker undoubtedly had plenty of reasons for disliking the Stakhanovites.

By June 1936 practically all heavy industries had worked out and put into effect the new norms, which for the most part were between 20 and 30 per cent above the old tasks,

---

[1] From a resolution of the Presidium of the All-Union Central Council of Trade Unions of 27th December 1935.

though in some cases increases up to 60 per cent were made. By the end of the year 75 to 90 per cent of the workers in the different industries were fulfilling their new norms, and in December in heavy industry as a whole the norms were exceeded by 30·8 per cent.[1] Just what this means is not clear, but the impression it is designed to give is that most of the workers were easily able to complete their daily task, while a large number were able to exceed it by so much that the realised daily aggregate output was 30·8 per cent more than the aggregate of all daily tasks.

Almost invariably, whenever particular stress is laid on any activity in Soviet economic life, a series of perversions or misinterpretations crops up. This sometimes is the result of the procedure laid down being too complicated for the ordinary official intellect, but often it seems that the people on the spot who have to transform instructions into reality, aspire to improve on the original. Anyone who has had much to do with Russians will understand. If one orders a Russian to do something in a particular way or make some arrangement, he is very likely to do it in another way or take upon himself to vary the arrangement on his own responsibility, because he thought his own way was the better, and then expects to be applauded for his cleverness. This is a genuine Russian trait and has nothing to do with Communism. One would naturally think that whatever might be the method of fixing norms, the norms themselves would be simple enough, but lots of rate-fixers were not content to fix a certain definite comprehensive task, they had to divide it up into a lot of parts. The worker had to complete a number of operations to each of which time was allotted to a fraction of a minute and pay to a fraction of a kopek. Consequently the worker was unable to calculate as he went along what his real output was or how much he had earned. Another perversion arose from the notion that norms were both practical and theoretical. The practical norm was the task expected from the worker judging by actual experience, the theoretical or technical norm was the output that should be realised if machinery and equipment

---

[1] *Labour in the Socialist Community*, p. 239.

were employed to full capacity. The planned output of a factory was based on this technical norm. Even if a margin was allowed for eventualities it was far from covering all interruptions, with the result that the factory's Plan came to a good deal more than the aggregate norms of all the workers : the workers on the whole might even exceed their norms by a considerable amount and still the Plan would not be realised. This introduced a lot of confusion into the finances of the enterprise, because one of the main principles of factory finance is that the planned wages bill must be conditional on planned output being realised. In theory the State Bank, which keeps the current accounts of all state enterprises, should refuse to pay out the full amount for wages unless production plans are realised. If the workers as a whole exceed their aggregate norms they will earn more than the planned wages bill, but if at the same time the factory itself does not fulfil its production Plan it cannot draw the full amount to cover planned wages, let alone the additional sum needed to pay the workers' premiums for over-fulfilment of their norms. In such circumstances the enterprise usually covers the deficit by depleting its working capital.

When the daily task is fixed, the next thing is to determine what it is worth in terms of wages. This is the job of *tarifikators*, or tariff-fixers. The standard official answer to questions about wage-fixing is that wage rates are determined by collective agreement between the industries and the Trade Unions. The easiest course would be to accept this without comment, but the matter is worth more attention than that. Unfortunately Soviet authorities seem to have decided to make the details of wage-fixing more or less of a mystery. At any rate no rules of procedure as for norm-fixing are available so far as I know. We are informed in *Labour in the Socialist Community* that production norms, tariffication and valuation of work were all prepared by the normalising apparatus. Which presumably means that one organisation undertakes the whole series of duties, viz. (1) fixing the daily task; (2) classifying each task; and (3) assessing the wage for each division or category of task.

In spite of attempts to reduce the inordinate number of wage scales there are still a very great many with very small differences between them. There is no standard classification for a whole industry : it seems a regional matter and the same work may be paid at different rates in different enterprises. For instance, " the basic wage of spinners producing twist No. 54 in two neighbouring cotton mills varies from R.8·61 to R.9·15 ".[1]

No less complicated is the system of premiums for exceeding the norm. In the Ural Machinery Works there were 270 different methods of calculating premiums ; in the Podolsky Machine Works there were 142 methods of calculating the premiums earned by the engineering and technical staff, 106 methods for the ordinary workers and 35 for the clerical staff.[2] Apparently under these systems, just how they work is not disclosed, it is impossible for the worker to know whether he is actually earning a premium or not. It is obviously not the simple matter of knowing that if he exceeds his norm he will earn a premium. For instance, in the cotton industry premiums may be earned even if the worker fails to produce his norm through work being interrupted ; whereas in the Ural Machine Works, already mentioned, the multiplicity of methods of calculating premiums was in a majority of cases used to deprive the workers wholly or partly of their premiums at the discretion of the management.[3]

Another feature of wages that has come in for criticism is the small differences between the salaries of qualified engineers and the foreman class and the relatively low pay of these compared with the workmen. As an example, in the Kirov Works the basic rates of pay for engineers in charge of smelting furnaces was R.700 a month, while shift foremen were paid R.500. At the same time an ordinary furnace workman of the seventh class earned R.1000 to R.1200, presumably including premiums. In the metallurgical and engineering industries it seems to be the rule that the most skilled workmen earn as much or more than

[1] *Labour in the Socialist Community*, p. 242.
[2] *Ibid.* p. 243.　　　　　　　　　　[3] *Ibid.* p. 243.

their foremen. The consequence is that the best workers refuse " promotion " to foremen. There will be more to say on the subject of foremen later on.

Apparently the Soviet wage system puzzled Sir Walter Citrine when he visited the U.S.S.R. in 1935. Wages were, naturally, one of the subjects he was chiefly interested in ; but from what he wrote in *I Search for Truth in Russia*, though he found it a simple matter to discover what certain people earned, it was quite another matter to find out the details of wage-fixing. He came up against that Russian obstructiveness which everybody has experienced who tries to investigate conditions on the spot. My own experiences have led to the conclusion that in a great proportion of cases one's informant or guide just does not know the answer, but refusing to admit his ignorance, takes refuge in repeating the official dictum on which one wants further explanation. Sometimes the real answer cannot be given because it is forbidden ; in such cases, oddly enough, one's informant untruthfully pleads ignorance. Finally there is a class of question that simply cannot be answered because it relies on the false assumption that official instructions are carried out or theoretical procedure put into practice. It is probable, one might say practically a certainty, that wage-fixing is a much more rule-of-thumb proceeding than the official theory indicates. That this is a reasonable supposition is indicated by a casual admission in *Labour in the Socialist Community* that although there were seventy tariff scales in the cotton textile industry the wages of 78 per cent of the operatives were fixed without reference to the tariff.

The complexity of the whole wage system may be gathered from the different factors that go towards determining the individual worker's earning power. First of all is his grade, of which there are seven or eight in heavy industry and more in light industries. The worker is graded according to the results of a test of skill. Secondly, the job he is doing ; thirdly, the volume of his output. I would not claim that the following interpretation is absolutely accurate, but it is, I think, a fair representation of the facts. The worker's basic wage depends on his grade, but two

workers in the same grade may be performing two different
sorts of work which may be paid at different rates. I am
not quite clear whether two workers of different grades
doing similar work would be paid the same wage, or whether
the higher grade worker would receive a higher wage. I am
inclined to the latter belief. But it would seem to be the
case that a high-grade worker set to perform a low-grade
job, that is one requiring less than his grade of skill, is paid
at a lower rate than his grade entitles him to. The ground
for this is the following passage from *Labour in the Socialist
Community* :

> The tendency towards equality in the payment of workers
> also renders possible the irregular employment of higher grade
> workers in work requiring inferior qualifications. If workers of
> superior qualifications cannot be set to a job in conformity with
> their skill, they will be paid at lower rates. Thus, for example,
> in the Kirov Works (formerly the Putilov armament works in
> Leningrad) a certain driller of the sixth grade had to work
> 29 hours at second-grade work, 42 hours at third-grade work,
> 521 hours at fourth-grade work, 10 hours at fifth-grade work
> and not a single hour at his proper sixth-grade work. (This would
> seem to cover about three months' employment.)

From this one might judge that it is rare for a worker in a
low grade to be given a higher grade job. On the other hand,
one hears so much about the dearth of skilled workers that
one would be inclined to say that the opposite is the more
common.

The total wages fund, that is the sum of all wage and
salary payments by the State and state institutions and
enterprises, is a very important item in the annual economic
Plan drawn up by the State Planning Commission. The
basis of the All-Union Plan is the individual plans, or rather
estimates, made by every individual employing institution
or enterprise of the total amount they will have to pay out
during the coming year, and this, naturally, depends on the
quantity of labour employed, the volume of output and
changes in wage rates. In theory wages should not increase
as much as productivity of labour, in order that production

111

costs should fall and prices be reduced. However, this result has never been achieved and prices have not shown the smallest tendency to fall since single prices and free trading succeeded rationing. In fact, retail prices on the whole were appreciably higher in 1939 than in 1936. While every productive enterprise aims at reducing the costs of its products by keeping wage increases below the increase in labour productivity, *Gosplan* has another aspect to consider. The total wages fund must be related to the volume of consumers' goods available on the retail market. Wages and salaries together with allied payments such as pensions, students' allowances, etc., account for all but a negligible percentage of the urban consumers' aggregate income and for some 70 per cent of the total income of the whole population. If the wages fund increased disproportionately to the increase in the supply of goods, prices would have to be put up to prevent stocks being sold out and shortages appearing.

Judging by references to wage-planning in Soviet publications it seems that enterprises to arrive at an estimate of their wage bills take their total labour and the average per head earnings. This at least seems a fairly reasonable way of tackling the problem. The question is, How does the collective bargaining, said to be undertaken by the Trade Unions on behalf of the workers, fit into the scheme ? It seems evident that the Trade Unions have no say in the total wage bill, which is determined above all else by the planned volume of production and planned production costs. The only question left open for settlement by negotiation is the allocation of wage rates to the different workers' grades within the framework of the Plan. That is to say, whatever negotiations do take place, they are confined to fixing the relative wage scales and not absolute wages, which are already determined by the Plan. Of course when one comes to go into the matter it is clear that the absolute amount of the average money wage has no bearing on the average real wage, which depends entirely on the quantity of goods available for distribution. If the average wage were doubled it could not buy more, nor would it buy less if it were halved. Prices would be doubled or halved as the case might be.

But a man earning twice as much as his fellow can buy twice as much, however the price level may move ; so wage-fixing amounts to a device for distributing an inelastic supply of goods among the population in proportion to the relative earning power of the individual. The workers as consumers have no influence whatever on the production of consumers' goods. The proportion of total productive forces to be allotted to manufacturing capital goods and consumption goods is decided by the inner council of the Party leaders, the details being worked out by the State Planning Commission. The Trade Unions, as representatives of the workers' interests, have a certain voice in the manner in which the supply of consumers' goods shall be distributed, but that is all.

CHAPTER IX

ORGANISATION OF LABOUR AND INDUSTRY

THE organisation of Soviet industry is constantly varying ; it is impossible to give a detailed and comprehensive description of the system, because different industries follow somewhat different principles, and rules in force to-day may be altered next week. For example, up to October 1940 it would have been correct to say that every industry supplied its own requirements of skilled labour through its own factory schools and training establishments. But the Law of the 2nd October at one stroke put all the schools belonging to individual organisations under a central body responsible directly to the Council of People's Commissars.

Up to 1932 the control of all industry was centralised in the Supreme Economic Council. In consequence of the expansion both in the number of enterprises and new branches of industry, some decentralisation of control became inevitable and four separate Commissariats were formed, viz. the People's Commissariats of Heavy Industry, Light Industry, Timber Industry and Food Industry. As industry continued to grow these were from time to time split up and subdivided until, in August 1940, 23 separate Commissariats had been formed. These were the People's Commissariats for —

(1) *All Union Commissariats*

Coal	Armaments
Petroleum	Heavy machine manufacture
Ferrous metals	Medium machine manufacture
Non-ferrous metals	General machine manufacture
Chemicals	Electric power stations
Airplane construction	Electric machinery and equipment
Shipbuilding	Building
Military supplies	Cellulose and paper

114

(2) *Union Republic Commissariats*

Light industry	Fish and fishing
Textiles	Meat and dairy produce
Timber	Building materials
Food	

In all forty-two Commissariats, including those in charge of the country's politics (foreign and internal affairs), social services (health, education and justice), defence, trade, finance, agriculture, communications and transport, were in existence at the end of 1940. All-Union Commissariats control industries of such general importance that they require centralised control by the Government of the U.S.S.R. ; Union Republican Commissariats apply to industries producing consumption goods and commodities for local consumption manufactured from local material. Each Republic has its own Commissariats for these industries, which are subordinate to the Central Commissariats in Moscow only in respect of matters of general policy. Precisely to what extent the Republican Commissariats enjoy independence is difficult to say. Certainly they all must conform to the general Plan ; large new factories cannot be built without the approval of Moscow, neither can a Republican Commissariat manufacture articles at its own discretion without reference to the standards and specifications fixed in Moscow. While general price limits for standard commodities are laid down in Moscow, some latitude is permitted to local Commissariats, particularly with regard to goods produced from local material for purely local consumption. It must always be remembered that whatever autonomy local administrations enjoy on paper, every administrative organ throughout the country, from a Republican Government to a village Soviet, is under the thumb of the Party, even though Party members may not be in a majority. Party instructions, official or secret, can always ensure that " autonomous " bodies will not take decisions conflicting with the Central Government's policy. If this be insufficient, Article 69 of the Constitution empowers the Council of People's Commissars of the U.S.S.R. to suspend decisions and orders of the Councils of People's Commissars of the Republics.

Every Commissariat contains a number of departments, or Chief Administrations, supervising a certain class of enterprise, or all factories in a certain district (for example, the Commissariat of textile industries includes separate Chief Administrations for linen, woollens and silks, and no less than seven Chief Administrations for cotton mills in different centres); other Chief Administrations deal with finance, raw material, disposal of finished output, equipment, staff, labour, etc. In addition there are numerous bureaus or sections for planning, social services, transport, legal questions, accounting, technical inspections, etc. From this it will be readily understood that Soviet industry requires an enormous number of administrative, technical and clerical workers who have no immediate concern with actual production. Nor is this all; in most industries the factories themselves are grouped under trusts, which exercise centralised managerial and co-ordinating functions and form a link between the actual factory and the Commissariat. A few of the very largest individual enterprises, such as the Magnitogorsk Metallurgical Works, are directly under the control of the Commissariat without the intervention of a trust. The manager of a factory is concerned almost entirely with the internal affairs of his enterprise. Market problems of procuring raw material and disposing of finished output are taken off his shoulders by the trust and the Commissariat. Neither has he much, if any, discretion in the matter of patterns, styles and qualities of his output. All this is settled for him and he is responsible only for producing the goods ordered. His real responsibility is the efficient working of his factory coupled with the maintenance of planned production costs. If he can reduce production costs, so much the better for himself and his workers, because part of the extra profits will accrue to their benefit.

According to the principle of single management, the managing director of a factory is supreme within the limits of his competency. But it is very difficult to say how far his supremacy is a reality in practice or to what extent he exercises it. A lot undoubtedly depends on his own character and his standing in the Party. So many directors are *vydvizhentsy* (*i.e.* promoted workers, see Chapter VII), who, conscious of their own limited technical qualifications and lack of administrative experience, may well feel diffidence in standing up to their assistant directors and the factory committee. The great defect in industrial administration seems to be, that while the principle of single responsible management is upheld in theory, there are too many checks on its exercise ; for in common with other dictatorships nobody is wholly and implicitly trusted. This naturally and inevitably inclines weaker characters to pass on responsibility, and with assistant directors and factory committees inside the works and local Party committees outside, not to mention Trade Unions which share the responsibility for factory discipline, it is fairly easy to throw the blame on someone else.

Whether managing directors of factories are appointed by the People's Commissariat or the trust I cannot say for certain. It probably depends on the size and importance of the enterprise. The technical staff, that is engineers and qualified technical experts, are engaged by the trust, as is shown by newspaper advertisements, while the ordinary workers are engaged by the factory itself. Neither Soviet publications nor foreign writers attempt to present a clear-cut picture of the hierarchy of authority in Soviet industrial enterprises. Possibly because the system is of infinite variety. At the seventeenth Party Congress in February 1934 L. M. Kaganovich, then People's Commissar of Railways, speaking on the question of industrial organisation, declared that " The foreman must be master in his section, the shop engineer in the shop and the director the sole head and controller of the works with full personal responsibility ". But this was a mere reiteration of the current theory of management and leads us nowhere. At that time a certain minority of leading Bolsheviks still upheld the principles of " democratic centralism " and collegiate control.

Factory directors are far less independent and have much less discretion than capitalist managers. Practically every contingency is provided for in government decrees, circulars issued by the Commissariat, or instructions from the Chief

Administration. And the director is supposed personally to see that the decree and instructions are carried out. When the Law of 26th June 1940 introduced the eight-hour day and penalties for workers absent without leave, factory directors were, naturally, supposed to see that the new rules were enforced. In an article " On Single Management " in *Planned Economy*, No. 8, 1940, a director of the Stalinsk Metallurgical Works was criticised because he " officially transferred to the manager of the staff department and the legal adviser the duty of combating breaches of the law of 26th June 1940 ". A mine manager was similarly criticised for entrusting his assistant with the duty of contending with loafers and absentees. If these men delegated their authority to subordinates and washed their hands of all responsibility, the criticism may be justified. But this is not expressly stated. One would hardly imagine that a director is supposed personally to check up time-sheets to discover which workers turned up late or failed to turn up at all. One would naturally assume it to be among the duties of the staff department ; and the head of that department would be responsible to the director for seeing that it was carried out. But if, as the passage quoted seems to suggest, directors are supposed to give their personal attention to details of this nature, it throws some light on the difficulties of factory administration. Either directors have altogether too many small details to attend to and cannot devote themselves to the broader aspects of management, or assistants and departmental managers cannot be trusted to carry out their responsibilities without close supervision.

The same article in *Planned Economy* goes on to declare that all productive activity in factory enterprises must be permeated with strict discipline so that all orders given by the chief are promptly and accurately carried out. This, however, can be realised only when the chief is energetic and stands no nonsense. Unfortunately this is by no means always the case. " For example in one of the largest metallurgical works, Azovstal, productive and technological discipline is shaky. The orders of the director and chief engineer constantly remain unfulfilled and are submitted to discussions." This seems to mean that orders are not obeyed until the staff and workers concerned have debated the matter ; sometimes, presumably, deciding that an order shall not be obeyed.

We have more information on the duties and position of foremen. During the first half of 1940 a press campaign broke out for improving the status of foremen, a number of whom thereupon wrote letters to the press about their grievances. They complained that —

(1) They had to give up too much time to filling in forms and office work generally, and thus were unable to give proper attention to the work of the men under them ;

(2) They had insufficient authority among the workers to maintain proper discipline, and their position was rendered still more equivocal by managers and engineers giving orders direct to the workers over their heads ;

(3) Their wages were less than the average earnings of skilled workers.

On account of these conditions most skilled workers preferred remaining workers and declined promotion to foreman status. Eventually a decree was issued removing foremen's disabilities and raising their standard of wages, but the decree was interpreted variously in different enterprises. " In different enterprises foremen have different rights and duties, which hitherto has hindered the establishment of proper relations between foremen and other persons in authority " (*Industriya*, 19th September 1940).

With the improvement of the status of foremen the Government directed that, before promoting workers without any technical and theoretical education, they were to pass a test or examination ; which seems a quite reasonable measure. But the Commissariat of Heavy Machine Construction decided that all existing foremen were to undergo a test, with the result that a considerable number failed and were degraded. For some reason or other the Commissariat decided it would be a good thing to have in its factories as many foremen as possible with technical engineering training and employed the test to get rid of the merely practical men. The new foremen with some theoretical training would be men, or youths, who had done a course in a factory school, or a part-time course in a technical high school, or perhaps had studied for a qualified engineer's diploma and had failed. Foremen may be classified under two headings : older workmen who have shown themselves possessed of natural ability and leadership fitting them to hold a measure of responsibility and exercise authority over others ; and young men with theoretical training, but not much experience of practical work nor of directing the labour of others. In fact the new type of foreman may in some respects be compared with apprentices in capitalist works, who having studied the theory of their profession are taken on by engineering firms and set to work in the shops for a year or two to gain practical experience before being given more responsible work. But in Soviet industry these ex-students are immediately given authority over the ordinary workmen, while the capitalist apprentice with an engineering degree has to start by being under the orders of a practical foreman. If Soviet engineering graduates ever do any practical apprenticeship in the shop, it is only a very short course. As a matter of fact, judging by the Soviet newspapers and journals, immediately a student has taken his degree he generally gets a responsible post as a full-blown engineer. In justice to the Soviet system it should be pointed out that students in the universities and technical colleges intersperse their theoretical studies with practical work in neighbouring factories, which would take the place of laboratory work in a capitalist engineering college; though I do not thereby imply that Soviet training establishments never possess laboratories. But that this practical work is a good and complete substitute for an apprenticeship seems more than doubtful. The Bolsheviks claim that, by carrying on practical factory work concurrently with theoretical study, they reduce the time necessary to produce a fully qualified engineer.

In comparing the Soviet system with our own we must always keep in mind that the origin and sentiments of factory

labour is different and that a class of skilled industrial workers
with a long history and tradition behind it does not yet exist.
Before the revolution the total number of factory workers
was below three millions, and at least half of these were still
peasants at heart with their roots in the country. The
number of genuine industrial proletariate was probably not
much more than a million. To-day industrial labour alone,
excluding building and construction, transport, trade, etc.,
amounts to ten millions. Few workers can have a long
record of family service in industry ; in fact the great mass
of present-day factory workers are of recent peasant origin
and a very large proportion were actually born in peasant
families. They have no inherited skill and experience in
factory work, which cuts in two ways. American engineers
with whom I have discussed the question generally agree
that Russian workmen are fairly intelligent and easy to
teach, but lack the instinctive knowledge how to do things.
The only way to get efficient work out of them is to work
with them, not merely explain by word and diagram what
you want of them and leave them to get on with it, but take
off your coat and show them how you do it. On the other
hand, their lack of tradition gives them a freedom from
conservative ideas and they are ready to use new methods
without any inhibitions against new-fangled notions. For
these reasons Soviet factory workers are less prejudiced than
the British workman against young and more or less inexperienced shop engineers and foremen provided they can
show that they really are capable of putting their theory
into practice. Unfortunately the Soviet youth, having
graduated from his university or technical college, all too
often aspires to become a white-collar worker and tries to
avoid the practical exercise of his profession. Not only are
the technical and planning departments in administrative
offices full of qualified engineers, where a certain number
are, of course, essential, but they fill posts in the accountancy,
staff, commercial and other departments where their qualifications are wasted. A good many even cut adrift from
their profession altogether and find their way into commercial enterprises, government offices and the like. From

time to time the authorities make a drive to prise engineers and technicians from their office stools and send them into the workshops and down the mines. As the process is constantly repeated, it looks as though the engineers soon drift back to their offices.

One reason for the employment of technical experts in clerical work is, no doubt, the enormous administrative and office staffs which seem essential to any sort of Soviet enterprise. In Soviet terminology the management and office staff of an enterprise are known as the *apparat*, or apparatus, another instance of the curious twist given to the sense of adopted words. The inflated apparatus of industrial organisations and enterprises was the subject of an editorial in *Pravda* of 21st November 1940, from which the following is taken :

In 1939 compared with 1937 the employees (*i.e.* broadly the salaried staff as distinct from the wage-earning workers) of the Commissariat of Medium Machine Construction increased by 25·1 per cent while the workers increased by only 1 per cent. During this period the number of engineers and experts increased considerably ; but very many of them, instead of being employed on productive work, gravitated into factory administrative offices, where they simply augmented the administrative staff. The same sort of thing happens in practically every branch of industry.

At a meeting of the Collegium of the Commissariat of Medium Machine Construction the People's Commissar himself said that, in the factories belonging to the three machine construction Commissariats having up to 500 workers and employees, the latter formed 30 to 40 per cent of the whole, while in England they would form 20 to 25 per cent and in America only 12 to 15 per cent. In a particular works in Moscow employing 151 productive workers there were 215 auxiliary workers. These would include gate-keepers, watchmen, cleaners and others not directly concerned with the works' manufacturing activities. The management comprised a director, chief engineer, assistant director, 10 departmental heads, 2 deputy departmental heads, 2 section managers and 80 persons in the offices of the 10 departments.

Thus it required just on 100 managers and salaried staff, not to mention over 200 people engaged on all sorts of odd jobs, to run a factory employing 150 workmen.

Nearly all tourists to the U.S.S.R., whatever conflicting impressions they receive, agree in one thing, that one never sees any work going on anywhere without about as many men standing around as are actually working. It is an old Russian custom, no doubt dating back to the days of serfdom when labour cost next to nothing, to have twice as many workers on a job as are needed. In unskilled work on roads, etc., which the tourist is most likely to see, the reason for idle labour is simply that it is the custom, and the ordinary Russian works best when he has an audience. One might often be excused for supposing that the audience are casual passers-by stopping a moment to exchange badinage with the workers ; but they are nothing of the sort ; they are just as much " on the job " as the workers who are actually working. A passage in my diary of my visit in 1939 reads : " We had to cross a level crossing. We stood 15 minutes or so while a succession of trains passed, each announced by a loud-speaker. The staff included one woman with a flag, another to operate the barriers, a policeman complete with revolver and one more woman and a man apparently attached to the group, but without any visible function."

The huge quantity of returns and statements demanded by Soviet bureaucratism partly accounts for the enormous clerical apparatus of all economic organisations. Attempts are always being made to cut down this clerical work, but without any appreciable success. The fact is, I think, that, apart from the normal appetite for paper possessed by the Soviet bureaucracy in common with capitalist public ser- vices, no Soviet official will do anything without a written order ; very often he does not do it then, but he always wants to be protected. Equally, everybody who gives an order puts it on paper for a record. Consequently every Commissariat issues floods of *postanovlenia* (decrees), *prikazy* (commands), instructions and circulars to its subordinate organisations ; the trusts issue similar documents to their enterprises and factory directors issue orders and instructions to their departments. In addition to all this, the State Planning Commission and its regional offices demand returns on every imaginable subject at intervals varying from five days to twelve months.

At one time a cause of redundant labour was the principle called *funktsionalka,* or functionalism. This is defined in *Labour in the Socialist State* as follows :

The essence of this consists in the fact that the completion of this or that task and the responsibility for it were divided among separate workers, each of whom performed one incomplete part of the work (one function), and no one was responsible for the whole complete result. Functionalism even penetrated into the system of-management, as well as production.

In the workshops this had much the same effect as our own trade-union system, which forbids, or used to forbid, for instance, a fitter or mechanic encroaching on the carpenter's province, even to the extent of unscrewing the wooden cover of a steampipe. In a Soviet factory the carpenter would, naturally, never be on hand when wanted, and so a great deal of time was lost waiting for him to turn up. In management functionalism meant that " one part of the apparatus was concerned with technical matters, another with finance, a third with labour questions, a fourth with production costs, a fifth with planning, a sixth with supply, a seventh with staff, etc., and no one single person either controlled or was responsible for the progress of the whole ".

That is to say, enterprises were not managed by a single responsible director to whom all departmental heads were responsible but each department was run as a separate and independent entity. The defects of such a system are obvious, and it was abolished in 1932. Nevertheless the idea that a workman is only responsible for and can only be expected to perform a certain definite task probably persists ; though officially workers are encouraged to learn two or more trades and to be ready to turn their hand to another job when necessary.

The reintroduction of the 7-day week and 8-hour day by the law of 26th June 1940 was designed mainly to improve the organisation of factory labour and reduce staffs. Factories previously working three 7-hour shifts in the twenty-four hours went over to two 8-hour shifts, thus not only reducing the number of shop engineers, foremen and others needed to supervise the work of the factory hands, but also the clerical work in connection with time sheets, etc. It was also expected that output would not fall as a result of the change, in spite of the dismissal of a certain proportion of the workers and staff. Under the three-shift system the numbers working on the night shift had in most enterprises been much smaller than in the forenoon and afternoon shifts ; the night shift, too, had usually been much less efficient than the others (which is the case in capitalist countries too) and was responsible for an undue proportion of spoilt output. The three-shift system meant that during the twenty-four hours only three hours in all were available to the maintenance staff to overhaul machines and do all the other odd jobs that can be done only when machines are standing still and the shops free of workers. As a result maintenance work used often to overlap into working time and workers were kept waiting. The present 8-hour interval between afternoon and forenoon shift should give sufficient time for repairs, etc., to be carried out. However, the immediate results of the change were not entirely satisfactory. In an article " Socialist Labour Discipline " in *Planned Economy*, No. 9, 1940, the following passage occurs :

The Decrees of the Presidium of the Supreme Soviet of 26th June and 10th July 1940, require from enterprises the introduction of system . . . for a decided improvement in the organisation of labour. The first months of work under the new conditions have shown that the possibilities of reinforcing and developing production, created by these decrees, have been far from realised. In numbers of enterprises, instead of organising technological processes in accordance with the new requirements for the quality of production, there has been a reduction in the volume of output, with an increase in the amount of labour employed, mainly in retouching and refinishing. A genuine effort to diminish *brak*, however, has not yet been organised. The volume of *brak* in some enterprises has increased.

The decree of 10th July rendered factory directors and chief engineers directly responsible for *brak* and substandard output. The decree was soon followed by a number of prosecutions in which penalties ranging from dismissal to imprisonment were imposed. Consequently the heads of enterprises took alarm and, according to the above paragraph, had their defective goods touched up and patched up so as to pass muster, instead of tackling the problem at the root and seeing that defective goods were not produced in the initial and intermediate processes. Their difficulties were no doubt increased by the fact that, despite the change to two shifts, they were expected to keep up, if not increase, their former rate of production. And though this may have been technically possible when the new system had been run in, at first the reduction in the time from 21 to 16 hours a day during which the machines were working must have tended to lower production.

While it would be incorrect to say that there is absolutely no element of competition between productive enterprises for the sale of their products, for practical purposes we may ignore it. The whole idea of planning is to do away with a competitive market, and this is summed up in the aphorism that goods are produced for consumption and not for profit. Price planning is one of the more important duties of *Gosplan*, which aims at fixing wholesale prices of goods at a level that covers all production costs with a comparatively modest margin of profit. If planning were perfect it would be possible to tell in advance exactly what it would cost to produce any article ; the quantity and price of the raw material consumed, the amount of labour employed and the wages earned in the manufacturing processes, the proportion of total overhead expenditure to be charged to each unit of production and every other item in the total cost would be known in advance. But no two factories producing the same sort of goods work with exactly the same efficiency ; apart from the human element one factory may be better equipped with up-to-date machinery and labour-saving devices than another. Therefore when fixing the price of a standard commodity *Gosplan* has to strike a fair average

that will allow the ordinarily efficient factory to dispose of
its output at a small margin over total production costs.
This margin is known as " accumulation " rather than profit,
because the word profit has a rather discreditable capitalist
savour. The amount of the accumulation of every manufacturing and commercial enterprise is planned in advance ;
a certain percentage is paid straight into the budget ; this
may be regarded as the State's dividend as sole shareholder,
or, as the Bolsheviks would prefer to put it, as trustee for
the whole community to which eventually all means of production and distribution belong. The rest is retained by the
enterprise to be devoted according to plan to increasing its
turnover or working capital and financing capital renewals
and extensions. Actually the expenditure of retained
accumulation by enterprises is largely controlled by the
trust to which they belong.

The above is a very short and summarised description of
industrial finance, which had to be introduced to explain
the origin and disposal of what is known as the "Directors'
Fund ". From the preceding pages it must have been
realised that in a very large number of industrial enterprises
there exists a considerable, often an enormous, margin for
economies. It is probably no exaggeration to say that
almost every manufacturing enterprise in the country could
vastly reduce overhead and working expenses and hence
production costs, and so show a large margin of accumulation
over and above the plan. To encourage all concerned, from
the director of an enterprise to the ordinary workman, to
increase accumulations, the Government decreed in April
1936 that a fund be formed, consisting of 4 per cent of the
net accumulation (*i.e.* profits after making allowance for
amortisation of capital and all renewals and replacements)
up to the planned amount, and 50 per cent of any sums by
which the net accumulation exceeds the plan, and placed
at the disposal of the director of the enterprise for the
following purposes :

(*a*) Not less than 50 per cent of the total fund to be used
to finance the building of dwelling-houses for the
workers and employees ;

127

(*b*) To the improvement and extension of the social services and amenities rendered the workers and employees, such as crèches, kindergarten, clubs, dining-rooms, etc. ;

(*c*) To bonuses to specially outstanding workers ;

(*d*) To supplementary capital construction ;

(*e*) To supplementary measures of rationalisation and technical propaganda.

The directors' plan of expenditure must be approved by the factory trade-union committee.

A supplementary order issued in the following June provided that expenditure on social services and amenities for the workers and employees should be exclusively financed by the fund : which meant that all former grants for such objects from the State, the trust or any other authority ceased, and that enterprises showing no profits were unable to do anything to improve the living conditions of their people. And that any expenditure from the fund for the housing and living conditions of the director himself, the deputy director and the head book-keeper must be approved by the trust, or the Chief Administration in the event of the enterprise not being a member of a trust. In 1938 the 4 per cent of the planned accumulation was reduced to 2 per cent.

The total sum paid into directors' funds in 1939 was R.1303·8 million, of which R.209·3 million only was derived from the 2 per cent deductions from planned accumulations. Thus a large number of enterprises must have made profits in excess of their plans. On the other hand, a considerable number did not make their planned profits ; for R.209·3 million is 2 per cent of R.10,460 million, whereas the total planned profits for all industrial and commercial enterprises was R.17,673 million. The industries benefiting most, that is those that made the greatest excess profits, were light industries and food industries, that is those producing for general consumption. The total sums paid in to the directors' funds in these industries amounted to an average of 1·73 per cent of total wages and salaries, whereas in heavy industries the ratio was only 0·43 per cent. This seems to indicate that more opportunities of profit-making are permitted to industries producing goods for popular consumption than capital and producers' goods for the State.

It was inevitable that some directors should abuse their authority to control the disposal of their funds. Allegations have been made by correspondents to the press that chief engineers, departmental managers and other senior officials were allotted flats rent-free in houses built through the fund, and that a disproportionate amount was distributed as bonuses to officials while the workers were neglected. A complaint vented in *Planned Economy*, No. 4, 1938, was that the amount spent on building dwelling-houses was far less than provided for under the original decree. In 1936, for instance, instead of 50 per cent of the aggregate funds only 3·7 per cent was allotted to this purpose. The explanation may very well be that building was impossible. Seeing that all sorts of government building schemes were held up for lack of material and labour, there can be no doubt that individual enterprises would have found the utmost difficulty in finding the means to carry out their building schemes. Rather naturally, the money that could not be spent on building was distributed as bonuses. This gave no trouble to the director. And it was also rather natural that he should be biassed in favour of his chief assistants, on whom he relied for the efficient running of his enterprise. In any case a large proportion of his ordinary workmen were just birds of passage, who would leave and be replaced within a few months. Directors themselves seldom stay in one post for any considerable length of time, and therefore cannot be expected to take the same interest in their enterprises and workpeople as they would if their appointments were permanent. It is a curious peculiarity of the Soviet Government to keep its higher officials and managers continually circulating from post to post. One example to my personal knowledge is the State Bank, which had five presidents between 1936 and 1940. One reason, if not the main one, is to prevent responsible officials from acquiring anything like a vested interest in their enterprises and too much influence and popularity with their subordinates. It is characteristic of dictators to demand the entire loyalty of their subjects to the exclusion of all other personal loyalties. And because the true Russian esteems the man more than his office, personal leadership is impaired if not almost destroyed. This I believe to be one of the gravest faults in the Soviet system and one that is responsible for a very great deal of the inefficiency and disorganisation in Soviet economy.

A note on the changes in the principle of industrial administration is given in the appendix to this chapter.

Appendix to Chapter IX

SOVIET MANAGEMENT

IN the early days of the Bolshevik revolution the departments of Government or People's Commissariats were administered by committees, or as they were called, collegiums. The principle of administration by committees was in accord with the theory of Socialist Democracy. And, since at that time the Central Government was in an experimental stage, each Department of State was of necessity more or less independent and had to carry out its tasks with but little direction and assistance. Lenin, explaining the obstacles to instituting single responsible heads of departments, said :

The collegiate system, as the basic type of Soviet administrative organisation, is a necessary preliminary stage in reconstruction. But when a more or less permanent form of government has been established the transition to practical work will be accompanied by single responsible administration, which above all ensures the greatest utilisation of human capabilities and a real, instead of a simulated, control of activity.

Lenin and the more intelligent of his colleagues realised that they were inexperienced in the art of government and were moreover breaking new ground in this field. The final Soviet system would emerge as a result of trial and error and after many discussions and consultations. Other considerations, which do not appear in Soviet histories, may be guessed at : few if any of the Bolshevik leaders possessed any practical training or experience in administration, rendering the choice of departmental heads both hazardous and invidious. In fact Lenin may well have determined that in such important matters as running Departments of State there was safety in numbers. But he was fully aware of the defects and inefficiency of corporate management. In March 1918 he decided that conditions warranted the appointment of single responsible heads, or Commissars. On 26th March the Government issued a decree concerning the centralisation of the Administration of Ways of Communication, which provided for the appointment of a People's Commissar of Communications at the head of the Commissariat, responsible to the Council of People's Commissars and the All-Russian Central Executive Committee of the Council of Workers and Peasants' Deputies. The collegium consisted of the People's Commissar as President and members appointed by the All-Russian Railway Convention and confirmed by the Council of People's Commissars and the Central Executive Committee. The collegium could not interfere directly with the orders of the Commissar, who exercised full authority in all matters relating to transport.

Clause 44 of the first Constitution of the R.S.F.S.R. (10th July 1918) provided that every Commissariat should have a collegium of which the People's Commissar was to be President. Clause 45 provided that every People's Commissar had the authority personally to take decisions on all matters connected with the conduct of his Commissariat, but had to bring his decisions before the notice of the collegium. In the event of the latter disapproving it had the right of protesting to the Council of People's Commissars or the Presidium of the Central Executive Committee, but could not arrest the execution of any action decided upon by the People's Commissar. Both the collegium as a whole and an individual member had the right of protest. The necessary reorganisation of the administrations of all branches of the national economy took some time.

Meanwhile, the ninth Party Convention (March–April 1920) submitted a choice of forms for the administration of industry. These were :

(1) An administrative (or managing) director chosen from among the worker professionalists (workers in the relative industry) with an engineer as technical adviser.

(2) An engineer-specialist as acting manager of an enterprise, with a Commissar from among the workers having extensive powers and the duty of participating in all sides of the business.

(3) A director-specialist (*i.e.* a qualified manager) with one or two workers as assistants, commissioned to investigate every aspect of the factory management, but without the power of vetoing the director's orders.

(4) In enterprises managed by a small collegium, the members of which have in actual practice proved their efficiency, the existing arrangement to be retained for the time being, with, however, a considerable extension of the authority of the President of the collegium and a heightening of his responsibility for all the acts of the collegium.

The first Constitution of the U.S.S.R. (1923) more precisely differentiated the advisory functions of the collegium from the executive functions of the responsible manager. It was only natural that the revival of industry and general increased economic activity should require a closer relation between economic management and industrial production and should call for an increase of personal responsibility and the elimination of " impersonality " in work.

In 1934 a government decree of 15th March dissolved all collegiums in government and economic organisations, except in the case of elected bodies where the collegiate principle was retained. In People's Commissariats the collegiums were replaced by Councils consisting of 40 to 70 members, of whom not more than half might be presidents of local organisations and enterprises. The chief function of these Councils was to maintain a close liaison between the Commissariats and their subordinate organisations and enterprises and to ensure a general exchange of information and experience.

From 1934 to 1938 the collegiate system was in abeyance. During the course of 1938 many of the larger People's Commissariats of industry were split up and reorganised, the reorganisation including the creation of collegiums which, however, were not to interfere with or detract from the Commissar's personal authority and responsibility. These were somewhat different, both in constitution and functions, from the collegiums before 1934. As an example, the relative clauses in the constitution of the Commissariat of Light Industry may be quoted :

A collegium will be formed in the People's Commissariat of

Light Industry under the presidency of the People's Commissar, which will hold regular meetings mainly to review matters of practical production, fulfilment of plans, the selection of staff, the reports of local organs, and the more important orders and instructions. The decisions of the collegium will be put into effect by orders issued by the People's Commissar.

In the event of disagreement between the collegium and the People's Commissar the latter will execute his decisions, at the same time reporting the disagreement to the Council of People's Commissars. Members of the collegium may in their turn appeal to the Council of People's Commissars.

The re-establishment of collegiums did not do away with the Councils, which continued to fulfil their functions of maintaining liaison between the People's Commissariat and its local organs and enterprises and arranging exchanges of technical information and experience.

Collegiums consist of between nine and eleven members all holding positions in the Commissariat. Besides the People's Commissar, who is *ex officio* President, the members include the Deputy Commissars and other administrative officials. Thus the modern collegium may be compared with a board of managers or a committee of departmental heads.

The official, and seemingly the real, reason for the revival of the collegium was the increased scope and complexity of economic Commissariats. The splitting-up of the former large Commissariat (for example the People's Commissariat of Heavy Industry has in stages been subdivided into a Commissariat of ferrous metallurgy, three Commissariats of machine construction, a Commissariat of Armaments and several others) meant that each Commissariat had much closer connection with its own enterprises, and supervised details that were formerly the province of the trusts and combines. Thus the People's Commissariat of Ferrous Metallurgy as organised in February 1939 is divided into fifteen main departments or chief administrations dealing with each branch of the industry and a variety of subsidiary matters such as transport, technical education and supplies ; and twenty-two sections for finance, accounting, staff, planning, records, etc.

Clearly the People's Commissar could not possibly keep in close touch with every branch of his industry and every activity of his Commissariat, and his collegium is in the nature of a board of directors, each responsible for certain branches or activities of the Commissariat. This appears in press reports of the meetings of collegiums at which members submit statements on the activities under their special care. A collegium to-day exists to advise and assist in administration, whereas an important, if not the chief, duty of the former collegiums was to check the work and conduct of the People's Commissar, particularly in the political field. Under the former system, collegiums must often have impaired the authority and hindered the initiative of People's Commissars, who if energetic and competent, were frustrated by criticism and interference, but if weak and incompetent, took the path of least resistance and shifted responsibility to the collegium. Of course it would be very optimistic to believe that every member of a collegium is both competent and loyal to his chief. Lack of personal loyalty of this nature is a fundamental defect in the Russian character which the Bolshevik system has encouraged rather than corrected ; but it seems probable that whereas formerly the average competent People's Commissar considered his collegium an unmitigated nuisance, to-day he finds it of real assistance.

The problem of management has from the first been one of the chief difficulties of Soviet reconstruction. Pure communist theory is opposed to the concentration of authority in one person. And even when this principle was seen in practice to be unrealisable, the lack of experience and training coupled with political reliability made it impossible for the Bolshevik leaders to find trustworthy heads to run the country's economy. Their dilemma is well illustrated in the choice of forms for industrial administration submitted by the ninth Party Convention and quoted above. If a good Party man were appointed he had to have an expert adviser ; while if an experienced and qualified manager were installed he had to be supervised and controlled by a reliable Communist. It was assumed as a matter of course that the combination of technical qualifications and political reliability in one man was practically non-existent.

To-day industrial management bears a strong similarity to capitalist management. Even recent legislation concerning the status and duties of foremen has approximated them to factory foremen in capitalist enterprise.

CHAPTER X

LABOUR SOURCES AND LABOUR MARKET

THE good Bolshevik becomes frightfully indignant if one ventures to compare the procuring and distribution of labour in his country with the capitalist idea of a labour market. He will at once point out the fundamental difference between labour under the two systems. In capitalist countries labour is a commodity which the labourer sells to the capitalist, each party to the transaction trying to get the best of the bargain. In the Soviet Union labour is collective toil for the good of the whole community. Certainly, he will admit, the worker receives a wage, but this is not the price paid for the labour he sells, but his share of the common income according to the worth of his contribution in producing it. I do not imagine many Soviet wage-earners trouble to contemplate the ideological niceties of this argument. I am sure that most of them regard their wages in exactly the same way as any capitalist worker ; that is as a remuneration, usually disgracefully small, for toiling so many hours a day at some more or less uncongenial work. In support of my conclusion I would point to the progressive premium system by which workers can increase their earnings by working harder and more efficiently than the others, and the frequent paragraphs in the newspaper telling how this or that Stakhanovite earns so many times more than the average wage during a given month. Like the capitalist worker, the Soviet citizen responds with much more alacrity to the stimulus of increased earnings than to any exhortations concerning the dignity of labour and his duty to work for the State.

The Bolshevik continues his argument by asserting that the capitalist worker is forced by hunger or fear of hunger to sell his labour in the labour market. In principle we must agree with him that economic necessity compels most people to work, irrespective of whether they work for a wage or in an enterprise of their own. But when he goes on to say that the Soviet citizen works not from economic necessity but from a sense of duty and because it never enters his head that work is something to be avoided if possible, we must join issue with him. Economic necessity is just as sharp a spur to the Soviet as to the capitalist worker. Knowing the Russian talent for indolence as I do, I should say if the economic necessity to work were removed, a smaller proportion of Russians than of almost any other European nation would continue to work from a sense of duty or because they found a satisfaction in working for work's sake.

Because the demand for skilled industrial labour is greater than the supply, there has always been a certain element of competition between industries and enterprises to attract workers. In spite of the protestations of the Bolsheviks it is impossible to deny that the market element still plays a part in the distribution of labour. I do not say that a labour market in the full capitalist sense exists, because the distribution of labour, like everything else, is planned. But this does not mean, as yet, that a certain number of workers are allotted by name to a certain enterprise, nor even that an enterprise is allotted a certain aggregate of workers. Planning affects an enterprise's power to employ labour through fixing the amount it may pay out in wages. In practice this control is exercised by the State Bank, with which all enterprises keep their current accounts. It is the duty of every branch of the Bank to see that the bi-monthly sum drawn by its customers for wages does not exceed the planned amount, but this may vary according to whether the enterprise has over-fulfilled or failed to fulfil its production plan for the preceding period. Thus the Bank is supposed to check up on its customers' output before honouring their wages cheques. As a rule enterprises try to draw more money than they are entitled to : firstly, because they so often employ more hands than are really necessary ; secondly, because the planned amount of their wages does not make full allowance for the extra sums earned by workers who exceed their norms. Wages, of course, are

138

calculated to allow for a certain ratio of premiums to the basic norms ; but, until recently at least, it usually happened that the workers as a whole earned a good deal more in premiums than was expected. If the rate of remuneration for every unit of output were the same, this would not matter, because when the workers as a whole exceeded their norms and the factory its planned output, the management would be entitled to draw a corresponding amount in excess of its normal wage bill. But under the progressive premium system the more the workers exceed their norms the higher is the amount of wages paid out in respect of each unit of production. So the rather odd situation arises, that in a factory in which the workers as a whole greatly exceed their norms and the factory itself earns approval for over-fulfilling its production plans, the wages bill will mount up disproportionately and the Bank may raise questions. In actual practice, judging by articles in the daily newspapers and technical journals, the Bank finds its job too complicated and often settles the problem by doing nothing.

To a certain extent industries or enterprises producing goods in great demand can extend their activities and so employ more labour. Soviet planning is not meant to be absolutely rigid and in practice is a good deal less rigid than it is supposed to be. Price control does prevent producers of scarcity goods putting up their prices and making large profits, but I am sure that it is more profitable to manufacture goods in great demand than goods of which the supply is more or less equal to the demand. This is partly due to the fact that the Soviet Government does permit, and in fact is practically bound to permit, the reaction of supply and demand to play a definite, though minor, part in determining the rate of expansion of different industries ; and partly to the fact that though prices are legally fixed, the manufacturers of scarcity goods usually manage in some roundabout way to circumvent the price control and pocket a little extra profit. One way of doing this is to invoice goods as of higher quality than they really are, and at a correspondingly higher price. Of course this involves the collusion of the purchaser, who, however, is prepared to pay the higher price in order to get the goods. The real checks on an unplanned expansion of scarcity industries are the shortages of material and the State's control of the greater part of the national savings available for capital investment. Soviet industry as a whole may be divided into industries manufacturing consumption goods for the public and industries manufacturing capital goods for the State. The State having control of by far the greater part of new investment capital, allots the bulk of it to industries producing the goods it wants, mainly armaments and industrial equipment, leaving consumption industries to finance their own development from that portion of their net profits they are allowed to retain for themselves. It is therefore not surprising to find that the average wage in capital industries tends to rise somewhat faster than in consumption industries. In other words, industries expanding rapidly and demanding a correspondingly rapid increase of labour or an increasingly higher quality of labour do attract workers by offering higher rates of wages.

Another way in which labour was distributed among different branches of the national economy was through the technical training institutions run by the different Commissariats. The following is an example of the advertisements such institutions publish in the newspapers :

THE MOSCOW ARCHITECTURAL-CONSTRUCTIONAL TECHNIKUM
OF THE PEOPLE'S COMMISSARIAT FOR CONSTRUCTION

announces enrolment for annual courses for training technician-mechanics in the mechanisation of structural production. (With withdrawal from production.) [1]

The courses are open to —
> Worker-Stakhanovites up to the age of 35, who have completed courses of mechanics for skilled workers in Socialist labour. . . .

Applications for admission must be made before 30th Sep-

---

[1] This means that the students attending the courses will be fully occupied and will not be able to continue their ordinary work during the period of attendance.

tember. Those accepted will be granted a subsistence allowance of from R.200 to R.300 (a month) with communal lodging.

The courses will commence on 1st October 1940.

Under the Law of 2nd October 1940 for the creation of a national labour reserve, described in Chapter VII, these training establishments have been transferred from the separate Commissariats to the Chief Administration for Labour Reserves under the Council of People's Commissars. This ends the competition between the training establishments of separate Commissariats to obtain students. The system was not altogether satisfactory, for some Commissariats, or rather the departments responsible for the schools, advertised extensively while others took little trouble to attract students, and the energy devoted to getting students did not by any means always coincide with the intensity of the Commissariat's demand for labour. In future the youths conscripted in the labour reserve will be distributed among industries and transport services according to current needs for labour.

So far I have dealt with the ways in which workers are drawn into different industries. Firstly, those industries whose rate of expansion causes their demand for labour, either in quantity or quality, to increase more than others offer relatively higher remuneration. Also, I think, an intangible factor that should be mentioned is the psychological one of the social standing accorded by public opinion to certain professions. The title " Engineer " has a peculiar distinction in Soviet Russia ; mainly because it symbolises the country's emergence from agricultural primitiveness to modern industrialism ; but also, I think, because to the masses of the Russian people an engineer is a person who is an adept in high mysteries. For these reasons enterprises such as machine manufacturing shops, motor-car and tractor works, power stations, iron foundries and even mining, in which the workers can claim to be connected with the engineering profession, are the most popular. Secondly, workers are enlisted and attached to a certain industry, profession or trade by education and training, and the conditions and facilities offered by training establishments must have

141

some influence in deciding a Soviet youth what career to take up.

The other aspect of distribution is the allotment of workers already trained in a certain trade among the different employers of that trade. It is obviously not enough to have enough electricians, machine-tool operatives, chauffeurs, etc., to supply the total needs of the country ; they must be distributed where they are wanted. Since the dissolution of labour exchanges this distribution has been left to the *laissez-faire* methods of personal application by the worker and advertisement by the employer. The Trade Unions do little if anything to act as employment agencies. It certainly is not among their official functions. Personal application for employment is just the same sort of business as anywhere else. On one of my visits to Moscow I had an appointment with one of the heads of Centrosoyus, the central organisation of the consumers' co-operative associations, which, according to an old Russian custom, was fixed for the evening after normal office hours. A girl entered just in front of me and I heard her ask the *shveitzar* (door-keeper) if there were any vacancies for typists. " Lots," he answered. " Come in the morning and apply at room number so-and-so."

When an enterprise wants hands it often advertises. The following, from *Industriya* of 16th August 1940, are typical :

(1)

The Trust " Uralenergostroi " urgently requires rate-fixers, chauffeurs, carpenters, stonemasons, locksmiths, electric fitters, etc. etc.

Apply to House of Industry, Sverdlovsk.

(2)

The Trust " Drevinet " of the People's Commissariat of Ferrous Metals, requires for work in sawmills in the Sverdlovsk and Chelyabinsk Provinces, engineer-timber-technologists or practical workers for duty in manual labour factories ; and engineer-mechanics or practical workers for duty in mechanised factories. Salary by agreement.

Also wanted, workers in all trades.

Apply — 8 March Street, Sverdlovsk.

(3)

Urgently required for work at the headquarters of the Trust "Sverdugol", mining electricians and mining engineers : and for work in outlying enterprises, mining engineers, electricians, surveyors and planner-rate-fixers.

Terms of payment by agreement.

Apply — 8 March Street, Sverdlovsk.

It was probably only a coincidence that all the advertisers of vacancies in that issue were in Sverdlovsk.

When an institution has vacancies for persons of higher qualifications, such as teachers at a technical college, it will advertise for competitive applications. Thus on 28th June 1940 the Mining-Metallurgical Institute at Alma-Ata, in the Kazak Republic, advertised in *Industriya* for applicants for the posts of professors of mathematics, physics, geodetic mechanics, mineralogy, crystallography, etc. Applicants were requested to submit their life histories, certificates of education, certificates of character from last place of employment, etc.

It is clear from the foregoing that Soviet citizens have, or had, freedom to choose where they shall work and whom they shall work for. How the latest laws will limit their choice remains to be seen. The idea that the life of the Soviet citizen is planned throughout is quite false ; though it must be admitted that the Law of Labour Reserves does look as though the State means to exert more control over him in future.

Between 1929 and 1939 the population of the U.S.S.R. increased from 154·3 millions to 170 millions, the urban inhabitants from 27·6 millions to 55·9 millions, while the rural population declined from 126·7 millions to 114·6 millions. Thus the total population increased by 15·7 millions, the urban population by 28·3 millions, while the rural population declined by 12·1 millions. The chief source from which industry satisfied its increasing demand for labour was the rural and agricultural population. The numbers of persons engaged in industry, transport, commerce, finance and the public services was 12·2 millions in 1929 and some 27·5

143

millions in 1939. Of this increase of more than 15 millions, probably somewhere around 10 millions was drawn from the rural population and 5 millions from the natural increase of the urban population and the recruitment of women into industry. Actually the number of women employed in industry and other branches of the national economy increased by some 6 or 7 millions, but of these a considerable part was included in the migration of rural population into industry. I shall deal with women's labour in a subsequent chapter.

The surplus agricultural labour, nowadays almost entirely from collective farms, is recruited into industry in two ways. Young *kolhozniki* can choose an urban and industrial career in preference to the less exciting life on the land and obtain employment as unskilled workers, or if they showed promise in their elementary school they could formerly enter a higher technical institution and become skilled workers ; to-day they would probably volunteer for the labour reserve. The other way is by recruitment or conscription for what is known as *othozhyi promysel*, which may be translated " industrial employment away from home ". The term is a very old one, for it was originally used in connection with serfs on *obrok*, who took employment away from their villages (see Chapter I). Because of the excess agricultural labour in most parts of European Russia, it was always the custom for large numbers of peasants to seek work in the towns, either seasonally or more or less permanently. In our cotton mills in St. Petersburg long before the last war many of the unskilled and semi-skilled workers were peasants, who came to us in autumn after the harvest and returned to their villages in spring when farm work began again, or at least in summer for the harvest. This migration from the land to factory and back again to the land was not organised in any way. It was simply a custom that had grown up from economic necessity. The Bolsheviks, however, organised the system and made it an important item in the supply of industrial labour. Naturally the *kolhozniki* are not skilled industrial workers. They are recruited mainly for work in the lumber industry, digging peat in the peat bogs, unskilled work in coal mines, quarries, making roads, etc. Whereas formerly it was the peasant who went out looking for work, now it is the employer who goes out to recruit labour in the villages. The republican or provincial Governments calculate the quantity of collective farm labour that can be spared for industry, then industrial Commissariats, trusts or separate enterprises are given the monopoly of engaging labour in different districts. They do not, however, approach the *kolhozniki* individually, but make a contract with the *kolhoz* to provide a certain number of workers for a certain time to perform specified work. Whether the *kolhoz* calls for volunteers, nominates the persons for the draft or uses compulsory powers only when sufficient numbers fail to volunteer, is not definitely clear. The Bolsheviks are always most careful to avoid direct reference to compulsion and maintain the fiction of free choice, as for instance in the case of subscriptions to the state loan. But all the indirect evidence tends to show that *kolhozy* are supposed to fill their quotas somehow or other, while the term used for the recruitment of *kolhozniki* is *nabor*, which definitely connotes levying or conscription. So I think it is fairly safe to assume that some sort of coercion or pressure is exerted when necessary to make up the quotas.

When a *kolhoznik* has been detailed for, or has volunteered for, a labour draft he has to sign a formal contract with the employing enterprise, which sets out that he undertakes to work for the said enterprise at a specified description of work for a period of time between specified dates ; to start out for the place of employment at a certain date ; to fulfil the tasks given him honestly and conscientiously ; take proper care of the tools, implements and installations belonging to the enterprise which are issued to him as well as of the dwelling quarters and special clothing allotted him ; and to observe labour discipline and obey all the rules and orders issued by the management. For its part the employing enterprise must pay the cost of transport from the *kolhoznik*'s home of the man himself and 240 kilograms of effects (this seems to indicate that he is expected to bring his own bedding, cooking utensils and possibly simple tools

145   L

such as spades, pickaxes, saws, etc.). Remuneration is the standard rate of wages for the work with the usual premiums for exceeding the norm. After twelve months' work the *kolhoznik* is entitled to a holiday on full pay ; if he leaves before completing twelve months he receives a gratuity in lieu of leave of one twenty-fifth of the total wages he has received up to date. If the *kolhoznik* contracts for not less than twelve months' employment he may receive from one to two months' leave without pay and without travelling expenses to return home for farm work. Presumably if his farm requires him for the harvesting season it has to foot the bill. When groups of ten or more *kolhozniki* travel together to their place of employment they are sent in charge of a politically trustworthy and reliable leader. Whether this is usually a representative of the employing enterprise sent to fetch the draft, or a person appointed for the job by some local authority, or a member of the draft itself, is not clear. Nor is it plain whether his main duty is to prevent his charges deserting *en route*, or to see that they are properly looked after on the journey, catch the proper trains, etc. In existing conditions on Soviet railways it is quite impossible to count on arriving at distant destinations at a fixed date unless furnished with a powerful document attesting that one is travelling on duty and demanding preferential treatment from the railway authorities. A batch of *kolhozniki* travelling unescorted, even if they were furnished with documents, would almost certainly receive scant respect from railway booking clerks and others. I can testify from my own experience that in Soviet Russia petty officials can be as insolent, obstructive and stupid as the worst in any capitalist State. Official documents covered with stamps and seals must be supported by an authoritative mien, a loud voice and lots of bluster to be effective.

In spite of what I have written above about compulsion of *kolhozniki* to join labour drafts, it does not follow that the planned number of labourers is obtained. According to *Labour in the Socialist Community*, the planned number to be procured in thirty-six republics and provinces of the R.S.F.S.R. in 1938 was 2,781,000, of whom 1,653,000 were

actually enlisted ; but of this number only 1,495,000 were
in fact despatched to the employing enterprises. What the
total number is of *kolhozniki* drafted to industrial labour is
rather uncertain. Some years ago the Plan provided for
about 2·6 millions, but this total was almost certainly not
reached. If thirty-six republics and provinces supplied about
1½ millions in 1938, the total must have been over 2 millions,
for there were forty-seven such territorial divisions in the
R.S.F.S.R. at that time (several provinces have been divided
in two since then), not to mention five autonomous republics
and eighteen provinces in the rest of the Union, though in
the Asiatic territories the scheme is scarcely operative. This
number, however, by no means absorbed the whole surplus
agricultural labour, which might be of the order of 8 to
10 millions if agricultural labour as a whole were fully and
efficiently employed. But it is not so much the question of
finding the labour as of employing it, for the supply of unskilled labour is adequate to the needs of industry. The
creation of the Labour Reserve, of which a large part is to
come from the agricultural population, will have the effect of
withdrawing a large annual quota of labour from agriculture
and converting it into skilled industrial labour, instead of
allowing it to become part-time farm labour and part-time
unskilled and more or less redundant industrial labour.

Before leaving the subject of the labour resources of the
Soviet Union mention must be made of convict labour, because this plays, or has played, a very important part in the
construction of canals, hydro-electric dams, roads, railways,
etc. Convict labour and prison camps have been the subject
of an immense amount of anti-Soviet propaganda. It is not
easy to get a really objective view of the system, because
foreigners are not encouraged to go and see for themselves,
and the Russians, such as the Chernavins and Solonevichs,
who have succeeded in escaping abroad from G.P.U. camps,
have written about their own experiences rather than dealt
with the economic aspects of the system. I think it has
been pretty well established that the G.P.U. did at one time
round up large numbers of humble citizens, mainly belonging
to the peasant class, on trumped-up charges simply because

147

they wanted their labour. I would not say quite the same about the scientists, engineers and specialists who fell into the G.P.U. net. Probably these had been indiscreet in their conversation or had afforded the G.P.U. some grounds for arresting them by unconsciously showing that they could not swallow Bolshevism. But it is quite possible that when the G.P.U. wanted an engineer or other technical expert they examined their dossiers to see who could be arrested on some plausible charge. In any case the quantity of labour at the disposal of the G.P.U. in their various convict camps throughout the U.S.S.R. ran into millions. This labour was employed in the forests and sawmills of Northern Russia and Siberia and in constructing canals, etc. The White Sea–Volga and Moscow–Volga canals were among those built with convict labour. The G.P.U. is also said to run manufacturing enterprises with prison labour. I cannot say much about this from personal experience, except that once in Tiflis, having been apprehended on suspicion of being about to photograph a forbidden building, I found myself in some G.P.U. officer's room in Tamara's Castle, admiring a display of coloured models of animals and flowers in compressed bread. These, my host or jailer said, had been made by some of his prisoners in the bakery. All the prisoners were usefully employed ; as far as I remember hats and boots and perhaps earthenware were among their products. This was only prison industry on a small scale compared with the big factories fully equipped with machinery which the G.P.U. is credited with running. But the point concerning convict labour on canal construction is that these enterprises would almost certainly prove to have been uneconomic to construct with free labour. The convicts were given the minimum food, clothing and shelter and lived under conditions that free labour would not have tolerated for a moment. The output per worker would almost certainly be much less than that of free labour, so the difference in cost per unit of work done by convict and free labour was perhaps not so great as one would think. The more important consideration, however, was not the cost in food and clothing but machinery, at a time when all sorts of capital goods were scarce and every sort of industry clamouring for equipment and machines. The convicts were made to do all the excavation work, etc., with the minimum of labour-saving and power-driven machinery. It did not matter much how long the work took, for supplying them with food was only a problem of transport, and it was no matter for regret if quite a large proportion succumbed to privation and disease. The use of convict labour in the 1930's has certain similarities with the use of serf and forced labour by Peter I, when he built canals and roads and drained marshes. In both cases free labour was difficult to procure either because it was not available on the spot or because it demanded supplies and equipment that were scarce. In Peter's day power-driven machinery had not been invented ; in the early 1930's it was not available, because Soviet industry was not yet able to make it or was fully occupied in producing other things, and the Soviet Government could not afford to import it from abroad.

I am inclined to think that the use of convict labour and the number of prisoners in G.P.U. labour camps has considerably declined during the past two or three years. The fact that one hears nothing fresh about it may simply be due to the increased veil of secrecy which conceals all activities the Bolsheviks want to keep out of the capitalist press, and because nobody has recently escaped abroad from the camps to tell their story. I base my opinion rather on two other facts : since 1938 there has been no evidence of wholesale arrests and deportations of peasants such as took place in 1930–2, nor arrests of workers, engineers, specialists, etc., on the scale of the purge in 1937 ; secondly, Soviet industry is now capable of providing sufficient machinery to render the employment of forced manual labour less economic than it was when these things were scarce. Also the two chief protagonists of forced labour, Yagoda and his successor Yezhov, were both eliminated, the former in April 1937, the latter in December 1938, since when the G.P.U. (or the Commissariat of Internal Affairs, as it is now termed) seems to have suffered a curtailment of its former extraordinary and despotic powers.

CHAPTER XI

TRADE UNIONS

TRADE-UNIONISM is one of the aspects of the Soviet State that has been intensively studied and described by foreign observers. I have not made a special study of it and am therefore somewhat diffident about my qualifications for discussing it. But as the Trade Unions, or Professional Unions to use the Soviet term, play an important part in the life of the Soviet worker, they cannot be left out. The fundamental difference between capitalist and Soviet Trade Unions may be summed up as follows : capitalist Trade Unions have as their chief function the protection of the workers' interests against exploitation by employers ; in the Soviet Union the workers themselves own the means of production and dispose of the products of industry, therefore it is the duty of the Trade Unions to take the lead in raising the productivity of labour through promoting " Socialist competition " and the Stakhanov movement. For this reason the Trade Unions share in the organisation of industry ; and this is the cause of important differences between the structures of capitalist and Soviet trade-unionism.

Capitalist unions are formed on a craft basis, wherefore the workers in a single industrial enterprise may be, and usually are, distributed among a number of unions ; all of which compete against one another in the sense that all are concerned to obtain the best terms for their own members, irrespective of whether the success of their efforts reduces the capacity of the industry or enterprise to increase the wages of other workers. Soviet unions, on the contrary, are interested in raising the productivity of labour as a whole, because in this way only can the pecuniary rewards of labour be increased ; for Soviet industry, in theory at least, does not make profits that may be diverted from owners and shareholders to the workers. For this reason the unit of

Soviet trade-union structure is an industry as a whole and not a particular craft. The whole staff and personnel of an enterprise, from manager to sweeper, are members of the same union no matter what particular trade they practise or what office they fill. Because all are interested in the same way in the prosperity of the enterprise there is no distinction between employers' men and the ordinary workers, such as exists in capitalist enterprises, where managers and those in authority are deemed to owe a loyalty to the employer which precludes them from association with the workers.

The total number of Trade Unions in 1938 was about 165 with a membership of over 22 million out of about 26 million wage and salary earners. In common with the Party, Consumers' Co-operative Associations and other social and political organisations the trade-union system is organised on the pyramid principle, the base consisting of factory committees and local committees, the apex being the All-Union Central Council, whose general secretary at the moment of writing, Comrade N. M. Shvernik, is also a member of the Central Committee of the Communist Party and a candidate (alternate number) of the *Politbureau*. That is to say, he is one of the inner circle of rulers of the Soviet Union. The intermediate organs are the republican, provincial and district councils composed in each case of delegates from the next lowest stage. The election of members to serve on the primary organs, the factory and local committees, is by secret ballot of all members. Every organ is responsible to and must report periodically to its constituents, while factory, shop and brigade meetings are held to discuss all matters affecting the members and to elect shop committees, organisers, collectors of dues, etc. Most of these are unpaid, or at least are supposed to be unpaid.

Originally the conception of the duties and functions of Soviet Trade Unions was not in principle different from the capitalist idea. In 1920 Lenin himself admitted that " Our present Government is such that the proletariat, organised to the last man, must protect itself against it. And we must use the workers' organisation for the protection of the workers against their Government."

During the period of N.E.P. the existence of private employers of labour gave the Trade Unions the opportunity to exercise their function of protecting the workers against exploitation, particularly that of foreign concessionaires. Through a system of persecution and provocation they made the work of concessionaires doubly difficult, and this as much as anything rendered them ready to yield without much of a struggle when the Soviet Government proposed terms for cancelling their concessions. M. P. Tomsky, President of the All-Union Central Council of Professional Unions from 1917 to 1929, upheld the principle that Trade Unions existed to defend the rights of the workers, for which he was accused of Right Wing heresies and expelled from the Party. He eventually committed suicide when about to be arrested in 1936. At the eighth Congress of Professional Unions in December 1928 the struggle between those who subscribed to the old ideas of the functions of Trade Unions and the new principles advanced by Stalin and his adherents came to a head. This was not mere chance, for this congress coincided with the beginning of the Five-Year Plans and the final eradication of private enterprise in industry. It is curious to note how closely the charges levelled by the Stalinites against Tomsky and his principles resembled the allegations made by reactionary conservatives against trade-unionism in our own country. The workers, they said, were taught to consider their labour a commodity to be sold to the highest bidder and the unions were concerned to force up wages and opposed rationalisation and mechanisation because these would cause unemployment. Unemployment relief and sickness benefits were awarded in ways that encouraged the workers to evade employment and to malinger. Which, presumably, meant that insurance benefits were too generous and awarded too easily.

After the disappearance of Tomsky the trade-union system may be said to have been completely transformed into a state organisation. In 1934 the People's Commissariat of Labour was abolished and all its duties transferred to the

Trade Unions, which thus became responsible for making regulations for factory hygiene, prevention of accidents, etc., and, through its inspectors, for seeing that its regulations were observed. The Trade Unions also took over the administration of social insurance funds and a great part of the cultural and recreational amenities provided for the workers. At the eighth plenary session of the All-Union Council in 1939 the duties and functions of the Trade Unions were re-stated. The following is a summary of the important parts :

The Trade Unions must do more to develop the principle of socialist competition. Instead of organising competitions from above, they must persuade the workers themselves spontaneously to organise competitions.

Factory trade-union organs must assist the workers to improve their qualifications and technical skill. They must also use the Stakhanov movement to develop the individual initiative of workers and the rationalisation of labour ; and share in the organisation of factory labour with a view to increasing efficiency and reducing waste of time.

One of the most important duties of the Trade Unions is to assist in maintaining discipline ; for instance, seeing that factory managements strictly observe the law of 28th December 1938 (see Chapter VII). The Trade Unions must also see that workers do not receive more sickness or disability benefits than they are strictly entitled to.

Trade Unions take a part in fixing wage rates. Their activities in this direction, however, are not concerned with securing the highest rates possible, but with removing anomalies in the existing schedules, fixing normal tasks and the premiums for exceeding these tasks.

The other side of trade-union duties is concerned with the provision of social services and amenities for the workers. The unions run nearly 6000 clubs, 13,000 libraries, 10,000 cinemas, 174 sports stadiums, 667 sports grounds, 621 rest homes and 216 sanatoria. It is also their duty to improve working conditions in the factory and living conditions outside by controlling the building of dwelling-houses, crèches, kindergarten, schools, shops and restaurants. The expenditure involved is financed by the levy of 1 per cent of the workers' wages and the social insurance contributions paid by employing enterprises. But it should not be imagined that all the amenities provided for the workers are given gratis. An order issued by the Secretariat of the All-Union Central Council, dated 28th April 1937, gave the charges for a month's stay at various sanatoria at sums ranging from R.750 to R.940, while instructions issued in March 1940 provided that members must pay 30 per cent of the cost of their holiday if their wages amounted to more than R.300 a month. A month's stay at a sanatorium would therefore cost between R.225 and R.282, even if the charges fixed in 1937 have not since been raised.

The United Budget estimates of the Central Committees, the intermediate organs, the factory and local committees in 1938, were —

REVENUE

	R. Millions	R. Millions
Total		2297·5
Of which the chief items were —		
1. Members' dues . . .	805·4	
2. Receipts from " cultural measures "	180·4	
(This, presumably, refers to payments by members for amenities such as holidays in Sanatoria as mentioned above.)		
3. Contributions from employing enterprises towards cultural work .	818·9	

EXPENDITURE

	R. Millions	R. Millions
A. *Administrative and Organisational Expenditure* —		
Total		460·8
Of which the items were —		
1. Wages and salaries . . .	312·2	
[4903 members of Central Committees at R.7000 (average).		

R. Millions   R. Millions

14,173 officials in intermediate organs at R.6000 (average).

28,321 workers in factory and local committees at R.5000 (average).

5973 inspectors at R.8000 (average).]

2. Office expenses, etc.	37·8	
3. Organising expenses	110·8	

Of the above, R.323·5 was covered by members' dues.

B. *Assistance to Members —*

     Total . . . . .   229·8

     Of which the items were —

1. Grants to loan co-operatives .	75·3	
2. Expenses of members visiting sanatoria, etc.	61·9	
3. Children's homes, summer camps, etc.	33·4	
4. Grants-in-aid to trade-union members	52·0	
5. Grants-in-aid to workers in the trade-union apparatus	6·8	

C. *Cultural and Social Services —*

     Total . . . . .   1387·9

     Of which the items were —

1. Political instruction and propaganda	283·1	
2. Elementary education	125·2	
3. Art schools, etc.	300·9	
4. Cultural recreation	49·2	
5. Radio	23·9	
6. Care of children	64·1	
7. Libraries	131·8	
8. Sport and physical culture	174·4	
9. Upkeep of clubs, etc...	124·8	
10. Grants to publications	32·4	
11. Anti-religious propaganda	21·2	
12. Other forms of cultural work	56·8	

D. *International Activities* . . . .   2·0

E. *Capital Expenditure —*

     Total . . . . .   26·4

     Of which the items were —

1. Clubs, palaces of culture, etc.	11·1	

		R. Millions	R. Millions
2. Physical culture (sports grounds, etc.)	.	2·3	
3. Craft schools . ʼ . .	.	1·7	
4. Union headquarters, etc.	. .	1·6	
5. Dwelling-houses . ˙	. .	9·7	

F. *Equipment and Installations —*
          Total .   .   .   .   .   96·1

Of which the items were —

1. Sports	.	13·0
2. Culture	.	66·9
3. Offices	.	7·2
4. Transport and clubs .	. .	9·0

G. *Appropriations to the All-Union Central Council* . . . . . .   24·9

H. *To cover Former Deficits* . . . .   6·4

I. *Balance to Reserve* . . . .   63·2

                                              R.2297·5

The Presidium of the All-Union Central Council, when adopting the budget for 1938, drew attention to the fact that in 1937 the collection of dues was very inefficient, with the result that only 85·5 per cent of the full amount was realised.

The budget gives a precise summary of trade-union activities and the relative importance attached to each particular form of activity. The salaried staff amounts to over 53,000 persons, whose total pay, plus other administrative costs, comes to just 20 per cent of the total revenue. This does not seem extravagant when compared with the working expenses of British Trade Unions, which came to over 34 per cent of total revenue in 1938, or over 37 per cent of members' dues. But while over 90 per cent of the revenue of British Trade Unions was derived from dues, only 35 per cent of Soviet trade-union income came from the same source ; so that the ratio of administrative expenses to members' dues alone was about 57 per cent.

The functions of Trade Unions as organisers of labour as

a productive force are exercised through factory wages commissions, which in spite of their name are concerned more with raising the productivity of labour than with obtaining higher wages and better conditions of work. In capitalist enterprises such commissions would be regarded as organs of the employers. Wages commissions are established by all factory and local committees from among their own members, and include Stakhanovite workers, engineers and technical workers and employees in numbers varying between three and twenty-one, according to the number of workers employed and the size of the enterprise. Their duties comprise :

Organising socialist competition among the workers and employees by fixing conditions calculated to raise the productivity of labour.

Controlling the management's classification lists of Stakhanovites, " pre-eminent workers " and " shock - workers " and the number of workers drawn into socialist competitions.

Organising the exchange of experience between Stakhanovites and employees by means of Stakhanovite schools, lectures, etc., and glorifying distinguished competitors in works newspapers, by radio, in the clubs and so on.

Disseminating particulars of new forms and methods of Stakhanovism.

Organising technical instruction.

Inculcating systems of wage scales to accord with improvements in labour productivity and in quality of output.

Co-operate with managements in perfecting systems of fixing task norms, control the revision of norms, organise instruction under Stakhanovites for those workers who fail to fulfil their norms, and assist the management in removing causes of non-fulfilment.

Combat waste of time and defective output by discovering the causes and removing them and bring to the notice of the factory committee the names of persons responsible for these faults.

See that proper relations are maintained between the wages paid in different trades and make recommendations to the factory committee for removing anomalies.

See that the workers are properly distributed among the various departments and that their labour is properly employed in accordance with their qualifications. Also assist the management in classifying workers.

Check the proper observance of government laws regarding wage payment and see that wage sheets are properly made out.

See that the total amount of wages paid out is in due relation to the fulfilment of the factory's production plan.

See that labour discipline is maintained, particularly with regard to the laws against absenteeism, idling, etc.

See that new workers are properly treated and assist them in mastering their new jobs.

Organise factory conferences on production and see that recommendations by workers are duly received by the management and given proper consideration.

Organise inspection and care of equipment, tools, etc., and supervision of the quality of production.

Generally co-operate in encouraging initiative and invention, in rationalising labour and providing technical assistance to inventors.

Wages commissions work to a Plan approved by the factory committee and carry out any special tasks entrusted to them by the latter. They must bring to the notice of the factory management any breach of factory law, regulations and wages agreements, and if the management fails to pay attention to the commission's recommendations, the latter refers the matter to the factory committee for appropriate action.

If the workers are in any real sense the owners of Soviet industrial enterprises, and if democratic control be an operative principle and not merely a theory, Soviet Trade Unions may be considered organs of the workers. The whole question depends upon whether the Communist Party and the Soviet Government are, as they claim to be, the representatives and guardians of the workers' interests. It is quite possible that though the short-term views of the workers do not coincide with the long-term policy of their rulers, the latter are the best judges of the ultimate good of the whole community. In any case, the Trade Unions are concerned more with carrying out the rulers' policy than advancing the workers' immediate interests. It is improbable, to say the least, that the workers, left to themselves, would instruct their delegates to advocate and assist in introducing " speeding-up " methods, revision of piece-work rates downwards and legislation designed to prevent the workers' freedom of movement. At the same time the rulers themselves find fault with the Trade Unions for neglecting their duties and for bureaucratic tendencies.

The seventh plenary session of the All-Union Central Council in September 1938 adopted a resolution containing the following passages :

The VII Plenary Session takes note that the Trade Unions have not fulfilled the most important instructions drawn up at the VI Plenary Session to pay attention to the daily needs of workers and employees, both in respect to their living conditions and their employment.

Active control has not been exercised over the fulfilment of the Plan for dwelling-house building, the construction of crèches and kindergarten. The question of communal feeding has received entirely inadequate attention, neither has the work of trading establishments nor of mending and repairing workshops been controlled.

The instructions issued by the VI Plenary Session for greater activity in the protection of labour and technical safety measures have not been carried out. . . . This is shown by the irregular working of ventilation plant in various enterprises, by defective enclosures of lathes and machines, by bad lighting, etc.

Some trade-union organisations continue to infringe democratic principles : they neglect rendering regular reports to their members ; questions are decided by a single person instead of collectively ; and officers are co-opted instead of being elected.

159

It is impossible not to reflect that in any sort of truly democratic organisation such derelictions of duty on the part of the elected officers and committee would not be tolerated by the members. It is quite understandable that the members of a factory trade-union chapel would not take their representatives to task for a certain laxity in prompting the management to punish breaches of discipline, or in advocating upward revisions of the workers' daily tasks. But it is difficult to imagine that they would not express dissatisfaction if their representatives showed indifference to their material welfare.

Other indications that the " democracy " of Soviet trade-unionism is something different from what we associate with the word are provided in the proceedings of the annual conference held in Moscow from 27th July to 9th August 1940. The chief defect then denounced was the inflated " apparatus " of salaried officials. In 1939 the total of paid officials in the central committees and the sports societies under trade-union control numbered 194,433 ; in 1940 it had risen to 203,821, with a salary bill of over R.1000 million. A considerable number of officials, oddly described as " organisers of leisure ", " workers with the population " and so on, apparently hold sinecures. As a result, the Trade Unions were not only failing to fulfil their functions as schools of government and schools of Communism, but were becoming alienated from the masses of trade-unionists. No use was being made of the seven million " activists " (voluntary propagandists and political workers) among the workers, who were positively discouraged from their voluntary exercises by the presence of so many paid officials.

The conference resolved that the paid staffs be reduced as follows :

Central committees . . .	from 13,803 to 7,372
Provincial and regional committees	from 28,773 to 15,947
Factory and local committees .	from 50,797 to 14,658
Social clubs . . .	from 87,150 to 32,647
Sports societies . .	from 33,145 to 8,717

The totals are not comparable with the figures disclosed

in the budget for 1938, since the latter did not include social clubs and sporting societies. But it appears that whereas in the budget for 1938 provision was made for 47,397 paid officials in central, intermediate, factory and local committees, the actual number of these in 1940 was 93,373. No doubt the actual numbers in 1938 were considerably higher than those budgeted for.

In the published reports of the proceedings of the conference no mention was made of any discussion on wages, hours of work or working conditions, which, one would imagine, are topics of vital interest to trade-unionists.

The trade-union system is an outstanding example of the Bolshevik form of mass organisation and mass participation in the administration of public services. But, as the annual conference in 1940 disclosed, the Trade Unions were in imminent danger of becoming bureaucratic institutions. Whether in the least bureaucratic trade-union organisation the workers possess any real voice in the conduct of affairs is questionable. It is possible that unimportant local questions without political significance may be decided by a free vote of members in primary organisations : but it is quite certain that no matter on which the Government or the Party has given a lead can be debated. For to question the wisdom of the rulers is heresy. Thus the Trade Unions afford no opportunity for the workers to voice their grievances. For it is one of the articles of communist faith that the workers cannot have grievances in the Workers' State. Dissatisfaction with the way in which factory managements and trade-union committees carry out the labour laws and government instructions is admittedly possible, for the Government itself often finds cause to criticise its own executives. But the fact that criticism always seems to come from above and that reforms are initiated and prescribed by superior organs convincingly suggests that mass participation has singularly little chance of effecting improvements from below.

M

CHAPTER XII

THE STANDARD OF LIVING (1)

Present Standards compared with Pre-1914

THE most disputed question in relation to the economic condition of Soviet Russia is the standard of living of the people. On the one hand Bolshevik propaganda endeavours to prove that Russia is a workers' paradise, on the other hand critics of the Soviet régime produce equally plausible facts to show that the Russians as a whole are little, if any, better off than they were before the revolution. The general standard of living depends not merely on the material consumption of the people ; social services provided by the State and public bodies must also be considered. And it is worth noting that this aspect is the one most commonly stressed by the Bolsheviks and their friends. The Soviet Government permits the publication of no index figures of the cost of living nor of retail prices, nor is it easy to find any information regarding the absolute consumption of food and clothing. Figures purporting to show the percentage increase in *per capita* consumption of various commodities are of little value. If the consumption had risen by a respectable amount the Soviet Government would certainly have made full information available. The fact that this information is withheld is *prima facie* evidence that the standard has risen so scantily, if at all, that the Government is unwilling to confess to it.

With regard to social services and the amenities of life there is no question that the Bolsheviks have done a very great deal. But that their claims are exaggerated goes without saying. If in this respect the Russian worker is better off than were his parents under the Tsar, the real test is how conditions compare with those in capitalist countries. In assessing the success or failure of the Soviet régime to improve the conditions of the Russian worker it is necessary to fix upon some standard for comparison. The Bolsheviks themselves support their claim of a greatly improved standard of living by comparing present with pre-revolutionary conditions, or with conditions prevailing at the close of the First Five-Year Plan, that is in 1932 or 1933. With regard to the former they make no allowance for the improvement that would have occurred had there been no revolution. During the period from 1906 to 1914 the conditions of the industrial workers improved very considerably, both in material consumption and, even more, in working conditions and social services. It cannot be doubted that this improvement would have continued. The second comparison is also vitiated by the fact that the standard of living in 1932 had deteriorated compared with 1929 and, in fact, had sunk to a level comparable with 1922 or 1923, when, as a result of the war, the revolution and the civil war conditions were worse than in 1913. For a true perspective of living conditions comparison should also be made with conditions in the industrially advanced capitalist countries. It will simplify matters to deal separately with the material standard of living, that is the purchasing power of the workers' income and their consumption of food, clothing, etc., and with what may be called the intangible items, such as factory conditions, health services, education and so on.

Statistical information concerning pre-revolutionary standards of living is too incomplete to enable an accurate comparison to be made. But an idea of the relative purchasing power of the workers can be obtained from the following. *Planned Economy*, No. 5, 1938, gave the average per head consumption of the principal articles of food by the families of St. Petersburg textile workers in 1908. This was, per month :

[TABLE

163

Commodity	Kilograms
Rye bread and flour .	14
Wheaten bread and flour .	5
Groats and pulse . .	1
Vegetables . . .	11·3
Sugar . . .	0·7
Meat	2
Vegetable cooking fats .	0·2

The value of these commodities in 1913, 1929 and 1937 were, in current roubles :

Commodity	1913	1929	1937
Rye bread	1·02	1·32	11·90
Wheaten bread . . .	0·61	0·86	8·50
Groats and pulse . . .	0·13	0·21	1·30
Vegetables	0·80	1·52	7·10
Sugar	0·20	0·43	2·66
Meat	0·60	1·45	15·20
Vegetable cooking fats . .	0·06	0·10	2·90
	3·42	5·89	49·56

Industrial workers' wages in 1913 averaged about R.25 a month, in 1929 R.77 and in 1937 R.245. The cost of the above quantities of foodstuffs was therefore about 14 per cent of the worker's wage in 1913, about 8 per cent in 1929 and about 20 per cent in 1937.

Prices of clothing are more difficult to compare, because in 1913 the working classes bought a lot of their clothing from *kustari* (handicraft workers) and a good deal in the second-hand markets. A good pair of new boots could be bought in 1913 for R.10 ; in 1937 a pair of men's leather boots cost R.160 to R.180 and the quality would have been very poor. Ordinary cotton calico, from which working-class women made their dresses and men their shirts, cost in 1913 from R.0·25 to R.0·30 the metre, and in 1937 about R.3·75. In 1929 the official retail price index for manu-factured goods was about 212 (1913 = 100), and average wages were about three times 1913. No price indices have been

published since 1929 ; in any case the introduction of
rationing would have rendered them practically useless.
Rationing was ended in 1935, and by 1937 retail prices were
governed by supply and demand.

Though the Bolsheviks try to deny that market principles
have anything to do with price-fixing, it is perfectly clear
that the prices of staple consumption goods must be fixed
at a level that restricts demand to supply ; for if prices were
fixed too low the shops would be in a chronic state of " sold
out ", while if they were too high, stocks would remain unsold. Therefore prices in 1937 may be compared with 1929,
when rationing had not yet dominated the distribution of
consumption goods. On an average, the 1937 prices of
essential clothing and foodstuffs were at least five times the
1929 prices, while the average wage was only slightly more
than three times the 1929 level. In other words, the purchasing power of the worker's income in 1937 was about
65 per cent of 1929. The retail price index for all consumers' goods in 1929 was about 200 (1913 = 100) and the
wage index about 308. This would seem to indicate that the
1929 wage purchased about half as much again as in 1913 ;
but as the 1937 wage had only about two-thirds of the purchasing power in 1929, it looks as though real wages in 1913
and 1937 were pretty well at the same level.

I do not insist that the above calculations are definite
proof that the workers' standard of living to-day is no better
than in 1913. On the other hand, they certainly lead to the
conclusion that there has not been a very noticeable improvement. My own observations in the country itself lead
me to think that on the whole the workers to-day, at least
the factory workers, are slightly better off than they were
in the Tsarist Russia I knew. But that was in 1905, and
conditions certainly improved between that time and 1913.

The average wage is, of course, not a complete nor entirely
satisfactory yard-stick for comparing standards of living.
The general standard depends on the family income, or the
income per head when divided between earners and non-
earners. On this basis of calculation the advantage is
undoubtedly with the Soviet population, because a larger

proportion of the family is productive. Figures given in the Soviet Year-book, *Labour in the U.S.S.R.*, for 1936 for the composition of the families of workers in large-scale industry showed that the size of families and the number of dependants supported by each worker fell between 1930 and 1935 as follows :

Year	Average Number in Family	Average Number of Dependants per Worker
1930	4·02	2·05
1931	3·96	1·73
1932	3·93	1·73
1933	3·87	1·69
1934	3·83	1·66
1935	3·80	1·59

This process may have been specially rapid during the period covered by these figures, because it coincided with the period of most rapid industrialisation and a deterioration in the general standard of living. But, though official statistics are lacking, there is no doubt that both the size of the average worker's family and the number of dependants to each wage-earner were greater in 1913 than in 1930, and that the family continued to decline after 1935.

Another approach to the problem of the standard of living, much used by the Bolsheviks, is to compare the total output of consumption goods before the revolution with the output at the present time. But this method is faulty because it leaves out of count the large pre-revolutionary production of goods by *kustari* working independently or in producers' co-operative associations. Neither is allowance made for imported consumption goods, which in 1913 came to 28 per cent in value of total imports. What proportion of the total supply of manufactured goods these sources provided cannot be accurately stated. A large part of the handicraft output was made by peasants during the winter and sold locally, which rendered any attempt to compile statistical information practically impossible. Footwear,

166

furniture, cutlery, earthenware, locks, nails, lace and textiles were a few of the innumerable handicraft products. And in the case of footwear and furniture the output was considerably greater in volume than the output of the regular factories. To-day cottage industry has almost ceased and nearly all the so-called *kustarny* products are made in co-operative workshops and factories, whose output is included in the published statistics of industrial production.

Housing is also an item in living conditions. The difficulty here is to arrive at a fair mean because of the vast difference between the best and worst, both before the revolution and now. It is certainly true that even in 1913 a large proportion of the industrial workers lived under very bad conditions in insanitary log huts and wooden barracks, in the basements or even cellars of city houses and in other nooks and corners. But such dwellings are by no means unknown to-day and overcrowding is still intense and worse than in the old days. The average floor space per head of population in Moscow is about 45 square feet, and since officials, Stakhanovites and other privileged persons occupy a great deal more than the average, the ordinary worker must be content with appreciably less. On the other hand, most of the very large industrial enterprises own large blocks of workers' flats sufficient for a considerable proportion, but by no means all, of their workers. All the same, the encomiums lavished on Soviet housing by admirers of the Soviet system are not justified. The flats are tiny — two rooms and a kitchenette is the usual lay-out — and it is practically a rule that every room is used for sleeping at night, whatever may be its fate during the day. It is almost superfluous to add that no worker's flat has a bathroom and very few a separate lavatory. Feeding privately at home is looked upon as rather a bourgeois prejudice. Most factories have communal dining-rooms in which the workers take their principal meals. This comes much cheaper than eating at home ; besides very many of the workers' wives also work in the factory and have little time for cooking. All the same, the workers almost always prefer to eat at home if it can be arranged, and those who earn enough to allow their wives to stay at home and look after the house and do the cooking consider themselves well off.

When in Moscow in 1930 I visited a large tenement building called *dom kommuna* (communal house) in one of the industrial suburbs. It was not, as far as I remember, a factory house, but belonged to the municipality. I wrote in my diary at the time :

August 13, 1930. Visited the *dom kommuna* in the Shabolovsky quarter. Eight hundred persons occupy 200 flats which consist of one to three rooms, not very big, but light and airy. Every ten flats share a small kitchen with gas-rings and some of the bigger flats have kitchenettes of their own. Two or three flats that we were shown were neat and tidy, the occupants apparently being of the better artisan or skilled worker class. It was impossible to find out what rents were paid, but it seems that there is some sort of premium system which the tenants have to pay before obtaining a flat. This payment may amount to R.500. Single people and childless couples pay more than those with families. The building includes a communal theatre, recreation rooms, dining-room, etc. We were invited to try the midday meal, consisting of a large portion of *shtchi* (cabbage soup) and some sort of fish with nudels, costing in all 38 kopeks. A glass of milk cost 8 kopeks. Nearly every flat has a wireless supplied on the hire-purchase system, paid in eight monthly instalments. The public rooms and corridors are cleaned by a special staff of workers employed by the house, the flat occupants having only to keep their own premises clean. The dining-room walls displayed a number of exhortations to good manners, such as " Sit with your hands in front of you ", " Do not take salt with your fingers ", " Do not put your knife in the mustard ".

This was one of the first workers' tenements to be built and was rather a show place. The tenants were certainly above the ordinary factory operative class.

In 1939 our party spent a day at Gorki, where we were entertained to a motor-coach drive round the environs of the great motor-car factory. This employs thousands of workers and houses them in a whole township of tenement blocks laid out in parallel rows. The pink members of the party, determined to admire everything they saw in Russia, were enthralled by these barrack blocks. But what there was to admire was a mystery, at least to the rest of us taking a more objective and detached view of Soviet achievements. We were not invited to see inside, so it was quite possible that the flats were admirable. The outsides of the buildings, however, did not give much promise of the interiors. Like all brick buildings of the last ten years or so, the courses visibly deviated from the straight and horizontal, while the absence of pointing did nothing to improve the impression. Doorsteps had sagged and bits had broken away from plaster window-sills, while all doors and other visible woodwork were crying out for a coat of paint. The building of dwelling-houses in Russia to-day is nearly always scamped and maintenance is bad.

That existence in a communal block of flats is more tolerable and more hygienic than in a damp basement or wooden hut, I do not deny. But that it represents a degree of comfort unknown by pre-revolutionary workers is quite a false notion. Naturally the Bolsheviks suppress the fact that a number of the big industrial concerns in the Tsarist time provided dwelling-houses for their workers quite up to the standard of the best Soviet tenements. Towards the end of the old régime the conviction was spreading among Russian employers that it not only paid in increased efficiency of the workers to provide them with decent living conditions, but that employers were under a moral duty to look after their employees. One reason for the bad conditions under which industrial labour lived up to the close of the nineteenth century was the seasonal nature of so large a part of the labour. No manufacturer could be expected to build houses and go out of his way to provide amenities for peasant workers who worked in factories for only part of the year and returned to their villages when farm work called them. But when the numbers of real proletarian industrial workers began to increase and seasonal labour to decline, it became worth while to treat the workers well.

Comparison between the conditions of pre-revolutionary workers and Soviet workers in the late 1930's is still more difficult because of the great differences between the incomes of different grades of Soviet workers. The average wage and salary income of all workers and employees was about R.245 a month in 1937, but the individual earnings of industrial workers ranged from R.115 to R.1000 or more. In fact monthly earnings of two or three thousand roubles by Stakhanovites were by no means rare. So far as I know, the Soviet Government has never allowed the publication of figures giving the total number or relative proportions of workers in various wage groups. I should say that skilled factory workers earn from R.350 a month upwards, while so-called technicians, or mechanics and fitters as we should call them, earn from R.600 upwards. That means that unskilled or semi-skilled labour earns a good deal less than the average income. Life on an income of R.200 a month or less in 1937 was a mere struggle for existence. On the authority of the worker I interviewed in the train from Moscow to Rostov on Don, whom I have already quoted in Chapter VII, the minimum income on which two people could live was R.400. He gave it as his opinion that an income of R.300 at the present day was about the equivalent of R.40 before 1914, which makes the Soviet rouble equal to $7\frac{1}{2}$ Tsarist kopeks, or just about twopence. Incidentally British visitors to Russia, especially those who make a point of collecting and comparing shop prices, agree in valuing the rouble at between 2d. and 3d. so far as its retail purchasing power is concerned. In Tsarist Russia the average wage of mechanics, fitters and highly skilled factory workers was at least R.40 a month ; it was the unskilled and semi-skilled labour such as women cotton-mill operatives who were paid R.25 or less. On the whole it would seem that there was not much difference between the purchasing power of money wages in 1913 and 1937. But owing to the progressive premium system of piece-work rates in Soviet factories I would give it as my opinion that the higher ranks of skilled labour to-day, that is approximately all those classed as Stakhanovites, earn wages representing an appreciably higher purchasing power than their prototypes in Tsarist Russia. On the other hand it is very doubtful whether the condition of the rank and file of unskilled and semi-skilled labour is any better if as good to-day as in 1914.

Although the industrial workers form the largest section of the Soviet population after the agricultural peasants, the intelligentsia, that is the clerical workers, scientific and technical workers and the professions, number some ten millions, and with dependants may comprise between 14 and 15 per cent of the total population. In assessing the improvement or otherwise in the general standard of living this class must be included. Our socialist admirers of Bolshevism nearly always concentrate on proving that the lot of the industrial workers has been changed for the better by Bolshevism and neglect the intelligentsia and the peasants. The pre-revolutionary salaries of office clerks, salesmen, etc., ranged from about R.75 to R.300 a month in Moscow and St. Petersburg, rather less in the provinces. These incomes may be compared with incomes of R.750 and R.3000 to-day. A list of salaries in force in 1937 or later is shown on p. 172.

All the data given in the table are taken from the official bulletin of financial and economic laws. My own investigations on the spot show that the earnings of shop assistants in large shops in the big towns run from about R.200 to R.600. I should also explain that managers of shops, shop assistants and many other persons employed in trade and industry receive bonuses according to the turnover of their whole enterprise or particular department ; while professors and teachers can earn supplements to their salaries by giving " consultations ", in other words private coaching, to students. However, the incomes of professional people and " white collar " workers generally are not much above the wages of skilled workers. The difference between the remuneration of manual labour and brain-work is far smaller than before the revolution, and the standard of living of brain workers is very far below that in Tsarist days. With an income of R.150 a month, about the equivalent of £15, before 1914 a Moscow or St. Petersburg clerk considered himself comfortably off. He probably lived in a small self-contained flat in one of the less fashionable streets or suburbs, whose rent would be R.25 or R.30 a month. In summer he would rent a small

Profession or Occupation	Monthly Salary in Roubles
Education —	
University professors . .	1100 to 1500
University lecturers . .	700 ,, 900
Directors of studies in technical	
schools . . .	475 ,, 570
Teachers in technical schools .	340 ,, 405
Directors of secondary schools .	400 ,, 600
Teachers in secondary schools .	310 ,, 425
Teachers in primary schools .	270 ,, 400
School inspectors . .	650 ,, 700
Legal — .	
People's Court executives .	300 ,, 375
People's Court secretaries .	250 ,, 325
Medical —	
Dentists	265 ,, 390
Dispensary manager . .	375 ,, 630
Qualified dispenser . .	325 ,, 450
Senior operating theatre sister .	240 ,, 365
Commerce —	
Managers of trading concerns .	750 ,, 1200
Post Office —	
Directors	1200 ,, 1800
Departmental managers .	480 ,, 850
Chief cashiers . . .	480 ,, 600
Engineers . . .	600 ,, 1000
Telegraphists in large centres .	240 ,, 440
Telephone exchange operators .	190 ,, 320
Agriculture —	
Technical experts in charge of	
departments of the Commis-	
sariat of Agriculture . .	850 ,, 1200
Art —	
Concert singers attached to musi-	
cal institutions and giving 10	
performances a month .	400 ,, 2000
For single performances else-	
where	50 ,, 600

dacha [1] or part of one. The essentials of living were exceedingly cheap, and house-keeping for a family of four would have cost certainly no more than R.50 a month. To-day a clerk working in one of the big industrial or commercial offices would most likely occupy one room in what was formerly a big flat and his wife would share a common kitchen with four or five other residents. A Soviet clerk having about the same qualifications and duties as a pre-revolutionary clerk earning R.150 a month, would be paid perhaps R.600 a month ; whereas to enjoy anything like the same standard of comfort he would need an income of about R.1500.

In the earlier years of the Bolshevik régime the situation of the brain workers was absolutely inferior to that of the industrial workers. Not only was their money remuneration relatively smaller in comparison with industrial wages than to-day, but when rationing was in force their rations were smaller than the rations of the manual workers. The actual amounts of food included in the rations varied from time to time and from place to place, but as a general rule non-manual workers received about half the quantities of bread and meat allowed to manual workers. In other ways, too, clerical workers were discriminated against, particularly in regard to education, for, generally speaking, secondary and higher education was reserved for the children of genuine proletarians. Both these disadvantages were removed some years ago, and there is now no difference between the legal status and rights of any class of workers. All the same I have the impression that in some ways, such as the provision of clubs and recreation, holidays at seaside resorts, etc., the office clerk is not treated quite so well as the factory worker.

A deterioration in the standard of living of the non-manual workers compared with pre-revolutionary times must be set off against any improvement there may be in the condition of the industrial workers. There remain the

[1] *Dacha* is literally a country house, but the word was generally used to indicate the bungalows, usually built of logs, that are found on the outskirts of every big town and which were inhabited by the city folk during the months of May to August. Owing to the present housing shortage most of the *dachas* are now occupied the whole year round.

peasants, forming over half the total population. I must confess that I find it most difficult to decide whether the *kolhoznik* of to-day is better or worse off than the independent peasant farmer of former times. The chief difficulty is that collective farms differ as widely as did the peasant farms : some are prosperous and some are poverty-stricken. The density of the agricultural population is less than thirty years ago, and the land as a whole produces rather better crops owing to the application of more scientific methods and the use of machinery. The production of foodstuffs and agricultural raw material per head of labour employed is certainly higher to-day than in Tsarist times. The *kolhoznik* ought therefore to be better off than the former independent peasant. But there are other factors that must be considered and which react to his disadvantage. Obviously the *kolhoznik* must pay for the machinery he uses in some way or other. It is useless for the Bolsheviks to pretend that the tractors, drills, harvesters and other machines supplied through the machine-tractor stations are a gift to the peasants. There is no attempt to conceal the fact that the collective farms pay for the use of these machines ; but it is always implied, if not openly stated, that the vast capital invested in the enormous agricultural machine works was found by the Government at no cost to the peasants. Actually, of course, all capital investments in Soviet Russia are the result of national savings, to which the agricultural section of the population has contributed more than a fair share. By requisitioning a large part of the surplus product of the collective farms (probably about 80 per cent) and paying a very low price for it, the Government restricts the consumption of the *kolhozniki* and appropriates the resulting savings. Apart from this, the working costs of mechanical farming are certainly unduly high, because of the high cost of machine maintenance, the high consumption of fuel, etc. In terms of grain and other produce the cost to-day of the manufactured goods needed by the agricultural population, textiles, nails, soap, kerosene, sugar, etc., is at least five times the cost in 1913. Another indication of the poor remuneration for agricultural labour is the decrees issued in the first half of 1939 compelling the *kolhozniki* to work a certain number of days in the year on the farm, and ordering all private plots to be strictly limited to the legal maximum size. These decrees were found necessary because in a very large number of farms the *kolhozniki* found that it paid them better to cultivate their own allotments, of a half-acre to an acre in extent, than to work on the collective fields, for which the rewards in money and kind were, and still are, very scanty.

A somewhat false indication of the Soviet peasant's improved prosperity, as quoted by the Bolsheviks, is his increased purchases of consumption goods compared with both Tsarist times and in Soviet Russia before the collectivisation. The natural economy of the individual peasant has been replaced by a money economy, for owing to the decline of home industries the *kolhoznik* to-day buys many things his parents used to make for themselves. For example, very many *kolhozniki* to-day buy bread from the village co-operative store ; in Tsarist days nearly every peasant household baked its own bread from flour made from its own corn. In those days nearly every village had a small flour-mill, often belonging to the largest farmer in the community, at which the peasants could have their corn ground. The Soviet suppression of private enterprise resulted in a great majority of these mills falling into disuse and ruin. In consequence *kolhozniki* often find it impossible to convert the grain they receive from the collective farm into flour, and in some cases, as reported in Soviet newspapers, are compelled to pound their wheat or rye into a coarse meal at home and eat it in the form of porridge. But in spite of the increased consumption of bought goods, the rural population still buys very much less per head than the urban population ; as a matter of fact the total turnover of retail trade in the country is absolutely less than in the towns, though the rural population in actual numbers is about twice as large as the town population. As I have already remarked, it is very difficult to determine whether the Soviet peasant is better off in material ways than his parents were under the Tsar, but I think it can be confidently said that the peasant to-day has a lower standard of living compared with the factory worker than in Tsarist times. From what I have written in this chapter the reader will have gathered that I am not in agreement with those who would make out that the Russian people to-day are definitely worse off materially than at the close of the Tsarist régime ; still less do I support the allegations of the admirers of the Soviet system, that the revolution has brought about an immense improvement of the lot of the people. For the sake of the argument I am willing to concede that it is possible that the Russian masses may on the whole be better off than thirty years ago, but is it not fair to expect that an improvement in their standard of living would have taken place had the Tsarist régime continued ? I do not think that anybody but the most bigoted Soviet propagandists attempts to deny that great advances in every way were made between 1905 and 1914. The World War naturally checked the progress that was being made ; but is there any reason to suppose that recovery would have been any slower than under the Bolsheviks, or that subsequent progress would have been any less ?

So far I have been dealing with the masses of the population, the industrial workers and the peasants. These, however, do not form the whole population, and to form a complete picture we must know whether the Bolsheviks have improved the conditions of any sections of the people and which sections, if any, have suffered. What, for instance, has been the fate of the upper classes in Tsarist Russia, the aristocrats, the gentry and the industrialists and merchants, with whom we should perhaps include the clergy ? The popular conception of the enormous wealth of the Russian nobleman and the merchant was a great exaggeration. Some of the old noble families and some merchant princes were certainly very rich indeed, but as a whole the upper classes were not extravagantly wealthy and lived simply. They, of course, have been exterminated, and few foreigners extend them any sympathy, which in my opinion is unfair. The ruling and upper classes were no worse, if no better, than in other countries. A very large proportion was public-spirited and liberally inclined ; many members of the

176

aristocracy gave both time and money to public service, though opportunities in this direction were limited by the policy of the Government, which did not approve of private enterprise in social work. The educational and health services of the *zemstvos*, which may be likened very roughly to our county councils, and of the urban municipal councils were hindered rather than assisted and encouraged by the Imperial Government. I fail to see how any reasonable person can regard the total elimination of the old Russian upper classes as an unqualified gain.

The upper middle class consisted, as with us, of professional men, civil servants, scientists and teachers and the leaders of private enterprise in industry and commerce. A very large proportion of this class was physically exterminated by the revolution and practically the whole was ruined. The comparatively small remnant that adjusted itself to Soviet conditions and now serves under the Soviet Government has a standard of living infinitely inferior to that enjoyed in the old days.

Even the industrial workers should not be taken as a whole, for they are divided among a number of groups from the highly skilled factory worker to the workers in the convict camps. I suppose some people might question the inclusion of the last-named. But as the great majority are not criminals in our understanding of the word and as they certainly form an appreciable part of the total industrial labour, I see no reason for excluding them. I am inclined to think that the top stratum of industrial labour is genuinely better off than in the old days. It is undoubtedly much better off in comparison with all other groups or sections of the population. The position of the ordinary factory operative or machine-minder is rather less certain. My own opinion is that there is not a great deal to choose between their standard of living to-day and formerly. It should be understood that I am thinking now only of the material consumption of food and clothing and housing conditions.

The condition of the unskilled workers, such as peat-diggers, workers in lumber camps, navvies and so on, can scarcely be any better than in the old days, for their wages represent a mere subsistence level. It is questionable whether even the convict labour is much worse off. Including these and the unskilled labour earning the minimum wage of R.115 a month, the total number existing on a bare subsistence level is probably not less than three millions. Nobody knows the number of convicts in the labour camps in North Russia and Siberia employed on railway and canal construction and similar works. Besides these a considerable number of prisoners are employed in factories run by the G.P.U., whose condition is certainly worse than that of the ordinary unskilled factory labour.

In Tsarist Russia the peasants were divided into three groups, the rich, average and poor. The rich peasants, rich only in relation to the mass, are called *kulaks* by the Bolsheviks, a term originally applied to that class of peasant who exploited and victimised their fellows by lending money at exorbitant rates of interest or, being the owner of a flour-mill, charged the poor peasant a high price for grinding his corn. The poor peasants were those who, owning no land or very little and no working animals, were compelled to eke out a scanty existence by hiring their labour to landowners or rich peasants. The average peasant possessed just about enough land to enable him and his family to exist without working for wages as a regular thing. In almost any other country they would have been regarded as poor, and as a matter of fact most of them lived on the borderline of starvation, which periodically overtook them when the harvest failed. Of course the average standard of living varied in different regions. In those parts of the country where peasant holdings were fairly large and the land fertile, such as in the south-eastern districts, now comprised in the North Caucasus, the average peasant would have been accounted rich in the densely populated parts of Central Russia. The same applies to the collective farms to-day. Generally speaking, those situated in regions where formerly the peasants were comparatively prosperous afford a higher standard of living to their members than those in the densely populated regions, where the standard of living of the peasants was low. Collectivisation has probably reduced the difference between the extremes. The most prosperous collective farms certainly do not afford their members so high a standard as that formerly enjoyed by the most prosperous of the independent peasants. At the same time there are probably few *kolhozniki* quite so poverty-stricken as the former *batraki* (landless agricultural labourers). I would venture the guess that the average standard of living of the *kolhozniki* to-day is about equal to that of the rather better off among the former average peasants.

Even if the Soviet régime has brought about some improvement in the condition of the manual workers and peasants, it is probably imperceptible to the people themselves because their desires have increased. The spread of education and culture, and by that must be understood the cinema, radio and sport, has made the ordinary man more aware of the possibilities of life and he is no longer content with the homespun existence of his parents. As a matter of fact very few Russians to-day have any vivid recollections of conditions before 1914 ; either they are too young or their memories have been overlaid by far more poignant experiences during the past twenty years. I have usually found that the ordinary Russian compares conditions to-day with those prevailing in the years 1930 to 1933. Certainly compared with those years a great improvement has been made. When the Soviet Government announced the First Five-Year Plan, it warned the people that they must be prepared for a few years of stress and hardships, in order that the country's productive power might be built up rapidly. But the Bolsheviks were too optimistic and committed the country to a programme of capital investment beyond its power of saving. No doubt, too, the world depression which caused a greater fall in prices of foodstuffs and raw materials than of the manufactured goods the Soviet Government had to buy abroad, added to its difficulties. The result was that the standard of living of the whole people fell even more than had been expected and allowed for. In fact even this was insufficient to cover capital investments, which were made partly at the expense of existing capital. It is now a matter of history that during the years 1929 to 1932 about half the country's total head of farm livestock disappeared. The usual explanation is that the peasants slaughtered their animals rather than pool them in the collective farms, and to a great extent this is true. But it is nonsense to imagine that the animals were entirely wasted. A great many were slaughtered, not to prevent them falling into the hands of the collective farms, but for food, and it may be taken for granted that practically all that were slaughtered for any reason whatever were eaten. Thus it is obvious that the capital represented by the animals that were killed was consumed and not merely wasted. And, it must be remembered, the years 1931 and 1932 were starvation years, so the food was urgently needed. It is also an acknowledged fact that during that famine some millions of persons (fairly reliable estimates give the number as about four millions) died from starvation or diseases caused thereby. The loss of so many workers and potential workers must also be regarded as a loss of capital to the nation. The industrial workers, though they did not die like the peasants, also consumed capital in order to live. In an article in *Planned Economy*, No. 8, of 1936, entitled " The Standard of Living of the Toilers in the U.S.S.R.", it is on record that in 1933 no less than 7·2 per cent of the workers' income was derived from the sale of their own belongings. In 1934 the proportion was 3·4 per cent and in 1935 1·6 per cent. A considerable part of these sales was of food rations, which the poorest of the workers were compelled to sell in order to buy other necessities. Finally the maintenance of dwelling-houses, the railways and almost any form of property whose repair could be postponed was neglected, which must also be regarded as consumption of capital.

In those years of the early thirties the supply of food was insufficient to provide the whole population with an adequate diet. Moscow, Leningrad and the industrial region of Donbass and the workers in the coal and metallurgical industries were given preference in the distribution of rations. Thus, while in Moscow and the other places mentioned the lower income groups of industrial workers were

able to satisfy 77 per cent in money value of their requirements with their rations, in other large towns rations supplied 68 per cent and in, so-called, second-category towns
only 46 per cent. The higher income groups bought 60 per
cent in value of their food in the open market in Moscow
and Leningrad, 70 per cent in other large towns and 87 per
cent in second-category towns. Since nobody then had
money to spend on mere luxuries, and moreover the prices
of non-rationed goods were exorbitant, it is safe to say that
purchases on the open market were confined to supplementary quantities necessary to satisfy quite modest food
requirements. In the preferred towns and occupations the
rations did not by any means provide a complete diet, while
in the second-category towns the poorer workers, compelled
to rely on their rations for most of their food consumption
must have existed on the verge of starvation.

When I visited Russia in 1930 the dearth of all sorts of
consumption goods was already acute, but not so catastrophic
as in 1932. People were not then so afraid of speaking to
foreigners. Several times I was the recipient of spontaneous
complaints by persons who, for some reason or other, felt
the urge to confide in a foreigner. In Kazan an ordinary
working man insisted on walking some way down the street
with us to tell us about the inadequacy of his rations and
the exorbitant prices of everything else. Unskilled labour
there at that time was paid R.30 to R.40 a month, which,
considering that bread cost about R.1 a kilogramme in the
open market and meat some R.2 to R.3, did not go far.
Kazan would have been a second-category town where the
ration scale was very low. Another man, carrying a port-
folio, the uniform badge of a Government clerk, stopped us
in the grounds of the Central Executive Committee building
to say that the population was almost starving. His own
private grievance was mainly the impossibility of getting
clothes. He was wearing the regulation Russian summer
suit of linen, almost indistinguishable from pyjamas, which
appeared to be his complete wardrobe ; and what he was
to do when winter came he was afraid to think. The chances
of being able to procure a warm suit and an overcoat were

so remote as to be practically non-existent. At Tikhorietz-kaya railway junction in the North Caucasus, where we had to change trains, the porter, who rendered us some slight assistance in carrying our baggage, excused his inability to carry a heavy suitcase by inadequate food. He did not look starved, I must confess, but, as he pointed out, no one can do hard manual work on a diet of bread and potatoes helped out with cucumbers and water-melon. Animal food was unobtainable by the ordinary folk. Our own experiences agreed with a general shortage of food. Not even in the best hotels in Moscow and Leningrad could one get more than one decent meal in the day, and even that was cut very fine. In the provinces conditions were generally far worse. Food was not only doled out in minute portions but was often nauseating. A young man who sat at the same table with us in the best restaurant in Novosibirsk cheered us up by opining that the so-called *goulash* was almost certainly horse. Fortunately we had provided ourselves, on the advice and from the stores of *Intourist* in Moscow, with a large sackful of tinned food, dried fish, sugar and hard biscuits without which we should more than once have been painfully hungry. Manufactured goods were equally scarce. In Moscow we found it impossible to buy one ordinary lead pencil. Clothing was just not to be seen in the ordinary shops ; the whole supply seemed to be concentrated in factory stores, whence they were doled out to the workers when their old clothes were finally and irrevocably past patching and mending.

Compared with 1930, conditions in 1937 were wonder-fully good. Food was abundant and the shops appeared to be well stocked with clothing, textiles, household goods, furniture and " cultural " goods, that is, musical instruments, toys, sports equipment and so on. Incidentally Soviet tennis racquets and balls must be seen to be believed, and anybody who dares use a Soviet shot-gun must be very brave. All the same, shortages of one thing or another were still chronic. At one time, at the beginning of winter of course, galoshes would be unprocurable, while at the beginning of summer the shops would be full of heavy overcoats and cloth suits, but quite innocent of cotton or linen fabrics. At any time it might be impossible to buy needles and thread, kerosene lamp chimneys or pocket torch batteries. But the Soviet citizen expects these minor inconveniences and orders his shopping with a view to future needs rather than immediate requirements. I remember two occasions in Moscow when the release of a stock of a certain commodity had a startling effect on the ordinary aspect of the streets. One was the sudden and inexplicable offer to the public of large quantities of pillow feathers. That day the odd spectacle was seen of hundreds of people passing along the streets with sacks, bolsters and pillows from which a steady trickle of feathers floated away in the breeze. The other was the sale of a large number of galvanised-iron wash-tubs, which led to processions of women carrying these cumbersome articles home to the accompaniment of the ribald jests of other wayfarers. For no Russian is ever in too much of a hurry, unless he be a Party official *en route* to a conference, to stop and stare and utter ribald jests at anything out of the ordinary. Then in 1939 our party was mightily entertained and intrigued by the simultaneous vision of thousands of yellow berets. It is no exaggeration to say that every other Soviet girl was thus bedecked : it was rather like one of those sudden appearances of clouds of yellow butterflies that now and again infest parts of the English countryside. I suppose at other times it might be blue or green berets, but the brilliant yellow ones were too obvious not to attract attention.

In reviewing recent years still fresh in their memories the Russians themselves are apt to forget the more distant years. Hence the Soviet régime gets credit for the improvements of the past few years, while its responsibility for the privations of the early 1930's is overlooked.

CHAPTER XIII

THE STANDARD OF LIVING (2)

Comparisons with Capitalist Conditions

IN the last chapter I gave my reasons for thinking that the material standard of living in Russia has not improved as much as Soviet propagandists would have us believe. Possibly I am too critical and sceptical, but as I took pains to make clear, there is very little precise information available, such as price and cost of living indices, working-class budgets and the like. If the Soviet Government chooses to keep such matters secret it cannot complain if other people interpret its reserve as evidence that there is something to hide. Though official price indices are lacking, it is open to anyone to collect prices for himself by going round the shops. I have been fortunate in having access to price schedules and other information compiled over a considerable period of time in Moscow by a resident foreigner whose job was to study economic conditions. These facts and figures were the result of personal enquiry and observation, and in the absence of official statistics may be accepted as approximately correct.

The Soviet Statistical Year-book gives the total annual wage bill and the average wage and salary income for all persons employed in the national economy. That includes the highly paid administrative and technical personnel as well as the ordinary workers. It is a simple matter to calculate the quantity of goods a given sum will buy and thus to arrive at some idea of the consumption power of various incomes.

In *The Times* of 15th February 1941 appeared an article on the standard of living of British working-class families, which may serve us as a standard of comparison with the purchasing power of a Moscow worker's family in 1939.

The Standard of Living

In 1938 the average wage and salary income in Soviet Russia was about R.3500 a year, or, say, R.70 a week. A factory worker in Moscow would earn somewhat more than this ; and, allowing for the usual annual increase in the average wage, we should not be far out if we put the amount at R.100 a week in 1939 for a skilled factory hand. *The Times* figures were based on a family containing 3·75 members, of whom 1·75 were wage-earners, with a total income of 86s. 3d. a week. A Moscow workman's family of the same size and with the same proportion of earners might enjoy a total income of R.175 a week. Actually this figure would probably be rather too high, since it is improbable that the subsidiary earners would receive the same rate of wages as the chief bread-winner. We must therefore bear in mind that R.175 represents a family income well above the average for all industrial workers.

The distribution of the two incomes according to *The Times* article and my Moscow informant would be :

Objects of Expenditure	British Working Class Family		Russian Working Class Family	
	% of Income	Actual Sums Spent	% of Income	Actual Sums Spent
		s. d.		R.
Food . . .	40	34 1	67	117·25
Clothing . .	9	8 2	14	24·50
Rent, rates and water	12	10 8 }	7	12·25
Fuel and light . .	7	6 4 }		
Direct taxes . .	..	⸲ ..	6	10·50
State loan ..	..	..	4	7·00
Union dues . .	2	1 4	1	1·75
Medical attention .	2	1 8	..	..
Insurance, savings and sundries . .	28	24 0	1	1·75
	100	86 3	100	175·00

It is very doubtful whether a Russian family with the above income would actually spend 67 per cent on food. Neither household goods, luxuries such as cigarettes, entertainment and holidays, books and newspapers are adequately

185

allowed for in the above scale. The R.1·75 for other items would certainly not go far. Besides a " voluntary " life insurance by the head of the family is practically compulsory. Supposing for the sake of argument R.117·25 were spent on food, it would be interesting to see how far this would go in providing about the same quantity and variety as the British family might be expected to consume.

Commodity	Quantity	Cost in England		Cost in Moscow
		s.	d.	R.
Bread . . .	13·5 lb.	2	8¼	7·14
Flour . . .	4·4 ,,		10	5·80
Cereals . . .	1·0 ,,		3¼	0·85
Meat . . .	4·7 ,,	6	2¼	25·20
Fish . . .	1·5 ,,	1	4½	5·06
Milk . . .	11·2 pints	3	0¾	10·25
Milk, preserved . .	.. ,,		6	3·45
Butter . . .	1·8 lb.	2	5½	14·00
Cheese . . .	1·0 ,,	1	0	6·66
Eggs . . .	1·0 doz.	1	10½	7·80
Bacon . . .	1·0 lb.	1	11	9·90
Lard . . .	0·3 ,,		2¾	11·75
Margarine . .	0·5 ,,		4¾	3·26
Tea . . .	1·25,,	1	7¾	50·00
Sugar . . .	4·8 ,,	1	0½	8·35
Vegetables . .	4·8 ,,	1	4½	2·50
Coffee and cocoa . .	..		2½	2·00
Jam . . .	1·0 ,,		7½	1·60
Fruit . . .	..	1	9½	5·00
	..	29	5¾	170·57

The quantities and English prices are taken from the article in *The Times*, while the Russian prices are those for the same quantities of the nearest available articles. The Russian would certainly not buy anything like such a varied choice of foods. He is accustomed to a very much simpler diet than the British working man ; he eats far less meat and animal food generally, his main consumption consisting of bread, cereals and vegetables. Butter, cheese, eggs and bacon would be considered great luxuries and if bought at all would be only to celebrate holidays. Though the Russian is quite satisfied with a simple and rather monotonous diet, it does not alter the fact that the standard of consumption of a Russian worker earning good wages is much below that of a British worker in more or less comparable circumstances.

A publication, *Towards a New Stage in Socialist Construction*, issued by the Institute of Economic Investigation in 1930, gives a lot of useful information on consumption standards in Russia during the latter part of the N.E.P. period. At that time statistics were compiled more honestly and far more expertly than to-day and were far more reliable. In any case no similar statistics have appeared since. The following is a list of foodstuffs and quantities consumed per head in workers' families in twelve months in 1927–8, that is just before the inauguration of the First Five-Year Plan :

Commodity	Quantity in Kilogrammes	Cost in Moscow in 1939 of Same
		R.
Rye flour . . .	29·23	46·77
Rye bread . .	35·67	30·32
Wheat flour . .	59·12	141·89
Wheat bread . .	58·46	99·38
Groats . . .	13·56	32·54
Potatoes . . .	95·76	47·88
Other vegetables . .	37·59	45·11
Meat and fats . .	49·21	590·52
Milk . . .	77·83	124·53
Butter . . .	2·70	47·25
Eggs . . .	4·82	65·00
Sugar . . .	15·58	59·20
Fish . . .	8·79	61·53
Vegetable oil . .	3·44	41·28
Salt . . .	5·86	0·29
Total cost in 1927–8, R.145·45		R.1433·49

The average wage and salary in 1927–8 was about R.703 and in 1939 about R.3800, thus, while income increased by 440 per cent, the cost of food increased by 888 per cent ; or, while in 1927–8 it took about 21 per cent of the average income to buy the above quantities of food, in 1939 it took nearly 38 per cent. It would appear then that the consumption of foodstuffs in 1939 must have been inferior to 1927–8. If we reduce the above to weekly quantities under the main headings, the consumption of the British and Russian working classes (supposing food consumption in 1939 to be about the same as in 1927–8) would be more or less as follows :

Commodity	British Consumption (Lb. per Head)	Russian Consumption (Lb. per Head)
Bread, flour and cereals . .	5·0	8·3
Meat and animal fats . .	2·4	2·2
Milk (pints) . . .	3·0	2·6
Eggs (pieces) . . .	3·2	1·6
Fish	0·4	0·4
Sugar	1·3	0·7
Vegetables . . .	1·3	5·5

Since the price of animal products has risen proportionately much more than the prices of vegetable foodstuffs since 1928, it seems likely that the Russian diet to-day contains relatively less animal and more vegetable food than the above indicates.

The consumption of textiles (including garments) and boots per head of working-class families in Russia was —

Commodity	Consumption per Head	Cost in 1939	Total
		R.	R.
Cotton (metres) . .	20·09	3·50	70·31
Woollens (metres) .	1·40	210·00	294·00
Other fabrics (metres) .	1·07	12·00	18·84
Boots (pairs) . .	1·39	175·00	243·25
Total cost in 1927–8, R.59·40			R.626·40

Like food, the price of clothing rose more than wages during the period. It must also be remembered that the above prices apply to the actual cost of the textiles in the piece and not the cost of the articles made from them. The British working-class family spending 8s. 2d. a week on clothing, say £21 in all, or £5 : 12s. per head in the twelve months, would be able to buy considerably more than the above quantities, the cost of which would be somewhere about £3 : 10s. At the same time the quality of British goods would be infinitely superior.

Consumption per head per week of food in the Russian peasant household in 1927–8 and of the British agricultural family in 1937–8 (*The Times*, 11th February 1941) compares as follows :

Commodity	British Purchases	Russian Consumption
	Lb.	Lb.
Bread and flour .	5·60	7·70
Meat and bacon .	1·47	1·00
Butter . . .	0·42	0·06
Other fats and cheese .	0·66	..
Tea . . .	0·16	..
Sugar . . .	1·55	0·14
Jam . . .	0·26	..
Potatoes . .	1·70	5·70
Other vegetables .	..	2·30
Apples . . .	0·30	..
Eggs (pieces) . .	2·20	1·00
Milk (pints) . .	2·90	4·40

These figures must not be taken too literally. The British family also bought a certain quantity of vegetables and fruit and produced some foodstuffs in its own garden. Except for a few things such as tea, sugar and perhaps sunflower seed oil, the Russian household lived on its own produce, for in 1928 the peasants had not yet changed over to a money economy. The situation is very different to-day ; probably a majority of *kolhoznik* households buy bread and various preserved foods at their village co-operative stores. For this reason it is difficult to compare conditions in 1939 with 1928. I should think that the food consumption of the *kolhozniki* to-day is different in kind rather than in quantity from 1928.

The distribution of agricultural family incomes according to *The Times* article and *Planned Economy*, No. 9, 1938, was :

Commodity	British, 1937–8	Commodity, etc.	Russian, 1937
	%		%
Food . .	48·4	Food . . .	27·5
Clothing .	9·2	Industrial goods .	38·4
Rent . .	8·2	Livestock . .	10·1
Fuel and light .	8·6	Sundries . . .	3·7
			——— 79·7
Sundries .	25·6	Taxation and savings .	5·8
		Cultural and social services, etc. . .	14·5
			——— 20·3
	100·0		100·0

The *kolhoznik* nowadays spends a considerable part of his money income on food, but not nearly so much as the British agricultural household. Taxation, cultural levies (*e.g.* for building and equipping club rooms, schools, crèches, etc.), subscriptions to the state loan, insurance, etc., all of which are in practice compulsory, account for over 20 per cent of the *kolhoznik*'s outgoings. Comparable expenditure by the British agricultural household on medical attention, national health, old-age and unemployment insurance, other insurance and union or society subscriptions comes to about 8·4 per cent. The Russian household spends about R.76 a year per head on clothing, equivalent to about 16s., the British about 71s. 6d.

Finally, here is an actual monthly budget for a married couple as given me by the Gorki mill foreman I have already quoted :

Commodity, etc.	Roubles	Commodity, etc.	Roubles
Rent . .	62·00	Sugar .	12·60
Bread .	23·40	Vegetables .	6·00
Meat . .	105·00	Vodka .	6·00
Tea . .	6·00	Sundries .	30·00
Milk . .	45·00		
Butter .	12·60		R.308·60

The quantities calculated on the basis of prices current at the time would have been (for the two persons) :

Commodity	Quantity
Bread . . .	1½ to 2 lb. per day
Meat . . .	¼ to ½ lb. ,,
Tea . . .	⅕ oz. ,,
Milk . . .	1⅛ pints ,,
Butter . . .	¾ oz. ,,
Sugar . . .	3 to 4 oz. ,,
Vegetables . . .	½ lb. ,,

The total income varied between R.500 and R.700 a month. So, if an average of R.600 be taken, rent came to about 10 per cent. If this seems a modest proportion of income to be spent on rent, it must be remembered that the " flat " consisted of one room with about 12·5 square metres of floor space (that is a room about 12 feet square). With vestibule, kitchen, etc., the total floor space came to a little more than double that of the living-room. Other expenses would include the premium on a R.5000 life insurance, subscriptions to the state loan, income tax and a contribution to the " cultural and building " levy, the total amounting to perhaps some R.75 a month. Thus day-to-day living expenses and compulsory outgoings in the nature of taxation and savings would absorb nearly R.400 a month, leaving R.200 to cover clothing, renewals and repairs, recreation, including an annual holiday. When I met him he was going for a month's holiday to Mineralny Vody, partly at the expense of his Trade Union. His wife remained at home. But a chance of a holiday in the Caucasus assisted by the State was a comparatively rare occurrence and he usually had to make his own arrangements. He considered himself comfortably off and was proud of the fact that his wife did not have to go out and work ; he had done better for himself than he could have expected under the old régime. Under the Soviet system he had opportunities of a technical training which enabled him to lift himself above the rank and file of industrial workers. He had for some years been attending, in his spare time, evening classes at the *rabfak*, or workers' faculty, which eventually would enable him to become an engineer earning from R.900 to R.1200 a month. Judged by Russian standards he was successful and prosperous, but compared with a British factory foreman earning £10 a week or more, his standard of living would be considered very poor.

THE SOCIAL WAGE. The people who declare that the life of the Russian factory worker is miserable and poverty-stricken err just as much as do those who insist that nowhere are the workers' conditions so good as in Soviet Russia. I would sum up the situation by saying that in present conditions the skilled Russian worker has a tolerable life : he is adequately fed and clothed, though his housing leaves a great deal of room for improvement. The cost of the necessities of life absorbs nearly all his money income and leaves him very little for luxuries and recreation. The condition of the masses of unskilled heavy manual labour are far worse. The Bolsheviks retort that the amenities of life are provided by the State ; they estimate the " social wage " as worth about one-third of the money wage. I shall return to this subject in a moment ; meanwhile I want to make two observations. First, it is obvious that the workers must in the long run pay for everything that they receive nominally free. The revenue of the State is entirely derived from the surplus product of the workers. A wealthy section of the population that can be taxed for the benefit of the poor does not exist. Everybody in the country is a worker in some way or other, and part of his labour goes to providing funds with which the State finances its social services. Second, the Russian worker, like any other, would certainly prefer to enjoy less free services and have more money to spend in his own way. For instance, is it possible to imagine that, given a choice, the Russian worker would prefer spending a holiday in a state rest home or sanatorium, with all sorts of rules and restrictions, to taking rooms privately where he was free to come and go as the mood took him ? Again, who would not rather go to a doctor's private consulting-room than line up with crowds of other people in a bare hospital waiting-room. The answer is provided by the Soviet aristocracy, who would not dream of staying at an ordinary rest home nor of seeing a doctor otherwise than as a private paying patient.

Social services may conveniently be placed under three headings : Education, Health (including physical culture, holiday resorts, etc., as well as purely medical services) and Social Insurance (including old-age pensions, disability allowances and sickness benefits). On each of these subjects a whole book could be written ; in fact books dealing exclusively with education and medical services in Soviet Russia have been written. I propose only to give concise statements of facts and figures with a few notes on personal observations.

Education. It is universally acknowledged that the Bolsheviks have created an educational organisation far surpassing anything known in Tsarist Russia. Nevertheless some observations should be made to correct popular misconceptions, due to an uncritical and indiscriminate acceptance of Bolshevik propaganda. It is quite true that even in 1913 somewhere about 70 per cent of the population over nine years old was illiterate. But it is also true that between 1906 and 1916 the number of elementary schools had been doubled and that at the outbreak of the World War the plan for compulsory education adopted by the *Duma* needed only eight years to be realised. Soviet statistics show that of the population which reached school age in 1914 nearly 92 per cent in the towns and 71 per cent in the country could at least read and write. Another misconception is that under the Tsarist régime higher education was almost an exclusive monopoly of the upper classes. The truth is that bursaries and scholarships to enable poor students to study at universities were granted on a more generous scale than in almost any other country. *Pravda* of 28th August 1939 contained the following particulars of the origin of students in eight universities in 1914 :

	Per Cent
Noblesse and state officials . .	38·3
Clergy	7·4
Upper bourgeoisie, merchants, etc.	11·4
Petite bourgeoisie, craftsmen, etc.	24·4
Peasants	14·0
Others	4·5

Thus over 40 per cent came from the lower middle and working classes and peasants. Including the clergy, who in Russia ranked as little better than peasants in the country and barely as gentry in the towns, it may be said that the university students were roughly half from the upper classes and half from the lower middle and lower classes. The idea that only the upper classes had access to higher education probably arose from the existence of special schools for the children of the *noblesse*, which was not by any means the same thing as the aristocracy, for it embraced all but the most junior commissioned ranks in the armed forces and all the senior and middle grades in the civil service. The chief advantage of these schools for the *noblesse* was not that they afforded a better education than the others, but that the fees were merely nominal. Though, for that matter, the cost of education in any state or public institution was extremely moderate. Without detracting from the educational achievements of the Bolsheviks, it must be pointed out that they inherited a useful foundation from the old régime. So far as the abolition of illiteracy is concerned, the census of January 1939 showed that of the population between the ages of 9 and 49 over 10 per cent of the total and nearly 6 per cent of the urban population alone was still illiterate.

Compulsory education starts at the age of 8, but many children come under the charge of the State almost from birth. Most large-scale enterprises have crèches for the babies of their women workers. In 1937 over 700,000 infants were accommodated during working hours in permanent crèches and, I believe, most of these are well managed and the children well cared for. State and collective farms provide crèches for the babies of the women summoned to work in the fields during the busy summer months. In winter, of course, the mothers look after their babies themselves. On a collective farm near Novorossisk visited in the spring of 1937 the crèche and kindergarten were amalgamated and housed in a substantial stone house set in the midst of a cherry orchard in full bloom. The children's ages ranged from a month or so to eight years and they were tended by three or four women, one to look after the tiny babies, another to prepare meals and a third to give lessons to the older children, some of whom were already beginning to read and write. One small girl with intense concentration and pride wrote her name in my notebook so that I might send her a copy of a photograph I took of them all. Some of the largest shops in the big towns have crèches where mothers can leave their children while they shop. The crèche in the big Moscow department store opposite the opera-house was a delightful place for children. The walls were decorated with mural paintings depicting Stalin and other Bolshevik leaders enjoying themselves at a children's picnic. A great variety of toys included dolls, model aeroplanes and wooden bricks, and if a child got tired of inanimate playthings it could play with a tame jackdaw or a squirrel in a cage. The nurse in charge, obviously very competent, said that it was often a difficult business to detach the children from the toys when their mothers reclaimed them, for few of them had such wonderful things at home.

Between the ages of 3 and 8, children may be sent to a kindergarten. It is not compulsory, but strongly recommended. Contrary to the general opinion that welfare services such as crèches and kindergarten are free, payment has to be made according to the parents' income. The cost, in 1939, of parking a baby in a crèche ranged from R.12 to R.65 a month, plus an additional 25 per cent if the child was left for the night. For a child sent to a kindergarten belonging to a factory in the Commissariat of Light Industry the payment ranged from 10 per cent to 35 per cent of the actual cost. These payments applied to the children of workers regularly deposited while their mothers were at work. As the children were fed, probably better than they would be at home, the charges were reasonable and justified. The point, however, is that this part of the social services on which propaganda lays so much stress, allowing it to be understood that it is free, is in fact not free. Even higher education is no longer free, as we shall shortly see.

Elementary education occupies the Soviet child between the ages of 8 and 12, " incomplete " or intermediary

195

secondary schooling lasts from 12 to 15 and full secondary from 15 to 17. In practice the whole gamut of the school curriculum comprises ten classes, of which the first four are counted as elementary, the next three as " incomplete " secondary and the final three as full secondary. Compulsory schooling ends with class 7. Formerly continuation into higher classes was dependent on attaining a certain standard in the passing-out examination from class 7, but was free. Since the beginning of the 1940–41 school year, fees amounting to R.200 a year in Moscow, Leningrad and the Republican Capitals and R.150 in provincial towns have to be paid for pupils electing to continue into class 8, except those who obtain " excellent " in two-thirds of their subjects and " good " in the remainder in their passing-out examination. The same fees are payable for pupils attending secondary specialised and technical schools.

Before the Law of 2nd October 1940 for the creation of the Labour Reserve, the child who acquitted himself satisfactorily had the opportunity, after completing his intermediate schooling, of continuing into the higher classes of the ordinary secondary schools, or of entering a *technicum* or factory school, or of entering a special secondary school in preparation for a professional career. From these secondary schools the student could pass into the university or a higher educational institute. The total number of persons attending all educational institutions in the scholastic year 1938–9 was :

	000's
Elementary schools (classes I to IV) .	21,202
Intermediate schools (classes V to VII) .	8,780
Full secondary schools (classes VIII to X)	1,404
Secondary technical and factory schools .	1,194
Universities and higher technical schools	603
	33,183

There were also 990,000 attendants at adult schools workers' faculties, etc.

According to the census of January 1939 the population

between the ages of 8 and 15 numbered 29·6 millions, of whom, judging by the figures above, some 79 per cent were attending compulsory schools. Of the age group 15 to 19 (some 15 millions), about 3·2 millions, or about 21 per cent, were attending the full secondary and secondary technical schools, the universities and higher technical schools.

Students have to pass a sort of matriculation examination to enter the universities and higher technical educational institutions. Formerly all those who needed support were entitled to a subsistence allowance of between R.100 to R.200 a month, which though small was probably just sufficient, considering that students could usually live very cheaply in students' hostels. The Law of 2nd October 1940, decreed concurrently with the Law of the Labour Reserve, not only abolished the general grant of subsistence allowances but introduced fees of R.300 in provincial towns, R.400 in the capital cities and R.500 for students attending schools of art and music. Why the fees should be highest for aspiring artists was not explained. Only those students who gain " excellents " in two-thirds of their subjects and " good " in the remainder in their matriculation examination are excused these fees and may receive the state subsistence allowance.

The precise effect of the Law of Labour Reserves on education is not yet quite clear. According to the law, as already explained, all factory schools and *technicums* belonging to industrial organisations and transport, with the exception of small factory schools and those training mass workers for the textile, light and food industries, were transferred to the Chief Administration of Labour Reserves. Admission to these is now confined to the 800,000 to 1,000,000 boys between the ages of 14 and 17 called up annually under the new scheme. Since the total number of pupils at all types of secondary schools, except those in classes VIII to X in the ordinary secondary schools, was less than 1,200,000 in 1939, it would look as though secondary technical education is to be considerably expanded. Apparently boys not included in the annual quota of the Labour Reserve will not have an opportunity of entering heavy industry nor transport except as ordinary unskilled workers.

I am inclined to think that the significance of recent changes in educational principles has not been fully appreciated. It is not merely that fees have been introduced, but a system of scholarships has been inaugurated to tempt the most promising youths to prolong their education and as rewards for outstanding research work. The official excuse for revoking subsistence grants and imposing fees was (*a*) that the increased prosperity of the workers enabled them to pay, and (*b*) the great increase in the State's expenditure on education. I would suggest the following additional reasons : the numbers of qualified engineers and scientific experts now being turned out annually is more or less equal to the demand, but the weak link in industry is still the intermediate foreman, or, so to say, non-commissioned class. This notion is supported by the evident motive behind the new Labour Reserves, to turn out a large number of skilled workers and technical experts, but not fully qualified university graduates. Secondly, it can well be imagined that with comparatively easy entrance to the universities and technical high schools and subsistence allowances during the period of studying for a degree, a comparatively large proportion of students of mediocre capabilities and lacking a high degree of zeal and industry to some extent interfered with and hindered the progress of the first-class candidates for honours. The average standard of Soviet university graduates is below that in capitalist industrial countries and the new rules, while reducing the quantity is certainly calculated to improve the quality.

To mark Stalin's sixtieth birthday the Council of People's Commissars at the end of 1939 established a series of annual prizes, fellowships and scholarships in the fields of art and science. A number of single grants of R.100,000, R.50,000 and R.20,000 are awarded every year for outstanding research work, artistic achievements and inventions, and a large number of scholarships from R.500 to R.1000 a month are awarded to students in certain universities, military academies, technical institutes, conservatoires and schools

of art. Fellowships of R.1500 a month are awarded to
graduates of the Academy of Science. The aggregate value
of all the above comes to more than R.34 millions a year.
In November 1940, in commemoration of Molotov's fiftieth
birthday, the Government founded 300 more scholarships
of R.400 a month for students at six higher educational
institutes in Leningrad, Kazan, Kirov and Molotov.

Free higher education is now virtually the privilege of
those who can best profit by it. The fees payable by those
who fail to qualify by examination for admission into the
higher classes of the secondary schools and the universities
will exclude the greater part of the mediocre students ; for
although the Government excused the new order by the
need of recouping part of its expenditure on education, it is
scarcely likely that any parents, except the well-to-do
official class, will be prepared to pay the fees for children
who fail in their entrance examinations. The total sum
collected in fees is not likely to afford the Government any
sensible financial relief. Of course, so far as the principle
goes, the Bolsheviks are doing precisely what they and their
socialist friends have always condemned ; for it cannot be
denied that higher education is now partly dependent on
the power to pay for it. It would not be surprising if the
payment of fees was really and truly adopted to provide a
back door into the universities for the children of leading
Party and government personalities unable to win free entry.

Candidates for admission to universities and the higher
educational institutions are examined in the following subjects : mathematics, physics, chemistry, the Russian language and literature, the history of the peoples of the
U.S.S.R., one foreign language (English, French or German),
draughtsmanship and geography. Not all of these subjects
are required for every faculty ; for instance, candidates for
the faculties of history, jurisprudence, geography and
librarianship are examined only in the Russian language
and literature, the history of the peoples of the U.S.S.R.,
and geography. From the omission of any reference to the
classics, either as a faculty or a subject of examination, it
would appear that they are ignored. Rather naturally, the

chief emphasis is laid on applied science such as engineering, agriculture and medicine. Out of 194,200 university and technical college entries in 1940 over 91,000 passed into industrial training institutions for engineering, metallurgy, mining, chemistry, technical schools for transport, communications, agriculture and medicine ; 88,900 took up the teaching profession and only 10,000 chose economics, law, art, etc. Regarding the quality of higher education I would not dogmatise, but I have been told that a considerable proportion of the theses and monographs that reach our own universities and research institutions show no originality nor deep knowledge of their subjects. On the other hand, there are several research workers of purely Soviet vintage whose work is acknowledged and esteemed internationally, perhaps in agriculture more than in anything else.

In 1937 I visited the Consumers' Co-operative High School at Moscow. Its organisation, no doubt, follows the general lines of all technical colleges. The official title is "The Moscow Institute of Soviet Co-operative Trade of the Tsentrosoyuz of the U.S.S.R." and its prospectus declared that its object is to " create a highly qualified cadre of economists in planning, accounting and in the science of staple commodities, to fill leading positions in economic planning and the exchange of goods in provincial and district consumers' co-operative unions ". In other words, the institute trains managers for wholesale and retail trading organisations. The full complement of students was 1300 and candidates could enrol between the ages of 17 and 35, having completed their secondary education. Those having " excellent " leaving certificates were excused the entrance examination, which for others included papers on the Russian language, mathematics, physics, chemistry, political enlightenment and geography. In the event of a surplus of candidates vacancies were filled according to the results of the examination. Successful candidates received free lodging and a subsistence allowance of R.111 a month with an annual increase of R.15 a month. Meals were provided at a very moderate cost in a communal dining-room. The living quarters were in wings off the main building, and though the rooms were tiny, about the size of an ordinary dormitory cubicle, they were clean and bright. Most of the inmates had gone to some pains to make their rooms attractive with curtains, pictures, etc., and had gay coverlets on their beds. I should say that the majority came from better working-class families or the lower ranks of the intelligentsia. The public rooms included a cinema theatre, a club, a gymnasium, a library, etc. There was also a shop for the sale of cigarettes, stationery, haberdashery, etc., and workshops where the students could have their clothing and boots repaired. In fact the place was very self-contained. There was even a country club with accommodation for 300, in which summer vacations were spent.

The full course lasted four years and was quite different from what one would expect of a commercial training college. During the first two years the students took a general course of instruction in political economy, the history of the national economy, the history of the science of economics, economic geography, commercial law, mathematics, physics, chemistry, foreign languages, some elementary mechanics, military duties and some other odd subjects. In their last two years the students specialised in one of two branches ; the art or science of commodities or planning and accounting. The science of commodities sounds rather a strange subject, but really it is quite simple ; it means the analysis of goods to discover adulterations, to determine actual composition, the preservation of foodstuffs, weighing and measuring, testing fabrics for strength and so on. All this involved a lot of laboratory work. Planning and accounting means studying the principles of Soviet trade, planning distribution (which corresponds roughly to the study of markets in a capitalist system), accountancy, etc. All students, needless to say, had to study Marxian dialectics, the history of materialism and Leninism, which might be compared with the compulsory study of logic, philosophy and divinity in an English commercial college. It will be noticed that book-keeping, accountancy, finance, etc., are omitted from the first part of the course, while in the second part these and kindred subjects take a minor place. Planned turnovers and fixed prices do away with the necessity of studying markets, while standard methods of payment and bank credit enormously simplify all financial questions. Nevertheless the fact that many trading enterprises are run at a loss seems to indicate that this aspect of Soviet retail distribution might with advantage receive more attention. It might also strike the impartial observer that the need for commercial experts to have an expert knowledge of food analysis and preservation, textile strains and so on is not complimentary to the honesty of manufacturing enterprises. As a matter of fact Soviet manufacturing enterprises need just as careful watching as capitalist manufacturers to prevent them passing off inferior goods as sound, or delivering goods under false descriptions.

At the conclusion of their four years the students take an examination, on the result of which diplomas are awarded. For three years afterwards they are bound to work in the consumers' co-operative system, after which they may at their option take positions in the state trading organisations, in the commercial departments of industrial concerns or wherever their training renders their services desirable.

I should add that the above applied to the institution in 1937. It by no means follows that the description is true to-day. Ideas and methods change so rapidly and so unpredictably in Soviet Russia that it is quite possible the whole system has been entirely reorganised, and it would cause me no intense surprise to hear that the college had been scrapped and the building put to some other use.

In theory every citizen of the Soviet Union has an equal right and equal opportunity of higher education, the sole qualification being natural ability and intelligence. But does this equality exist in practice? In 1938 the composition of students in the universities was : workers and peasants 50·2 per cent, employees and specialists 47·3 per cent, handicraft and other " free " workers 2·5 per cent. The Soviet intelligentsia (which broadly comprises the professions, public services, clerical workers and qualified experts in industry, agriculture, etc.) numbered between nine and ten millions, or less than 6 per cent of the total population. But it supplied very nearly half the number of university students. One would perhaps expect a somewhat higher average standard of intelligence among the children of educated parents, but nothing like the superiority over the manual worker class such as the above figures indicate. There seems no reason to doubt that the children of the better educated and higher income sections of the community stand a better chance of a higher education than the children of the labouring classes. The explanation, at least in part, may well be somewhat as follows : the youth who has spent his childhood in more or less cultured society and intellectual environment starts off with an advantage over the child of a working-class family. Also the child of a worker or a peasant probably spends a lot of his out-of-school hours in performing some sort of family chores, working in the cabbage patch, running errands and so on. It may also be imagined that he finds it difficult to study at home, even if he wants to, because it is very unlikely that the family dwelling contains a room where he can work in peace. Well-to-do officials and professional men tend to live in the larger towns and usually in the central residential quarters, and not in the industrial suburbs. Their children therefore tend to have much better chances of visiting museums, libraries, etc., than the children of the factory worker living on the outskirts. It may be assumed that the teachers in the central and, if one dare use the word in this connection, more fashionable schools are on the average somewhat superior to the teachers in factory quarter schools, and even more superior to rural teachers. Finally, the higher income of the intellectual class parent enables him to buy more and better text-books for his children and, maybe, pay for private coaching. Thus, all things considered, wealth has an appreciable bearing on the question of education. In this instance at least the principle of equality of opportunity and the principle that those whose services to the community are the most valuable shall receive the highest rewards seem to conflict. For undoubtedly a very powerful motive, and one that even the Bolsheviks must applaud, towards increasing one's income is the prospect thereby of giving one's children a better start in life. But the child of wealthy parents, who as yet has done nothing to earn his good fortune, starts with an undeserved advantage over the less fortunate children of the less ambitious and less talented parents.

Health Services. In 1938 the total number of hospital beds in the country was 672,000, or about one to every 250 of the population, compared with 175,500 beds in 1913 ; the number of qualified medical practitioners was 110,000 compared with 19,785 in 1913. Enormous progress has undeniably been made by the Bolsheviks, but when exaggerated claims are made it is as well to check them by a comparison with the most advanced countries. The following table will show how far the Bolshevik assertions that they have the best health service in the world are justified :

	U.S.S.R., 1938	Germany, 1934	England and Wales, 1936
Total number of hospital beds	672,000	457,358	260,819
Beds per 1000 of the population	3·9	6·8	6·5
Beds in maternity hospitals .	81,342	14,264	8,626
Beds per 100 births . .	1·6 *	1·1	1·2

* Assuming the annual number of births to be about 5 millions.

Owing to the housing shortage in the Soviet Union and the cramped quarters of most families, there is, naturally, a very intense demand for accommodation in maternity hospitals, and mothers are turned out as soon as possible after the birth of their babies.

Conditions in Soviet hospitals vary very greatly. Judging from occasional " self-criticism " in the newspapers, some are badly managed and the patients neglected. Foreign visitors are shown only the better examples. Hospitals for the privileged Party officials and the higher bureaucracy are much superior to those for the rank and file.

All doctors, dentists, etc., are public servants with fixed salaried jobs in a hospital, clinic or similar institution, but they are permitted to take private patients in their spare time. What proportion of them do so I have no idea, but wandering through the streets of any big town one notices their door-plates giving their consulting hours. I have also noted shops selling medical and dental appliances, which obviously are for private purchase. At least it seems highly improbable that a state hospital or dental clinic would get its equipment over the counter of a retail shop. There used to be a shop at the lower end of the Gorki street in Moscow, and it may still exist, at which any Soviet citizen with a preference for gold teeth could buy a small bit of gold for the purpose. I cannot say whether a state dental clinic would condescend to make a gold denture, supposing a patient arrived with a lump of gold, but I rather suspect that gold fillings are the mark of employing a dentist in his private capacity. In 1939 I noticed that most artificial teeth seemed to be made of stainless steel, and I have no doubt that this was the material supplied by the State. It would be a graceful and subtle compliment to Stalin.

Nearly all large villages and a good many of the bigger and most advanced collective farms have their own cottage hospitals. As I have already indicated, these are brought to the notice of the inquisitive foreigner only if they are a credit to the place. However, my impression is that on the whole they are fairly well run, of course rather primitive, but an enormous advance over conditions in the old days, when the only medical assistance to be found in most villages was a *feldsher* (literally a surgeon's dresser, usually a peasant who had picked up a smattering of elementary doctoring through serving in the Army medical service as a dresser. He would compare with the barber-surgeons of an earlier age.). On the other hand, all private enterprises employing above a certain number of hands were compelled by law in Tsarist times to provide a medical service. I remember visiting a colliery in the Donbass region in 1904 which maintained a very good hospital for the miners in charge of a fully qualified doctor, who was somewhat of an enthusiast. He had formed a little museum of his own containing exhibits of the curious diseases to which his patients were victims and some frightful monstrosities he had helped bring into the world and promptly assisted out of it again. Russians are rather morbid. In 1930 I was shown over the polyclinic in Kharkov, rather a show place, which had a museum for the edification of the patients. The idea seemed to be that they would be more impressed by ocular witness than by verbal exhortation to observe the ordinary rules of hygiene. Certainly the plaster models of the visible effects of Siberian plague, anthrax and other loathsome afflictions were calculated to terrify anyone. The instructional films on such matters also leave nothing to the imagination. I saw one on the subject of abortion and its evils, which in most countries would have been strictly confined to professional audiences. That was before abortion was made illegal.

I have heard it said that in Soviet Russia they do not take much trouble to cure people injured or diseased in such a way that they will never again be efficient members of the community. I cannot say whether there is any foundation for this, but human life is not regarded with anything like the sanctity it is in our own country. It will be remembered that during the Finnish war the Soviet Government claimed that a very high proportion of the wounded (75-85 per cent) were restored to complete health and activity. Some foreign correspondents alleged that the Russians only picked up those wounded whose injuries were comparatively slight and who stood a very good chance of complete recovery. But it must be remembered that in the temperatures experienced in winter in those latitudes a severely wounded man would succumb very soon if not picked up.

Since the Soviet Government publishes no public health returns, it is impossible to say whether epidemics are still frequent, or what is the incidence of deaths from different diseases. The sanitary services in big towns are good on paper ; the question is whether the measures prescribed are efficiently carried out. I can say from my own observation that the rules for the inspection of foodstuffs offered for sale in the peasant markets and the regulations for the maintenance of cleanliness in the market buildings are very thorough. The chief market halls in Moscow, and,

I imagine, in other big cities, have laboratories with trained workers to examine meat for trichinosis, test milk for adulteration and infection and so on. On the other hand, one not so very infrequently hears of food poisoning from eating canned food ; and there have been more than one or two cases of persons being tried in the courts for allowing food to become poisonous, or even of deliberately poisoning food, in institutions such as children's summer camps or factory kitchens. Foreign visitors nearly always suffer from alimentary troubles in the first two or three weeks. Sometimes the symptoms definitely indicate a mild form of food poisoning. In my opinion the trouble is probably more often than not due to the immoderate use of not very good preservatives. Tourists are often advised to be inoculated against enteric, cholera, typhus, etc., before going to Russia. Unless one intends travelling in out-of-the-way parts of the Caucasus or Central Asia, such precautions are not necessary. Naturally a prudent foreigner refrains from drinking plain water, but he would be just as well, perhaps better, advised to take the same precaution, say, in Italy or Spain. Unless Soviet statistics are deliberately faked, the general health of the people, and particularly the infant mortality rate, has definitely improved of recent years.

Sanatoria and rest homes are included under the head of health services. It may be as well to explain that in Soviet Russia a sanatorium is not a place for the sick or convalescent. The difference between a rest home and a sanatorium is that the former is probably near a centre of population or industry and the workers visit it for a short time only, or possibly just for the day on their day of rest. The sanatoria are institutions in some recognised health resort or watering-place, most of which are in the Caucasus or the Black Sea coast. Both rest homes and sanatoria as well as holidays generally are the province of the Trade Unions, but all, or nearly all, large industrial and commercial enterprises run their own rest homes for their own employees. While most of the sanatoria are directly run by the Trade Unions, it is possible that some of the very largest industrial enterprises have their own sanatoria in the Crimea or Caucasus, I cannot say definitely ; certainly the Red Army has its own sanatoria for officers, and there are super-sanatoria, or rather private hotels, on the Black Sea coast for members of the Government and high Party officials. The Trade Unions have nothing to do with these. In 1938 nearly 2·3 million persons spent the whole or part of their holidays at rest homes, and 439,000 were sent to sanatoria. These figures indicate the difference between the two institutions. A holiday at a sanatorium is rather an event in the life of a factory worker and, seeing that the total number of people employed in large-scale industrial enterprises is somewhere in the region of ten millions, it is obvious that on the average such a treat comes only about once in twenty years.

Life in a sanatorium for the ordinary workers is pretty thoroughly regulated : not by any means a go-as-you-like existence. Hours of meals, getting up and going to bed have to be strictly observed. The days are filled up with organised excursions to places of interest, cultural improvement and very likely lectures or talks on the history of Bolshevism and other improving subjects. How far the inmates are allowed to do what they like, go to the pictures or make an excursion on their own, I cannot say. In any case, that is the sort of thing one simply cannot find out. I can, however, describe my own observations at Yalta, in the Crimea, during a stay there in the spring of 1937. For instance, staying at the *intourist* hotel were two Russian girls who looked what they actually were ; that is, superior typists or office workers from Moscow. I asked our *intourist* guide how it was that they were allowed to stay at the hotel, and in any case how they could afford the charges, which would be pretty stiff for anyone earning probably R.400 or R.500 a month. The answer was that at that time of the year the tourist business was very slack (the Crimea season is the summer) and that the hotel was willing to accept private Russian guests to keep the staff occupied. Secondly, they had probably saved up for a year or two just for this holiday ; and they did not go to a sanatorium because of the irritating and cramping restrictions. Another time we were in the grounds of the Livadia palace, the former Crimean residence of the Imperial family, and I noticed a party of obvious sanatorium inmates being escorted round and lectured at intervals on the architectural features or history of the place ; anyhow it does not matter what they were being lectured about, the point is that they were being lectured and looked thoroughly bored. I asked whether it was a *prinuditelny* (compulsory) outing, to be told, rather unconvincingly I thought, that holiday-makers were never compelled to take part in officially conducted excursions. The palace itself, an ornate building erected in 1911 of marble in the Italian renaissance style with a suggestion here and there of Moorish, was a sanatorium for ordinary workers or peasants. It is, of course, characteristic of the Bolsheviks to convert a former residence of the Tsar into a home for the toiling masses. The special sanatoria for the Soviet aristocracy are in less pretentious buildings, but for that reason more comfortable. The palace appeared to contain no furniture except what one might expect to find in a barracks, and the holiday-makers seemed to be lounging about in the last stages of bored misery. The sole recreation seemed to be contemplation of the sea varied by contemplation in the opposite direction of certain pieces of genuine or imitation classical sculpture. As far as I remember the inmates were exclusively men. They may have been enjoying themselves, but they gave no outward evidence of it. I should perhaps make it clear that this particular lot were either peasants or from the lower ranks of industrial labour. As I hinted above, I am pretty sure they were housed there for propaganda purposes, to show the visiting foreigner that even the late Tsar's palace is not too good for the Soviet working man. Now, it is pretty clear that casual foreigners would not be welcomed if they went snooping round a sanatorium inhabited by the better educated and more or less superior class-conscious city worker or skilled factory hand. After all, even Russians have a right to privacy, a fact that so many foreigners seem to overlook when they complain that they are not allowed to invade clubs, hospitals or even private dwellings at will. So I cannot say from personal experience what the middle-class sanatoria are like. But I should guess they are better furnished, and probably something is done for the recreation and amusement of the inmates besides improving talks and official excursions. I can at least testify that some of them run to tennis-courts, of a sort.

It is quite a mistaken idea to think that holidays in a sanatorium are free. The All-Union Central Committee of Trades Unions in two decrees of 29th February and 7th March 1940 laid down that all workers earning more than R.300 a month must pay 30 per cent of the cost of their holidays, while those earning less than that sum pay a sum fixed by their own local Social Insurance Council or their factory insurance committee. Another thing to be noted is that if about three million persons enjoy holidays partly at the expense of the State, or rather the Social Insurance Fund, it is only about 10 per cent of the total number of workers and employees in the national economy. Also a certain number of this three millions are peasants, who do not count as state workers.

I do not want to minimise this part of what the Bolsheviks call the " social wage ". It is a great thing to give something like three million people, not including the children in the pioneer camps, an annual holiday in healthy and restful surroundings, but it must be realised that the whole cost is paid by the workers in the long run, for it must come out of the " surplus value " they produce. Another point to remember is that hotels, private boarding-houses and lodgings in holiday resorts are almost non-existent. The State having done away with private holiday catering, together with all other forms of private enterprise, was bound to put something in its place. Compare these conditions with England, where hundreds of thousands of middle-class families and industrial workers spend their holidays at the seaside or in the country at their own expense and can afford to do so because their incomes are relatively so much higher than the incomes of the same classes in the Soviet Union. Neither should we leave out of account the holiday camps run by such organisations as the University and

Public School East End missions. And now that holidays with pay are becoming the rule, I think there can be little doubt that the British workers are just as well provided for as the Soviet workers.

Social Insurance. Social insurance provides benefits during temporary incapacity to earn through illness or accident, pensions for permanent disability and for old age. The fund also provides grants of clothing and food for new-born infants, children's camps and other amenities not provided by the schools, part of the travelling and living expenses of workers sent to sanatoria, and finances the upkeep of these institutions, finances the building of hotels and hostels for Soviet tourists in the mountains of the Caucasus and some other places (mountaineering is a popular holiday pastime among the younger people), makes grants to workers' and employees' mutual aid societies, to en-courage physical culture (that is, to build gymnasia, equip sports grounds, etc.), to create and maintain parks of rest and culture, also to further political education and certain services such as labour inspection and medical control. There is no unemployment relief on the grounds that (*a*) there is no unemployment and (*b*) if anybody is unemployed it is his own fault.

The administration of social insurance has been in the hands of the Trade Unions since 1933 and is now one of the principal functions of the trade-union organisation. The funds are provided by payments by all employing enterprises of sums based on their total wage bills. The wage-earner pays no direct contribution. The social insurance budget for 1938 as approved by the Council of People's Commissars provided for a revenue of R.6323 million and expenditure of R.5900 million. The total wages bill for the whole country in 1938 was R.96,400 million, so contributions by employing enterprises averaged 6·6 per cent of wage pay-ments. Expenditure was distributed as follows :

[TABLE

211

	R. Millions	R. Millions
Pensions, sickness relief, etc., including —		
Temporary disability . . .	2136·6	
Maternity allowances . . .	991·5	
Funeral grants	22·8	
Pensions	314·7	
		3465·6
Medical control		19·5
Children's services		654·4
Sanatoria, rest homes and health resorts, including —		
Travelling and subsistence . .	836·3	
Maintenance, equipment and building .	197·9	
		1034·2
Tourism		50·0
Medical dietary		99·6
Mutual assistance societies		104·2
Parks of rest and culture		27·0
Physical culture		147·9
Education		84·1
Labour inspection		78·5
Administration, etc.		80·0
Bonuses to insurance propagandists . .		5·0
Expenditure by Central Committees on temporary relief		50·0
		R.5900·0

Social insurance is a weapon for inculcating labour discipline. The principle of reducing or refusing relief to workers guilty of breaches of discipline is foreign to our notions, but it forms part of the armoury of the Bolshevik leaders in their constant struggle with the workers. The following is a summary of the Law of 28th December 1938, which introduced this system.

A worker becoming temporarily incapacitated receives the full scale of relief, 100 per cent of his average earnings, only if he has been six years in one employment; when his length of continuous service is between three and six years he receives 80 per cent, between two and three years 60 per cent, and less than two years 50 per cent. Workers in some dangerous or particularly trying trade, such as underground work in mines, receive the full scale after only two years' employment ; while workers less than 18 years old receive 80 per cent when they have been employed for two years, and 60 per cent before that. Non-trade-unionists receive half the rates accorded to trade-unionists. Workers dismissed from their employment for misconduct or leaving a job of their own accord must serve six months in a new job before qualifying for any relief at all.

Because of the great liquidity of labour in Soviet industry and the comparative youthfulness of the workers, a very large proportion of the total labour employed must have worked for less than six years in one employment, and very many have not been working for six years in all. The average age of all workers in many enterprises is between 25 and 28, and the earliest age at which they can start work is 16. A large number of those with less than six years' continuous employment are therefore in that position through no fault of their own.

The maternity allowance for women, that is, leave of absence from work on full pay, was reduced from an average of 50 days before and after confinement to 35 days before and 28 days after.

Free railway travel to rest homes was restricted to workers with not less than two years' continuous employment.

Permanent disability pensions are granted to workers only when they have had a total period of employment varying according to their age when disability occurred. A man of between 55 and 60 must have been employed for at least a total of eighteen years during his lifetime and a woman of the same age fourteen years to qualify for a pension, while a young man or woman of 20 to 22 having the misfortune to become crippled will only get a pension if he has worked three years and she two years. An increase in the standard rate is allowed to workers who, when disability overtook them, had been in the same employment for a certain number of years. An underground miner, for instance, receives a 10 per cent increase after three years' continuous employment, 20 per cent after five years and 25 per cent after ten years. In less dangerous and trying trades the conditions are less generous, workers in heavy industry being required to have had at least twelve years' and in all other industries fifteen years' continuous employ-ment to qualify for a 20 per cent increase. However, permanent disability pensions are granted unconditionally when the disability is the result of maiming or disease directly attributable to the employment. The pension is based on the late earning power of the pensioner. I believe that the maximum rate is two-thirds of the wage or salary immediately prior to the grant of a pension, but I have not found an authoritative ruling on this point.

The minimum rates of pension are : [1]

	Roubles per Month		
	A	B	C
Underground miners and workers in dangerous industries .	50	60	75
Workers in heavy industry and railways	40	50	60
Workers in all other industries .	Not less than 25 in any cir-cumstances		

Note. A = When the pensioner has no dependants. B = One dependant. C = More than one dependant.

A family with one non-earning member receives R.30 a month, and with two or more non-earning members R.40 for the loss of the chief bread-winner.

The value of these pensions may be judged from the fact that the purchasing power of the highest rate, viz. R.75 a month, is no more than £1. Disabled pensioners are per-mitted to earn money, for instance by working in co-operative associations of the disabled, up to R.100 a month without any loss of pension. If they earn more than that sum their pensions are reduced by the amount earned in

[1] These minimum rates were introduced to alleviate the position of workers retiring on pension in the past when wages were much less than to-day.

excess of R.100 up to a maximum of 50 per cent of the pension. Old-age pensioners are not penalised at all for earning additional money.

State Insurance.—All other insurance is undertaken by the State, so that in a sense it may be included among the social services provided by the State. The citizen may insure his life and chattels voluntarily, and some particulars of the various schemes may be of interest.

A life endowment policy maturing in any period between five and twenty years may be taken out by any citizen between the ages of 16 and 60, the assured sum being payable at death, total disability due to accident, or at maturity. In the event of partial disability, amounting to more than 35 per cent of the assured's working capacity, occurring during the currency of the policy, the assured receives a corresponding proportion of the full sum assured. The balance is paid on death, on complete disability intervening, or at the maturity of the assurance if neither death nor complete disability occurs first. No further premiums are payable after the date on which partial disability occurs.

The premiums are rather high and there are no bonuses, profits nor any other addition to the sum assured. The annual premiums range from R.50 per R.1000 assured, payable by a person aged 16 to 22, for a policy maturing in twenty years, to R.239 payable by a person aged 60 for a policy maturing in five years. Except in the first case, every person taking out a policy which runs its full course pays a total amount in premiums that exceeds the sum he eventually receives.

Annual policies to cover death or disablement by accident or act of God (of course this is not the term used) may be taken out by enterprises in favour of their employees, by groups of workers collectively or by individuals. No medical examination is required. Individuals and enterprises pay premiums ranging from R.2·50 to R.12 per R.1000, according to the nature of the employment ; the premium for collective insurance is R.12 per member.

In none of the above schemes is any payment made when (*a*) an assured's death is encompassed by his beneficiaries, (*b*) the property of the assured or of his beneficiaries has been confiscated by order of a court of law. This latter rule is, of course, simply a somewhat euphemistic way of saying that policies of persons liquidated by the G.P.U. are thereby cancelled.

Should the holder of a life policy commit suicide, the surrender value at the time of his death is paid to his heirs and assigns at the date when the policy would normally mature.

Property and personal chattels may be insured against fire, flood and other convulsions of nature, but not against theft or burglary, except when the loss is occasioned by looting during a fire, etc. In towns and urban areas the premiums range from R.1 to R.4 per R.1000, according to the nature of the building. In the country, where cottages are as a rule thatched or shingled, the premiums range from R.2 to R.9.

Insurance of buildings, tools, implements, livestock, growing crops and stores is compulsory on *kolhozy* and *kolhozniki*. The premiums range from 0·3 per cent on machinery and implements, 0·8 per cent on buildings, to 6 per cent on horses and 8 per cent on tobacco crops against damage by hail and frost. The premiums payable by *kolhozniki* on his private property are 25 to 30 per cent higher. The amount of the indemnity is fixed by the State, and it is interesting to note that the value set upon property for insurance purposes is from one-half to one-tenth of the value when assessed for taxation. For instance, a pig for taxation purposes is assessed at R.300, but the State pays only R.60 indemnity if it dies from an insured risk.

CHAPTER XIV

TAXATION AND SAVINGS

In the last chapter we investigated the social services provided for the population by the Soviet Government either free or at reduced rates. This, so-called, social wage is claimed to amount in value to about one-third of the money wage. It is obvious that the means to provide social services must be acquired by the State through direct or indirect taxation ; for of all Governments the Soviet Government possesses the least in resources of its own. It has few, if any, investments abroad ; it certainly admits to none. The international services it performs, such as transport by sea or land for third parties, are insignificant.

In common with capitalist States Soviet taxation is both direct and indirect, but compared with the revenue from indirect taxation direct taxation is almost insignificant. Indirect taxation consists almost entirely of a turnover or sales tax on goods, and mainly on goods of popular consumption. In the budget for 1940 the turnover tax accounted for R.108,300 million out of a total revenue of R.163,300 million, or nearly 60 per cent ; direct taxation brought in R.9700 million, or about 5·9 per cent ; while subscriptions to the state loan and savings bank deposits were worth R.11,200 million, or nearly 7 per cent. Thus over 70 per cent of the State's revenue came directly out of the pockets of the people. The balance was derived from the profits of state enterprises, insurance and the earnings of the machine-tractor stations, that is, payment in kind and money by the *kolhozy* for the use of the tractors and machines supplied by the machine-tractor stations.

The turnover tax may be regarded as the State's monopoly profit on the sale of goods manufactured by state enterprises ; for in effect it consists of a sum added to the price at which an article could be sold to bring the price up to a level at which demand is restricted to supply. Because such a large part of the available labour is devoted to producing capital goods, the quantity of money put into circulation through wages is far in excess of the sum needed to purchase the whole output of consumers' goods, if these were sold at prices sufficient to cover all production and distribution costs.

Before giving examples of turnover tax rates, it should be explained that the tax on some articles, mainly foodstuffs, varies according to price zones, for the retail prices of bread, sugar, meat and other staple foodstuffs are not the same everywhere. The differences seem mainly to depend on the abundance or scarcity of local supply and the cost of transport, but according to the official explanation the differences are also due to political reasons. Though what this means is not quite clear. In some cases the tax on manufactured goods varies according to the factory, or type of factory producing them, in order to equalise differences in production costs. In the following list when two rates are given they may represent the highest and lowest price zones or the maximum and minimum rates on the goods of different factories :

Commodity	Rate of Turnover Tax
Rye bread . . .	5 per cent
Fancy bread . . .	15 ,,
Meat (beef) . . .	67-72 ,,
Meat (mutton and pork) .	60-67 ,,
Butter	60 ,,
Cheese	30-66 ,,
Sugar	78 ,,
Soap	20-30 ,,
Cigarettes . . .	75-88 ,,
Tea	25-60 ,,
Calico	48 ,,
Silk	21-37 ,,
Woollen cloth . . .	15-24 ,,
Boots and shoes . . .	12-35 ,,

On many articles the final tax is not the whole burden the consumer has to pay ; for instance, there is a turnover tax on flour when sold by the flour-mill to the bakery, while there is an intermediate tax on cotton when sold by the collecting organisation to the cotton-mills. The average total tax on all consumers' goods is about 50 per cent of the retail price. In other words, the price to the consumer is about double the price necessary to cover all production and distribution costs plus a reasonable rate of profit to the various manufacturing and distributing enterprises.

The total value of retail trade in the whole country in 1938, including restaurants, co-operative and open-market trading, amounted to R.163,000 million, and the yield of the turnover tax was R.80,400 million, and of this probably about 88 per cent was collected on the sale of goods to the consuming public. The tax on capital goods is very small; in 1937, for instance, the proceeds of the tax on the products of heavy industry was only 11·5 per cent of the gross yield.

Income tax is paid by everyone with an income of over R.150 a month, with the exception of certain privileged classes, such as " Heroes of the Soviet Union ", soldiers and students, and peasants who pay the agricultural tax instead.

A law of 4th April 1940 fixed the rates of the tax as follows :

Monthly Income	Rate of Tax		
R. R.	R. %		R.
151 to 200	1·20 + 3 of amount over		150
201 ,, 300	2·70 + 3·3 ,,	,,	200
301 ,, 500	6·00 + 4 ,,	,,	300
501 ,, 700	14·00 + 5 ,,	,,	500
701 ,, 1000	24·00 + 6 ,,	,,	700
Over 1001	42·00 + 7 ,,	,,	1000

The above applies to wage and salary earners employed in state enterprises. Co-operative workers pay 10 per cent more, while independent handicraft workers and others engaged in private enterprise pay a steeply graduated tax which begins at 4 per cent on an annual income of R.1200 and rises to R.8952 plus 60 per cent of any income in excess of R.24,000.

Writers and artists on income from royalties, etc., pay a tax ranging from $\frac{1}{8}$ to 1 per cent on sums up to R.1800 a year, but if they earn over R.300,000 they pay R.86·364 plus 50 per cent of the amount over R.300,000.

The tax on fees earned by doctors from private practice, by lawyers, tutors, etc., is 1 per cent on the first R.1000, rising to R.3975 on R.20,000 plus 38 per cent on any sum over that amount.

Interest on savings bank deposits, interest or lottery prizes on state loan bonds, sums realised from the sale of private property and money inherited or received by way of alimony are free of tax.

An idea of the relative incidence of the tax on various classes of income may be gained from the following :

Annual Income	Rate of Tax as Per Cent of Income from Different Sources				
	Wage and Salary	Royalties etc.	Co-operative Production	Free Handicraft	Private Practice of Professions
R.					
2,400	1·35	1·35	1·49	6·00	1·76
6,000	2·80	2·80	3·08	13·40	3·58
12,000	4·20	4·20	4·82	24·10	11·46
24,000	5·60	5·77	6·16	37·30	22·90
50,000	6·33	7·73	6·96	49·10	30·75

Income from private enterprise is taxed very much higher than income from employment in state enterprises. The incomes earned by writers and artists, which at first sight might seem to come under the head of private enterprise, are treated more as salary than as private enterprise, the reason no doubt being that their work is performed for and paid by state institutions almost exclusively. Free handicraft workers and professional persons in their private practice deal direct with the public and so are, according to communist notions, tainted with exploitation. It is also curious to note that while the highest amount specified in the schedules for wage and salary earners and co-operative workers is only R24,000 a year, provision is made for taxing writers and artists up to an income of R.300,000.

This seems to suggest that literature and the arts are very much more highly remunerated than professions and trades. The Soviet writer, Alexis Tolstoi, in an article contributed to *Pravda* in 1937 dealing with the earnings of authors, gave the following information. According to him there were at the time —

				R.		
14 authors receiving over				120,000 a year		
						R.
11	,,	,,	between	72,000	and	120,000
39	,,	,,	,,	24,000	,,	36,000
114	,,	,,	,,	12,000	,,	24,000
137	,,	,,	,,	6,000	,,	12,000
4000	,,	,,	up to	6,000		

through an organisation which collects and distributes the fees payable by concert halls, theatres, clubs, etc., for the right of performing the works of Soviet composers, dramatists, etc. Successful novelists, publicists, painters, etc., no doubt earn about on the same scale or even more. Whether the earnings of popular singers, actors, dancers, etc., who earn big fees as " guest " artists in theatres other than those to which they are officially attached, are taxed as salary or as royalties I cannot say.

A second direct tax is the Building and Cultural Levy, a sort of additional income tax to provide funds to build dwelling-houses, schools, workers's clubs, etc. The tax is levied on the net income remaining after income tax has been paid. The rates on wage and salary incomes are :

Monthly Income			Tax			
R.	R.		R.	%		R.
151 to	200 .	. .	1·05 plus	2·5 of amount over		150
201 ,,	300 .	. .	2·3 ,,	3·0	,, ,,	200
301 ,,	500 .	. .	5·3 ,,	3·5	,, ,,	300
501 ,,	700 .	. .	12·3 ,,	4·5	,, ,,	500
701 ,,	1000 .	. .	21·3 ,,	5·5	,, ,,	700
Over 1001	.	. .	37·8 ,,	6·0	,, ,,	1000

Members of co-operative societies pay an additional 10

per cent. On incomes from private enterprise the rates
are :

Annual Income	Tax
Up to R.1200 . .	2·5%
R. R.	R. % R.
1201 to 2400 . .	30 plus 4 above 1200
2401 ,, 4800 . .	78 ,, 6 ,, 2400
4801 ,, 10,000 . .	222 ,, 7·5 ,, 4800
10,000 and over . .	612 ,, 8 ,, 10,000

The yield of the levy was about R.1900 million in 1938.
In the Second Five-Year Plan the average sum spent on
dwelling-house construction was R.2700 million a year.
Even if this amount is considerably larger to-day, the taxpayers certainly provide a material part of the cost. This
should be remembered when the Bolsheviks protest that the
Soviet worker pays a very low rent for his dwelling space.

The sum of these two direct taxes on a few typical
incomes in different classes of the population works out
as follows :

Class	Sum of Both Taxes	% of Income
	R.	
Industrial worker earning R.300 a month	11·30	3·76
Skilled factory worker earning R.500 a month	26·30	5·26
Stakhanovite worker earning R.1000 a month	79·80	7·98
Official earning R.2000 a month . .	209·80	10·49
Independent worker earning R.300 a month	38·50	12·83
Independent worker earning R.500 a month	93·00	18·60
Independent worker earning R.1000 a month	305·30	30·53
Author, artist, etc., earning R.1000 a month	79·80	7·98
Author, artist, etc., earning R.5000 a month	699·80	13·99

These rates, except in the case of the independent

workers, do not at first sight look burdensome, but when we consider that R.500 a month, which is if anything rather above the average wage and salary, is equivalent to about 30s. a week in England, a deduction of what would amount to about 1s. 6d. a week is by no means trivial.

Another drain on the money income of the Soviet citizen is his contribution to the state loan. The pretence that subscription is voluntary has long since worn threadbare. Every worker is expected to buy bonds to the amount of two to four weeks' wages ; high salaried officials probably find it advisable to subscribe more. In 1938 the loan realised R.7593 million and the total planned aggregate of all wages and salaries was R.96,400 million. Loan subscriptions thus were about equal to one month's total wage and salary income. As a matter of fact, the average subscription would be somewhat less, for the above does not take into account the amount subscribed by the peasants, but this is not a great deal.

According to an article, " The Wages Fund and its Calculation ", in the Soviet monthly magazine *Money and Credit* early in 1940, the deductions at source from wages and salaries passing through the books of the State Bank in 1938 were :

	R. millions
Income tax	1952·4
Building and cultural levy . .	1857·1
State loan subscriptions . .	4072·6
	7882·1

The total sum of wages and salaries actually drawn from the bank accounts of employing enterprises was R.103,166·7 million. Thus it would appear that the loan subscriptions of the wage and salary earners came to about 4 per cent, or, roughly, an average of two weeks' earnings per head. The total of the sums deducted at source came to 7·6 per cent of the total wages and salaries.

The agricultural tax is paid by all collectivised peasants

and others whose livelihood is mainly derived from agriculture. The taxable income consists (*a*) of an arbitrary assessment of the yield of the land, (*b*) the actual money earned by the sale of produce on the open market and other ways, except wages in outside employment. The *kolhoznik's* dividend from work performed on the collective farm itself is not taxed, but he pays a flat rate of 3 per cent on the turnover of all sales in the collective farm market, that is, on the proceeds of the produce he himself takes to market, in addition to the agricultural tax.

The assessed income from crops and livestock varies in different regions. The schedule for the R.S.F.S.R. in 1939 was —

Crops	Assessed Yield per Hectare
	R.
Grain . . .	540
Potatoes . . .	1200
Flax . . .	500
Cotton . . .	750
Tobacco . . .	1700
Vegetables . .	3500
Vines . . .	7000
Animals	Assessed Yield per Head
Cows . . .	600
Sheep and goats . .	40
Pigs . . .	300

It is impossible to say whether these are fair estimates. It would, for instance, be a very poor grain crop that yielded so little as R.540 gross worth of grain per hectare, but when cost of production, reservation of seed and provision for the peasant's own consumption are taken into account, the value of the marketable surplus might well be no more than R.540.

The rate of tax on the money income calculated according to the above assessment is :

Annual Assessed Income		Rate of Tax		
Up to R.700 . .	R.50			
R. R.	R.	%		R.
700 to 1000 . .	50 plus	8 above		700
1000 ,, 2000 . .	74 ,,	9	,,	1000
2000 ,, 3000 . .	164 ,,	11	,,	2000
3000 ,, 4000 . .	274 ,,	13	,,	3000
Over R.4000 . .	404 ,,	15	,,	4000

These rates are much higher than the income tax rates paid by the workers. For example, a worker earning R.200 a month pays only 1·15 per cent in tax, but a *kolhoznik* with an estimated money income of R.2400 a year pays 8 per cent. The assessed income of independent peasants is calculated in the same way, but the rate of tax is much higher ; on an income of R.1000 a year it is 11 per cent, on R.2400 14·2 per cent and on R.6000 23·5 per cent. At the same time both *kolhoznik* and independent peasant have to surrender to the State at the latter's arbitrary purchasing price a fairly large proportion of the produce they grow. These prices, being much lower than those obtainable on the open market, render these compulsory deliveries a modified tax in kind.

The total money income of the whole Soviet population in 1938 may be put at R.197,000 million. This estimate is based on the article in *Money and Credit* already quoted and is not necessarily accurate. The figure is made up of the following :

	R. Millions
Wages, salaries and similar payments .	134,000
Private enterprise, including the yield from the private enterprise of *kolhozniki*	34,500
Kolhozniki's " labour-day " dividends .	7,000
Sale of produce by *kolhozniki* . .	13,500
Co-operative society dividends . .	5,000
Loan and savings bank interest .	3,000
	197,000

Q

The total revenue from direct taxation, loan subscriptions, savings bank deposits and insurance premiums, collectively known as the " mobilisation of the means of the people ", as given in the budget estimates for 1938, was R.19,807 million, or almost exactly 10 per cent of the aggregate money income of the population. The yield of the turnover tax on consumers' goods sold in retail distribution was about R.70,000 million. Altogether, therefore, it would seem that the population returned to the State in one way or another about R.90,000 million, or over 45 per cent of its gross money income.

The preliminary budget accounts for 1938 show that, of the total state revenue of R.124,000 million, R.35,300 million was expended on social and cultural services, R.51,700 million on the national economy, R.34,800 on defence and administration. If the above estimate of R.90,000 million as the direct contribution of the population to the national revenue be correct, then nearly 40 per cent was returned in the form of services provided by the State, and about 39 kopeks in every rouble contributed was expended on defence and the general administration of the country. The difference between the total budget revenue and the direct contributions of the population consisted mainly of the profits of state enterprise, so it may be said that a considerable proportion of the R.51,700 million spent on the national economy was not directly derived from taxation and popular savings. About half this amount, R.25,500 million, was invested in state industry, together with another R.9500 million of industrial profits not passing through the budget. Thus of the total national income about R.35,000 million was reinvested. Actually the real total of capital investment was a good deal more, because the above does not include capital investments by collective farms out of their own income, nor investments in local and co-operative industrial enterprise, nor in housing. The ratio of national savings to national income is obviously high as a matter of fact it amounts to at least 25 per cent.

CHAPTER XV

THE PLANNED ECONOMY

THE Soviet system is indissolubly bound up with economic
planning. It is my aim in this chapter to describe the
general principles of planning and its effects on the life of
the people. First of all, it is clear that a socialist State in
which all the natural resources of the country, the means
of production and of distribution, belong to the community,
must plan its economic activities. Capitalist economics are
based on private enterprise and markets : goods are produced to sell at a profit, and capital is attracted to undertakings according to the prospects of earning profits, which
will benefit the owners of the capital invested. In the
socialist State the owners of the capital are the whole community, whose interest it is to produce for consumption
the maximum quantity of goods. Money profits have no
meaning because no amount of money can enable the people
to buy more goods than are produced. Profits being excluded as a means of directing capital into this or that
industry, it remains only to plan the investment of capital
so as to give the greatest benefit to the whole community.
Obviously it is impossible to ascertain the collective opinion
of 170 million individuals, so the decision must be left to
their leaders, who, it is assumed, can accurately estimate
their will. The Bolshevist leaders believe that they know
better than the masses what is best for the ultimate good
of the community. This is a matter on which it is impossible
to pronounce an opinion. But in consequence of this conviction, the rulers of the country have taken upon themselves to plan the development of the country's resources.

The primary step is to decide what proportion of the
annual national income or net production of wealth shall
be saved, that is, used for the further development of the
national resources. The second step is to decide what

proportions of this new capital shall be devoted to the expansion of industries manufacturing further means of production and industries manufacturing consumption goods to increasing and improving means of transport and to the development of agriculture.

These appropriations must next be further subdivided among the capital industries producing fuel, iron and steel, machinery, munitions of war, etc. ; among the consumption industries manufacturing textiles, boots, household goods, food, etc., between roads, railways and shipping, and between different branches of farming to expand the production of foodstuffs, industrial raw material, etc., and so the process continues down to allotments of capital to individual enterprises. It must not be imagined that the Central Government decides all the minute details. After the main outlines of the Plan have been drawn, the details are filled in more or less automatically.

Output must also be planned. In the first place, the total amounts of raw materials to be produced are planned, or rather estimates of production are made, based on the known productive capacity of the industries concerned : and these must be allotted to the needs of the manufacturing industries. For obviously when there is no market the distribution of coal, metals, cotton, etc., cannot be effected by offering these commodities for sale to the highest bidder. Secondly, the output of partly manufactured materials must be planned according to the needs of the enterprises using them in their own processes. Finally, the output of finished goods must be planned ; in the case of capital goods, such as factory equipment, according to the demand for replacements and for newly created factories ; in the case of consumers' goods, according to the needs of the population. All this planning is inevitable in the absence of a market, which is regulated by prices, which in turn originate in the profit motive. In actual practice the distribution of materials and goods between enterprises is effected by direct negotiation and contracts, with a superficial resemblance to capitalist methods. But such contracts are really a method of implementing the Plan ; the producing enterprise is a planned supplier of the consuming enterprise and the negotiations are confined to fixing dates of delivery and specifications of the goods. Prices are fixed and are not subject to bargaining. As we shall see later, the form of buying and selling for money is retained, though the money is a mere unit of amount and not a measure of value.

It will be gathered from the above that there must be a radical difference between prices in a capitalist economy and in the socialist economy. What I am about to say applies to wholesale prices at which goods are exchanged between state enterprises and organisations and not to the retail prices of goods sold to the public. Wholesale prices are formed by the aggregate of all wages paid to the labour concerned in all processes from procuring the raw material to the final manufacture of the finished goods, including all transport costs, to which is added at different stages small percentages to provide a profit to each enterprise concerned. The word profit is not strictly a fitting term to translate the Soviet word, whose precise meaning is accumulation. This signifies that part of the price received, over and above the bare production cost, covers amortisation of capital with a small margin for capital increase. The prices of most goods also include a percentage of planned profit which is paid direct to the State. This is not a genuine profit so much as a sort of tax or levy collected by the State towards the budget revenue. Since actual production costs often, in fact almost always, differ in some degree from planned production costs, some enterprises make more than their planned profits and some less. Generally speaking, the more efficiently managed a factory is the higher will be its profits ; but it by no means follows that an enterprise making a loss is inefficient or uneconomic. The capitalist test of bankruptcy does not apply.

So far I have been trying to show how planning is inseparable from a socialist economic structure. There is no alternative, though the planning may be centralised in a greater or less degree. It might almost be said that the Bolsheviks made a virtue of necessity : in any case they maintain that planning is their deliberate choice and invention and was not thrust upon them. First, we must see what they claim for it. I think we may divide their claims under two heads : a planned economy is far more efficient and productive than a capitalist economy ; a planned economy ensures a far more equitable distribution of the national wealth among the people than the capitalist system.

In a planned economy waste, overlapping and un-productive effort are eliminated or reduced to a minimum. For examples, raw material, partly manufactured goods and finished goods are passed on and consumed without delay, whereas in capitalist economies stocks of this or that may be held for a rise in price or will accumulate because purchasers are not forthcoming at the prices demanded. This means idle capital which is equal to waste. In a planned economy the manufacture of commodities of all sorts is undertaken by factories of the most economic sizes and situated in places chosen with due regard to supplies of raw material and labour and consumers. In capitalist countries there are often many small competing enterprises all trying to sell practically identical articles distinguished only by small superficial differences (*e.g.* soap, tooth-paste, etc.). A smaller variety produced in larger factories should cut out a lot of redundant overhead costs and competitive advertising. It is uneconomic for several small shops selling the same kind of goods to be crowded together in one small area. This adds to distribution costs and among other things causes an unnecessary amount of unproductive em-ployment : large or medium-sized shops evenly spaced in residential areas can serve the public equally well and sell cheaper as well as releasing labour for productive employ-ment. Planned distribution can ensure economy in the transport of goods from place of production to place of con-sumption, cutting out unnecessary handling and redundant middlemen. This is not a complete list of the concrete advantages of planning, but they · indicate the general argument. To them must be added the advantages of a system in which goods are produced for consumption and not for profit.

Production for profit means that goods are produced

only if they can be sold at a price which yields a profit. And this applies not alone to luxuries. This may, and often does, result in unsatisfied desires and incomplete utilisation of productive capacity, including labour. Hence in the capitalist world occupations giving employment even of the most useless and unproductive kind are tolerated if not actively promoted. In the planned economy all unnecessary and redundant unproductive employment is bad because it reduces the total output of goods. Since prices are composed of the aggregate wages paid to the labour concerned in production, and a material part of the total labour is devoted to the production of capital goods, the purchasing power of the consuming public will always be sufficient to buy all the consumers' goods produced and services provided. In fact, retail prices have to be artificially raised by a sales tax to restrict effective demand to the actual supply of goods, although purchasing power is reduced by direct taxes and saving. Therefore there is no fear of producing too much, or more than can be bought. It is implied without question that the greatest happiness of the community consists in the enjoyment of the greatest possible amount of goods, which in Soviet Russia in present circumstances would no doubt be the verdict of 99 per cent of the inhabitants.

The notion that it is impossible for production to outrun effective demand is the basis of the claim that unemployment has been completely and permanently eradicated in the Soviet Union. It is admitted that the production of certain commodities of unelastic consumption might, through very faulty planning, be in excess of desire. But at the first signs of satiety the forces of production would be switched over to manufacturing something else. Eventually, if and when the productive forces of the nation produce goods to saturation point, the hours of toil will be reduced and the population will enjoy more leisure in which to consume its plethora of riches. This will mark the complete realisation of Communism ; but the dawn of that era is not yet predictable.

Meanwhile the distribution of the consumable portion

of the national income has to be planned as equitably as possible, having regard to the principle that the worker is worthy of his hire and that those who contribute most to the nation's wealth and well-being deserve the highest rewards ; among whom are included the High Priests of Bolshevism, whose exertions for the common good are perhaps not always appreciated at their face value by the common herd. This is not an exclusive peculiarity of Soviet Russia. The total absence of private ownership of capital precludes the enjoyment of unearned income by Soviet citizens. They must earn by their own toil all that they spend ; thus differences between the incomes of different persons are strictly proportionate to the results of their labour, which depend on their skill, intelligence and manual dexterity. It is true that some people are born with natural abilities of a superior order, others are subnormal. Unfortunately this natural inequality cannot be rectified. On the other hand, differential remuneration finds sufficient justification in the ability of most individuals to improve their natural ability by study, practice and application and in the voluntary choice of working long hours and industriously or taking life easily. In the first phase of the revolution the remuneration of state employees was regarded rather as the reward of devotion to the socialist cause and disinterested service in the common weal. To-day the emphasis is more on self-interest, which stimulates the worker to raise his earning power and thus gratify his mundane desires.

Soviet wages are different in kind from capitalist wages, which are the price paid by employers for labour bought on the market. His labour is the capitalist worker's sole capital and stock-in-trade, which he sells to the highest bidder. Labour in fact is a commodity bought and sold like anything else. Soviet labour is not a commodity. The Soviet worker is a member of the community, which theoretically owns the capital he sets in motion, and since as a worker he serves the community he is collectively his own employer. His reward consists of the value of the wealth he creates, part of which he enjoys collectively in association with all the other citizens of the commonwealth, the remainder being his personal remuneration, consisting of his money wage which alone varies according to the productiveness of his labour. As a concrete illustration, every worker engaged in the building of the monstrous temple called the Palace of the Soviets, from the Chief Architect to the humblest bricklayer's labourer, has as a citizen the same theoretical proprietary title in the edifice as 170 million other citizens, which may afford him some spiritual but scarcely any material gratification. But as a worker the Chief Architect's salary is many times greater than the labourer's wages because his contribution to the work is so much more important. And he is entitled to his high salary because he would not be the Chief Architect unless he had worked long and hard to acquire proficiency in his profession.

The total material remuneration of all Soviet labour is the amount of the consumption goods produced and services provided ; the individual's wage enables him to buy just that fraction of the total remuneration to which he is entitled as the reward of his toil. Thus money wages are a convenient method of distributing the total amount of consumable wealth in a way that gives the highest degree of satisfaction to the consumers. Money wages have this great advantage over distribution of goods by rationing or soup tickets, the wage-earner can spend his money as he likes or he can save it for further enjoyment. These qualities make Soviet money in the pockets of the people indistinguishable from capitalist money. And those workers who are old enough to have earned wages in Tsarist times are not conscious of any difference between their wages then and now. But, in fact, the Tsarist roubles they were paid before 1917 represented a claim on the products of third parties transferred to them by their employers, while their Soviet roubles to-day represent their dividends in an immense national co-operative concern.

As I pointed out above, the total amount of wages paid out, including the money payments to the peasants, which for this purpose have the same nature as wages, should, after deductions for taxes and savings, be approximately equal to the total value at retail prices of consumers' goods and services made available to the public. Planning ensures this equation more or less successfully from two directions : the total sum in wages to be paid out is fixed by the Plan, and the price of retail goods is controlled by the planned turnover tax, which raises wholesale prices to the level necessary to keep supply and demand in equilibrium.

When I say that total wages, or as a matter of fact the total money income of the population, is planned, it must not be imagined that the State Planning Commission works out a new plan each year unrelated to previous years. In all its aspects planning is the control of ordered economic development rather than a hard-and-fast scheme. So planning does not mean that wages are arbitrarily raised or lowered or that the retail price level fluctuates in order to maintain equilibrium. There is seldom violent interference with normal development, but the average annual increase in wage rates is consciously related to the rise in the average productivity of labour, which depends partly on the rising skill of the workers, partly on the increased use of labour-saving machinery and partly on improvements in organisation and administration. The task of the planners, therefore, is not to say the total income of the population in the coming year must be restricted to such-and-such a figure, but to foretell, in the light of their knowledge of the probable increase in industrial employment, increased productivity and other circumstances, what it should amount to. The output of industrial production should automatically increase *pari passu* with the increasing wages bill, and planning should have only to see that the proper relation is maintained between the production of capital and consumers' goods.

The control of the relative level of wages in different industries is subject to rather more arbitrary planning than the amount of the total wages bill. The progressive development of the country's economy causes differences to arise in the relative demand for certain commodities. For example, the mechanisation of agriculture brought about a very rapid increase in the consumption of oil, necessitating a relatively large expansion of the oil-producing and refining industries. This required a rapid increase in the quantity and also in the quality of labour employed in these industries. Consequently the average wage and salary paid in the oil industry was increased proportionately more than in most other industries. This was necessary in order to attract more labour, particularly from the annual contingent of youth making its debut in industry, because the individual citizen still enjoyed free choice of a career. This freedom has been materially restricted since 1940 and the distribution of labour has become much more a matter of direct planning than indirectly controlled by differential wage rates.

While strict socialist theory would recommend the remuneration of labour in accordance with the degree of skill demanded, the danger involved and the amount of energy exerted by the worker, irrespective of the utility of the product, differential wage rates between different industries might be defended on the ground that the worker employed in producing an article of high utility to the community is entitled to a high rate of wages, because he is of greater value to the community than the worker producing an article of less utility. But this seems to me rather an opportunist if not a purely capitalist doctrine, because it is only a certain confluence of temporary circumstances that decides whether, in the view of the Planners, a given commodity is of more immediate value to the community than another. At the moment the oil industry pays the highest average wage rate, therefore it may be concluded that oil is the most valuable commodity being produced. But the most necessary and indispensable commodity to any community is bread. The Soviet agricultural labourer receives a much smaller reward for his labour than any industrial worker, because the production of grain is sufficient for all and there is no call to attract more labour to the fields. Can it be said that in strict equity the oil worker should enjoy a larger share of the nation's consumable wealth than the farm labourer ? So under analysis it seems that the Soviet worker's personal remuneration is determined on much the same principles as that of the capitalist worker. That is, it depends very largely on the relative utility of the goods he produces. When labour is compulsorily distributed, wages presumably will differ solely on account of the qualifications of the worker and the demands on his physical constitution. The methods of fixing wage rates for different jobs were described in Chapter VIII.

The economic developments achieved in Soviet Russia since 1930 are impressive. Whether, on the whole, they surpass the progress made in England or the United States during any decade in the most feverish periods of their industrial revolutions is not to be taken on trust. The Soviet achievements are more spectacular because they transformed a rather primitive and industrially undeveloped country into one containing a large number of very large, imposing and up-to-date industrial enterprises in a very short space of time. But the Bolsheviks borrowed their technique and bought a lot of their equipment abroad ; they took their experience at second hand and did not acquire it by their own efforts and by trial and error, as did the industrial pioneers in the West. Neither can we accept their claim that the labour and materials needed to fulfil their great industrial schemes were provided by planning, and that a planned economy alone could have gained these results. The simple truth is that the Soviet Government was able to compel the population to save, that is, lend its labour for a very small material reward. Any dictatorship disposing of all the natural resources of a whole country, and able to conscript labour for capital construction without paying much attention to where the wages were to come from, could achieve astonishing results. What Democratic Government, except in a great national crisis, could compel its people to save 25 or more per cent of their gross incomes year after year without any end in sight and invest their savings in new economic enterprises. This is what the Bolsheviks have done. It may be granted that planning directed the investment of these savings, but it certainly did not create them.

If the Soviet experiment of a planned economy be accepted as a reliable test of planning as a principle, it has

not unequivocally established the superiority in all directions
of planning over private enterprise and markets. The
verdict, naturally, depends on what is expected. Most of
those socialistically inclined people who hold the Soviet
Union up as a model of what society should be are rather
apt to consider the abolition of private ownership of capital
as an end in itself, and the ownership of capital by the community as an undiluted and absolute gain. It is, I submit,
not the private ownership of capital that is inherently bad,
but the abuse of that ownership. Most socialists would
without a moment's consideration reply that the two terms
are synonymous, at the same moment indignantly repudiat-
ing the suggestion that the abuse of power by those in
authority in the socialist State produces just the same
consequences. It is not safe to conclude that those responsible for the administration of a socialist country are invariably characterised by wisdom, prudence and integrity.
Among the responsible Soviet leaders there have been foolish,
rash and even dishonest men. May it not be deduced, from
the large number it has been found necessary to shoot, that
the incidence of dishonesty and disloyalty is higher than in
any democratic capitalist country, where it is rarely found
expedient to imprison much less shoot cabinet ministers,
important civil servants or commercial and industrial
leaders ?

Upon the assumption that the Soviet planned economy
suffers equally with our own democratic capitalist system
from human errors and failings, we may now try to examine
the case for and against planning.

Unemployment has been overcome, to the extent at least
that Russia contains no " hard core " of unemployed. But
would our democracy consent to the abolition of unemployment on the same terms as the Russians ; namely, the
employment of a material proportion of the population at
bare subsistence wages ? Planning may have put every
able-bodied worker to work, but has not found means to
pay them all a decent living wage. Since every Soviet
worker receives that share in the national consumable
income to which his labour entitles him, the productivity

of those paid the minimum money wage must be extraordinarily low.

Planning may direct the productive forces into the proper channels to provide the greatest satisfaction of the greatest number irrespective of individual differences in income. That is to say, the wealthy individual has no more power to influence production than the poorest labourer. But is this true ? Can anyone conscientiously deny that the high salaried Party officials are proportionately much better catered for than the masses of unskilled and low wage labour ? Of course they must have luxuries to buy, otherwise their high salaries would be meaningless. To illustrate what I mean, there is seldom, if ever, a shortage of luxury goods, but quite often a severe dearth of ordinary everyday necessities. In other ways, too, life is rendered much more easy and comfortable for the wealthy Soviet citizen, and he enjoys a number of unofficial privileges compared with the ordinary worker. In other words, money talks the same language in Soviet Russia as anywhere else.

Planning is no improvement on competition between private enterprises in stimulating economy in consumption, interest in technical improvements and inventions, and system in management. In capitalist industry the standard of efficiency is set by the most enterprising and proficient of competing undertakings. Every rival tries to undersell the others by reducing the cost of his products or providing a better article for the same money. The manager of a Soviet enterprise works to a plan and has but a qualified interest in reducing production costs so long as they do not overstep his plan. He is apt to be suspicious of new ideas, and hesitates to experiment with new inventions lest they prove vain and interfere with orderly and proved processes and endanger the fulfilment of his plan. Thus he will try to avoid manufacturing a new type or pattern of article because he knows that he can comfortably complete his plan with existing output. In fact, the plan is apt to stifle initiative. This is no mere subjective induction on my part. It is amply proved by constant articles in the Soviet press, of which I have a typical one in front of me (*Planned*

Economy, No. 9, 1940), which points out that the consumption of copper in Soviet industry is proportionately much higher than in other countries, because there is no great urge to reduce the weight of castings or to use cheaper but efficient substitutes in bearings, etc., when circumstances permit. A Soviet factory manager may refuse an order for a consignment of goods slightly different from his standard product because it would cause some trouble to manufacture, and being able to dispose of all his planned output at fixed prices; it is no advantage to secure new customers, nor is he particularly interested in meeting the extraordinary wishes of old ones.

Whether state ownership or planning is the more to blame for the bureaucratism and red tape that are the chronic disease of Soviet industry is hard to say. But as planning in some degree is inseparable from state ownership, there is no profit in trying to separate the effects of each. It is, however, obvious that planning calls for a large amount of statistical and co-ordinating clerical work whose cost must be added to total production costs.

When plans fail to agree with reality, another set of defects arises. Because of faulty planning, the demand for certain raw materials or, still more probably, partly manufactured goods may exceed supply and a factory manager may find his work in danger of interruption through lack of some essential. This is not accepted as a good excuse for failure to complete his plan, so he will try to obtain what he wants by unconventional means. That is by a private deal with a supplying enterprise, which usually takes the form of offering the latter an addition to the fixed price, either in money or kind. For example, a watch and clock factory might offer a number of timepieces to a factory supplying brass stampings or spring steel or glasses. This is known as *blat*, and many factories retain the services of so-called commercial travellers whose chief occupation is to negotiate such transactions.

I am far from suggesting that the whole of Soviet industry is badly managed or that all Soviet managers are inefficient and unenterprising. The point I want to establish is that planning does not remove all the difficulties and problems of capitalist management, while introducing some new ones peculiar to itself. All the same, I am sure that there is a great danger of forming an exaggerated estimate of the defects of the Soviet system for the following reasons. I have before me a summary of press reports on the activities of the Commissariat of State Control over a period of some months in 1940–41. The Commissariat's investigators brought to light all manner of breaches of discipline, inefficiencies and even cases of deliberate misuse of state property by managers of enterprises. The most frequent charge was of producing substandard and defective goods ; some managers had neglected to install and utilise expensive foreign equipment allocated to them years ago. Over-consumption of raw material and over-payment of wages were also among the malpractices unearthed ; there were even cases of the illegal sale of material and goods. From all of which one might be tempted to conclude that Soviet industry was in a very bad way. But, in the first place, the Soviet newspapers do not habitually carry comprehensive lists of the enterprises that are working efficiently ; and even if they did they would not attract our attention to anything like the same degree as the black lists. I fear that a large proportion of foreign experts on Soviet Russia, quite unconsciously, suffer from what the Germans call *Schadenfreude* and pay too much attention to evidence of faults and failings. I except, of course, " authorities " like the Webbs, George Bernard Shaw and others whose panegyrics contribute nothing to an unbiassed and objective study of Soviet Russia. Secondly, it should be remembered that in economic matters the Bolsheviks like to wash their dirty linen in public. In our own country, if a manager proves unequal to his job or of less than rigid integrity, he will probably be allowed to retire in dignity and decency.

A fair conclusion is, I think, that a great deal of the inefficiency and mismanagement in Soviet enterprise is really due more to the inexperience of Russian managers, so many of whom are young and appointed more for their political trustworthiness than technical skill and experience, and to the Russian national character or mentality which is very apt to be deficient in method and tedious accuracy, than to inherent weakness of planning *per se*. On the other hand, the fact that serious imperfections continue to exist in the Soviet economic system belies the claims that planning is a cure for all the evils in capitalist economy. To perpetrate an aphorism, both a capitalist and a planned economy are good in proportion to the integrity, disinterestedness and wisdom of those responsible for their administration.

A problem that still awaits solution is the reconciliation of a price system with planning, or to discover the proper use and place of prices. The Bolsheviks early discovered that the production and exchange of goods must be controlled by some standard unit of account. Their experiment during the period of War Communism, to conduct distribution by direct exchange, ended in chaos. They returned with relief to money, and having established a Central Bank to issue an orthodox gold-secured currency, have never shown any inclination to renew their search for a moneyless economy. Industrial and commercial enterprises keep accounts similar in appearance to the accounts of capitalist enterprise and with practically the same ends. If state enterprises have to prepare balance-sheets and profit-and-loss accounts to enable the Commissariat of State Control to judge of their efficiency and to enable the State Bank to regulate its credit relations, it is inevitable that the profit motive will creep in. Though it is not money profits that determine the real utility of an enterprise or whether a new undertaking can be advantageously established in this or that locality, they certainly do influence a local governing body in its decision whether or no to develop a local industry. District and Municipal Soviets enjoy a large measure of financial auto-nomy ; they cannot draw unlimited credit from the Bank, and when considering investments must enquire whether they will pay. This depends on whether the price received for the product or services it is proposed to provide covers production costs. And, of course, the price is that fixed within limits by the State. The final result on the whole

R

has been to stifle local initiative and hinder the developmen
of local natural resources.

To remedy this condition a decree was issued on 9th
January 1941 removing local and co-operative industry from
the control of the Central Government and placing all such
local enterprises directly under the republican and pro
vincial governments. Prices of locally manufactured goods
unless included in the category of staple goods for which
All-Union prices are fixed, were in future to be fixed by
local governments. In the explanatory introduction the
decree explained that, mainly owing to price difficulties
local industry for developing fuel resources, for manu
facturing farm wagons and harness, for converting loca
textile fibres into fabrics and so on, were languishing
Certain industries, for example the manufacture of farn
wagons from local timber, which were traditional to certair
localities were still supplying distant regions which had al
the requisites for supplying themselves if only given en
couragement. Planning would dictate that, supplies o
material and labour being available, different regions shoul
supply their own wants if only to save unnecessary transpor
from other regions. But, it seems, price planning often cut
right across this policy. From this and other indications i
seems that the Soviet Government is moving in the directio
of abandoning planned price control in the lower strata c
the price structure and allowing market conditions to pla
an increasing part.

In retail trade price is necessarily determined by suppl
and demand, the State having no means of planning th
desires of the consumers. In order to prevent an apparen
shortage of goods or the accumulation of unsold stock:
shop prices must be fixed at a level that will restrict deman
for any commodity to the available supply. This, one ma
note, is not always realised, hence shopping queues [1] an
speculation (*i.e.* buying with the intention of reselling at

[1] A masterly piece of equivocation is attributed to Molotov, who
reported to have rebuked certain sceptics with the assertion that queue
were not evidence of a low standard of life ; on the contrary they prove
that the Soviet citizen was much better off than his capitalist counterpa
because he had so much money that he had to queue up to spend it.

profit). The difference between production and distribution costs and retail selling price may be regarded as the State's monopoly profit and, except for a small profit allowed to the retail organisations, is collected in the form of a sales or turnover tax added to the wholesale price.

When I was in Moscow in the spring of 1937 a party of prominent Dominion Ministers was staying at the same hotel. One of them, appropriately enough the Minister of Finance, at lunch one day held up a Chervonetz note asking what it really represented. He was apparently doubtful whether it was strictly entitled to the epithet of money. I forget what answer he received from the party's expert; it was at any rate not particularly helpful. In fact it is not easy to place the Soviet currency. Without going into technicalities I think one may say that it possesses a dual entity. In the hands of the people it fulfils all the functions of money, it is the medium of exchange which enables the ordinary citizen to satisfy his needs ; it is a measure of value since the differences in the prices of different articles reflect the relative value attached to them by the consumers ; it is a store of value because it can be saved for future expenditure. Roubles in the Treasury or in the bank accounts of state institutions and enterprises are primarily, if not exclusively, units of account. Though state enterprises settle their accounts by the transfer of bank assets from one account to another, it can hardly be said that the roubles concerned are a true medium of exchange, because they can be used only for specified purposes in specified amounts. They serve as a convenient common denominator for implementing and controlling the planned distribution of material and goods between state producing and distributing enterprises. Neither are they a measure of value ; they indicate the total amount of labour that has gone into the production of a given article, but not the relative utility of or demand for different articles. Marxian theory, of course, holds that the value of an article is the amount of human labour applied to its production and not its power of satisfying human needs. Reduced to its logical conclusion, this theory means that a dry hole in the ground

243

dug by four men in four weeks would be of precisely the same value as an identical hole that tapped a spring of water. Neither can roubles in the Treasury constitute a store of value. The State directly plans the production and consumption of wealth. The money collected in taxes and levies from the population simply represents that part of the national income not consumed by the population, it is not purchasing power transferred from the taxpayers to the State as in capitalist countries. The difference is — the capitalist Government taxes the nation in order to claim a share of the national wealth and labour to enable it to carry on its administrative functions ; the Soviet Government first decides how much of the national wealth and labour it needs and reduces the public's purchasing power to correspond. This disquisition on the content and functions of the Soviet currency rests on the capitalist view of money. In fairness the Soviet version should be studied.

Stalin himself should be the highest authority. Once, in rebuttal of insinuations that the Soviet rouble was not a stable currency, he retorted : " Is it not a fact that with this currency we built Magnitostroi, Dnieprostroi, the Stalingrad and Kharkov tractor works, the Gorki and Moscow automobile works, hundreds of thousands of collective farms and thousands of State farms ? " This profound observation is, of necessity, accepted and quoted by all Bolshevik economists without question or scrutiny. But we are free to enquire what it really means. Before the factory can be built the State Planning Commission must ascertain that the materials required are available. The money would be perfectly useless unless the bricks, cement, etc., were available. In fact the Government, owning all the resources of the country and able to conscript labour, could build a factory without using money at all ; but billions of paper roubles in the Treasury would not build a factory if the materials were not first produced. Construction is sometimes (formerly very frequently) held up because of shortages of material, never through lack of funds. Of course, if Stalin intended to imply merely that his roubles were a convenient form of counters to facilitate the distribution of material and labour, there is nothing to criticise.

Stalin was also once responsible for asserting that the Soviet rouble was the most stable currency in the world because it was backed not only by the enormous quantities of goods held by the Soviet Government, but also by all the capital represented by industrial enterprises, railways, etc. This was a reply to foreign insinuations that the rouble currency was being inflated. The fallacy is obvious, for Soviet factories and railways are not for sale and so cannot counteract inflation by redeeming surplus money.

The Soviet view of gold is a commodity that can be exported like grain or oil to provide means of paying for imports. It does not now serve as a backing for the rouble currency ; [1] which is understandable when it is realised that the rouble is exclusively an internal currency, so the question of redeeming foreign holdings cannot arise. But it is interesting to note that a writer in *Planned Economy*, No. 12, 1940, admits that gold may in certain conditions assist in maintaining the stability of the rouble " since potentially it represents a quantity of goods which at a suitable moment can be procured on the world market ". This is the first instance, to come under my notice, of a Soviet economist even indirectly confessing that it might be desirable to import goods in order to check a rise in prices. To paraphrase the Bolshevik dictum about consumers' goods being manufactured for use and not profit, it might be said that Soviet imports hitherto have been not for consumption but for use. That is to say, they are almost exclusively machinery and industrial raw material whose importation has no influence on internal price levels.

Soviet economists are not always consistent in their arguments to prove the differences and consequently the superiority of their system to the capitalist system. For example, industrial wages are not, as explained above, the market payment for labour as a commodity. The workman's wage is in the nature of a voucher or certificate entitling

[1] The State Bank ceased in 1932 to pay even nominal heed to the clauses in its charter enjoining a 25 per cent firm cover for the currency circulation.

him to a certain share of the national income for his own
use, which theory is not impaired by the existence of shops
and fixed retail prices as a means by which the due dis
tribution of the national income is effected. But (I am
quoting from the article in *Planned Economy* mentioned
above) on the next page the distinction between industrial
wages and the *kolhozniki's* labour-day dividends is described
as follows :

The money wage of every individual worker and employee
reflects the relationship between him and the socialist State
and consists of a fixed amount previously determined by the
State, depending on the quantity and quality of his labour and
not on the total results of this or that enterprise.

According to this definition the State's relation to the
worker seems indistinguishable from that of a capitalist
employer. The passage continues :

As regards the money income received by the *kolhozniki* for
their labour-days, this reflects the relation between any given
kolhoz and its individual members and does not consist of a
previously fixed amount, but depends on one hand on the total
money income of the *kolhoz* and on the other on the individual
share performed by each *kolhoznik* in the total work of the *kolhoz*

This definition of the *kolhozniki's* remuneration as a
dividend from the results of co-operative labour is essentially
the same as the description of industrial wages as " the
measure of the worker's share in that part of the national
income set aside for personal consumption ". Both are by
nature dividends, the one from the co-operative labour of a
small community, the other from the labour of the national
community. But for some reason of their own the Bolsheviks
in distinguishing between the two discover a radical dif
ference in kind. They may have been led into seeing a
difference, because the variation from year to year in *kolhoz*
dividends, due to the natural vicissitudes of farming, seem
to differentiate them from the wages, or dividends, of the
industrial workers which are relatively stable because there
are no extraordinary fluctuations in the total production of
the whole country.

The Planned Economy

Soviet economists distinguish in theory between physical money in circulation, that is notes and coin, and money represented by entries in bank accounts. The former is a medium of exchange in the acquisition of goods or in payment for services, the latter is used in settlement of debts and claims between state organisations and in the allotment of credit by the State Bank to other enterprises. The distinction is not very clear at first sight, because in capitalist financial systems money represented by bank balances is convertible at any moment into cash and serves identical purposes. But this is not so in the Soviet system, except in the case of private savings bank deposits. State enterprises cannot draw on their current accounts at the Bank for cash except for the payment of wages and till-money for petty outgoings. Therefore the amount of bank credit issued cannot affect the amount of cash in circulation and so lead to an inflationary expansion of consumers' purchasing power. It might be objected that as a manufacturing enterprise buys its raw material, etc., from other enterprises and sells its finished products to other enterprises by means of debits and credits in its bank account, an excessive issue of bank credit would lead to an inflationary expansion of bank balances and a rise in wholesale prices. But there is a rather important distinction between retail buying and selling and wholesale trade. Exchanges between state enterprises are planned, that is, regulated according to estimated requirements, and are not market transactions. The subsequent payment is only in the nature of a recording book entry for accounting purposes. Perhaps it will make it clearer if I put the matter this way : when one enterprise pays another for goods or material supplied it does not transfer an equivalent value, it only remits a certain number of units of account in token of receipt. The principle is somewhat similar to accounting between a number of separate factories belonging to a single capitalist company, whose mutual transactions are recorded in terms of money in the company's books, but between whom money does not actually change hands.

One may imagine Soviet money divided between two

compartments, one containing cash roubles and the other rouble units of account. Between these compartments there is a narrow and controlled channel through which a small stream flows from each to the other. From the unit of account compartment roubles flow into the cash compartment through wage and salary payments and the money paid to collective farms for their products and distributed among the *kolhozniki* in the form of labour-day dividends. The reverse stream consists of the taxes, etc., paid by the population and their subscriptions to the state loan. Substance is given to this illustration by the wide differences between wholesale and retail prices. We can calculate the approximate purchasing power of the cash rouble by noting prices of goods in the shops, but it is quite impossible to obtain any information on the accounting prices of machinery and capital goods ; so that when we see in the budget that over R.70,000 million are allotted to defence, we are entirely at a loss to know what this means in terms of guns, tanks, aeroplanes, etc., or to draw any comparison with the expenditure of other countries on defence. I should add that a certain amount of money escapes from its proper compartment and becomes pirate money. Sometimes this is the result of sheer embezzlement ; but more often to dubious manipulation of bonuses, commissions, etc. I think that the increasing efficiency of the system of economic control is probably rendering self-enrichment more difficult and risky than it used to be. But it is well known that equivocal financial transactions have accounted for the very large and quite inexplicable resources of certain members of the Soviet aristocracy, which usually led in the long run to their official if not physical extinction.

A large number of persons, in no way inclined to the red end of the political spectrum, are coming more and more to the conclusion that the *laisser-faire* conduct of capitalist economy is becoming obsolete in the complexity of modern civilisation and they naturally turn to Soviet Russia to see how a planned economy works. An investigation of Soviet planning is more fruitful of lessons in what to avoid than in constructive guidance. Probably the greatest single source of frustration is political interference, both in respect to actual planning as well as in the choice of persons responsible for the construction and execution of the Plan. It is also clear that planning has been too rigid and too centralised, which was at first perhaps inescapable owing to the lack of intelligent and experienced local officials fit to be entrusted with initiative. Latterly decentralisation seems to have become a definite aim. In assessing the Soviet experiment we must also bear in mind the enormous extent and physical variations of the U.S.S.R. which make central-ised control so much more difficult ; and the natural character of the Russian who is irked by discipline and monotony and is apt to find relief from the boredom of carrying out a set routine in introducing surprising novelties on his own re-sponsibility. Finally, one will come to the conclusion that Soviet planning has not resulted in any novel discoveries ; the whole of the Soviet economic system is founded on adaptations of capitalist methods.

CHAPTER XVI

WOMEN IN INDUSTRY

THE Constitution says that " Women in the U.S.S.R. are accorded equal rights with men in all spheres of economic, state, cultural, social and political life" (Article 122). This means that women may rise to any position, receive the same pay as men for the same work and perform the same sort of work as men.

The last time I visited Russia, summer 1939, was the first time I had gone with a party on a conducted tour. Previously I had been a free-lance making my own arrangements. The party might, I suppose, be termed intellectual, if by that one understands people with a serious mission and not mere sightseers. Politically we were of miscellaneous tints. Some of the younger members affected a pinkish hue ; one or two were blue, if that be the antithesis to pink ; the majority were grey or neutral and wary. Those of us who knew our Russia were about equally divided so that the tyros had both sides about equally forcefully presented. In Moscow we were taken to see, among other sights, the passenger port, or steamboat station as the Russians call it, on the new Moscow-Volga canal. It lies some way from the centre of the town, and *en route* we passed a gang of women engaged in laying stone blocks at the side of the roadway. One of our younger and pinker comrades found the scene very stimulating, for it afforded him an ocular demonstration of the equality of the sexes. When asked whether he would approve equally heartily of his own female relations performing navvy work on English roads, he was understood to say something about the cases being quite different. It transpired that his approval of heavy manual labour for women was confined to the principle in theory and in Russia only in practice. He was quite sure the Russian women liked their work and undertook it by choice and not from economic necessity. The point of this story is that many perfectly well-meaning and honest people with socialist leanings cannot look at Russia objectively. For some reason, mainly I suppose confusion of thought induced by overmuch reading of propaganda, they have come to regard Russia and the Russians as belonging to another world in which social laws and human nature are quite different from what they are at home. Thus they really believe that Russians do not mind living in conditions of overcrowding that they would be the first to condemn at home, that Russian women experience some spiritual gratification in performing hard manual labour and that the Russian people enjoy real intellectual and moral freedom.

The sight of women in Russia doing what we consider man's work does not intrigue me, because it is no new thing. Long before the revolution women worked on the land and on the roads and carried heavy burdens, worked in mines and in factories, though I am not sure whether they were actually employed underground. The real difference is that whereas in the old days women's work was unskilled, to-day they have the right and the opportunity to become skilled workers. Women are found among all the professions and trades, as engineers, doctors, agricultural experts, ships' officers, railway locomotive drivers and miners.

As I pointed out a couple of paragraphs above, admirers of the Soviet Union attribute the large share women now take in Soviet industry to the emancipation of women under the Bolshevik régime and their natural ambition to work side by side with men for the glory and advancement of Communism. Opponents and critics of the Soviet system dismiss the employment of women as due to economic pressure. As usual the truth lies between the extremes. I have no doubt that very many women are imbued with the crusading spirit and do take up all sorts of work with the intention of doing their bit for Communism and the Socialist Fatherland. Like women all the world over, the Russian, when she feels the call, is more fervent, fanatical and less critical than the male. I have generally found that even the most confirmed male Communist in Russia is willing to discuss his creed objectively and to listen to the other side, but a woman Communist takes the bit between her teeth and deluges one with Soviet slogans and fantastic statements about capitalism, refusing to listen to any argument or explanation. One of the *intourist* guides we met in 1939 was like this. We were all very modest people, not wealthy nor aristocrats, but working in various ways for our livings. But because we were much better dressed than the average Russian and were quite obviously accustomed to a much higher standard and more civilised way of living, she insisted that we were exploiters of the working classes, living in the lap of luxury while others toiled for us. She was quite pleasant about it, but let us understand quite plainly that she considered us bourgeois parasites. She had been brought up by Bolshevik propaganda in the belief that capitalist society consists of rich and poor, exploiters and exploited, and that the latter are always destitute and hungry and that the former always live in luxury. In my experience the Russian man, even though a convinced Communist, usually takes his Party's propaganda with a certain amount of reserve and when he gets hold of a Russian-speaking foreigner is more interested in asking questions than in expounding his own views.

A good many Russian women adopt an industrial career because it really appeals to them. Russian women are intelligent ; I would say that in comparison with their menfolk they are more enterprising and intelligent than most other women. At the same time, and for this reason, they are, on the whole, less domesticated than Western European women. I do not mean to imply that Russian women make bad housewives, but they do not allow housekeeping and family cares to occupy their faculties to the exclusion of everything else. Besides, housekeeping in Russia to-day is neither a whole-time nor a stimulating job, since it must be conducted at best in a tiny flat in a tenement building, at worst in a section of one room. The State, too, takes care that children shall not be an obstacle to a career by providing nurseries, kindergarten and children's institutes in which they probably get better care and attention than the mother could give them at home. And, though I would not for a moment suggest that Russian mothers are careless or indifferent nor take their parental duties lightly, I do think they are apt to be less wrapped up in their children than others. Certainly in the old days Russian parents interfered less in their children's lives, particularly in their intellectual lives, than English parents. And in present conditions children become independent at an earlier age and decide on their own careers with less deference to parents' ideas than before the revolution.

If the present state of affairs under the Soviet régime at once removes many of the inhibitions against women adopting industrial or professional careers and provides an incentive to them to do so, partly through public opinion and partly because of the lack of other interests, the main stimulus remains economic necessity. The earnings, not only of the bulk of the industrial workers but of the professional classes and clerical workers, are too small to support a married couple in comfort, let alone a family, unless the woman is also an earner. For the same reason children as soon as they leave school must start to earn too. The Soviet working-class husband has no rooted prejudice against his wife working, in fact he takes it for granted, and quite often she earns more than he. And the Soviet father is most emphatically in favour of his daughters as well as his sons starting to earn their living as soon as they attain the legal age of employment, namely, sixteen. If they aspired to a profession and became students at a university or technical high school, they used to become independent with their state grant. In November 1940 subsistence allowances for all students were discontinued and tuition fees introduced (see Chapter XIII), so except they win a scholarship they now have to go to work, unless the parents can afford to keep them at home and pay their fees.

So far as my experience goes, the wives of high officials and important functionaries do not as a general rule work. An outstanding exception was Madame Molotova, or Zhemchuzhina (Pearl) as she preferred to be known administratively, for most Russian women retain their maiden names when they pursue independent careers. She was at one time head of *Teje*, the scent, cosmetic and toilet preparations trust, and subsequently became People's Commissar of Fisheries and Fish Industries. Quite a number of the most prominent ballet dancers are married to important officials ; for instance, Semionova, generally credited with being the best dancer of the day, was at one time married to a vice-president of the State Bank. He was liquidated in the great purge. But dancers and theatrical artistes are very much members of the Soviet *élite* and mix socially with the members of the Government, the heads of the military services and directors of the most important state undertakings, and being far more attractive than the average run of Soviet women, naturally get snapped up by the most influential men. They cannot be placed in the same category as women employed in industry.

The Soviet system has caused a curious sort of detachment between husbands and wives. One may see quite a lot of a Russian and even get on friendly terms with him and never discover whether he has a wife and family. He never mentions them and would consider it rather odd of you to ask after them : and he never by any chance asks you to his home. But that is largely because home entertaining has practically ceased. Of course one must also remember that it is very indiscreet, not to say perilous, for a Russian to have anything to do with a foreigner except for official contacts. Even resident foreigners like diplomatic officials and newspaper correspondents practically never see the inside of a Russian home to-day, though up to 1936 a few long-resident foreigners had Russian friends whom they may have visited at rare intervals and who, perhaps rather more frequently, visited them. But such calls were strictly private, not to say surreptitious. In such circumstances and because the wife usually works under her maiden name, it is difficult to discover who are the wives of Commissars and government officials and whether they do a job of work or not. They seldom or never appear with their husbands at public functions and they never perform any public duty, like addressing a political meeting or opening a new kindergarten, as wives of leading politicians. If they do so, it is in their own capacity as Commissars or heads of government departments and in their maiden names. But, as I have already said, I do not think many of the wives of leading men hold any official positions. They have comfortable, not to say luxurious, homes and servants to do the housework. Any morning you like to visit the toilet salon at the Hotel Metropol in Moscow you will find several (for Russia) rather smartly dressed women undergoing a manicure or mysteries in a cubicle. They all seem to know one another, address the manicurist familiarly by her first name, and their conversation seems mostly about shopping, entertainments past and future and appointments to meet again. If you ask the manicurist who they are she will probably tell you *Gorodski Dami* (town ladies), which however is not what you might think, but means the feminine belongings of rich citizens who have plenty of money and leisure to amuse themselves. Some may be dancers and actresses of course, but evidently they form a society of their own and succeed in having a good time.

I feel that in order to remove possible misconceptions it ought to be explained that neither public opinion nor Soviet doctrine definitely insist on women working, nor is there any stigma on those who do not work if they have husbands able to support them. The Gorki mill foreman I have already quoted in Chapter XIII was obviously proud of the fact that his wife did not have to work. He belonged, being nearly sixty years old, to a pre-revolutionary generation and so may have retained some of the old prejudices ; but he certainly gave the impression that in his own class a man considered himself more worthy and successful if he could keep a wife to look after his home who was not compelled to work to help balance the family budget.

The following figures show the extent of women's share in industrial occupations. In 1932 six million women were employed in industry, or 27·4 per cent of all industrial workers ; in 1939 the total had risen to 10·5 millions and the proportion to 37·4 per cent. Of the urban population between 16 and 17 millions are women between the ages of fifteen and sixty, so it may be concluded that about three out of every five women of working age are employed in industry.

The proportion of women to total workers in heavy industries in 1938 was —

Coal mining	24·5	per cent
Metallurgy and engineering	31·1	,,
Power stations	20·6	,,
Petroleum	30·2	,,
Chemicals	38·9	,,
Building	20·6	,,
Peat digging	46·4	,,
Transport	18·3	,,

In light industry, particularly textiles, and in food industry, consisting very largely of canning factories, women are, as one might expect, in the majority.

In transport there were 4500 women engine-drivers and firemen, 3000 points-women and 5000 conductresses. On Russian railways every passenger coach has a conductor or attendant to keep the corridor and compartments in some sort of habitable condition.

Even more remarkable was the increase in the number of women engineers, specialists and technical experts in industry, from 3600 or 4 per cent of the whole in 1930 to 140,000 or 18 per cent in 1938. It may be that the intrusion of women into the ranks of industrial technical experts will be checked as a result of the Law of Labour Reserves (see Chapter VII). The exclusion of girls from conscription under this law may mean that on the whole women have not proved an unqualified success as engineers and technical experts, though I would hesitate to form an opinion on this slender evidence. There may well be other reasons. It is by no means impossible that some parallel scheme will be announced for girls to prepare them for professional careers, such as medicine, teaching and office work, for which they are naturally better fitted than for engineering, etc.

Personal observation, especially when one has a background of previous experience, is a valuable check on hearsay and theory. In my visits to Soviet Russia I have seen women working at all sorts of jobs ; usually it did not strike me as incongruous or abnormal for Russia. On my first trip in 1930, I travelled by sea to Leningrad in a Soviet ship. The second or third officer was a girl who had received a good deal of notice in the London press when the ship was in port. She was the first, or one of the first, Russian women to break into the peculiarly male profession of seamanship. Incidentally she was plagued by our passengers, mainly a party of very pink intellectuals on a visit to the communist paradise under the leadership of a very hard-boiled Clydeside Communist. They had no reticences nor manners, and pestered the poor girl about her origin, her job and why she had chosen the sea as a profession. Fortunately for her, none of them had any Russian and she only a smattering of English. I soon decided that the sea was not a profession for women, and in this the captain was in agreement with me. Firstly, few women have the physical strength to do the things that an ordinary ship's mate has to do. I am, of course, not talking about crack liners whose officers are not normally expected to lend a hand with ropes and things. Secondly, a woman's voice is no good for shouting orders from the bridge ; and thirdly, there is always the fear that she may lose her head in an emergency. The captain admitted that he never left the bridge or its immediate neighbourhood for long during the girl's watch, especially at night. During her watch on deck she wore the ordinary mate's uniform with trousers. We never saw her during her watch below.

Among the deck hands were three or four girls, who, I understood, were students putting in a sort of vacation job without any serious intention of becoming professional sailors. Their job was to wash down the decks and look after a large number of pedigree poultry travelling as deck passengers. They were not asked to do any real work about the ship and evidently looked on the whole thing as rather a lark. They always changed into skirts during their watch below and flirted with the regular sailors. The cooks and most of the stewards were women, and they did not seem at

257   s

all out of place. I may add that, for the benefit of the foreign passengers, the ship was run according to the communist theory of equality. In the evenings the crew assembled in the lounge for music or political debate, and off duty the captain was just one of the crowd. He himself said that he had the right to give only orders necessary to working the ship, and if he wanted anything done that was not strictly connected with the safety and navigation of the ship, it had to be approved by a meeting of the crew. This was all eyewash, for in other ships not catering specially for foreign passengers discipline is much the same as in capitalist vessels.

Wherever building is going on, women will be found acting as builder's labourers. Russians do not put up scaffolding in stages, like we do, with ladders between. They build a sort of spiral scenic railway around the work and use an incredible quantity of timber. When a house is being built one can see nothing except an outer casing of boards, behind which the bricklayers are working. The women in pairs carry bricks and mortar up the ramps on wooden stretchers ; the ramps are too rough and steep for wheelbarrows, while the absence of ladders makes it possible for two to work together. I have never seen a woman actually laying bricks, but no doubt some do. In any case, the bricklayer seems to have the easier job. Sir E. D. Simon in *Moscow in the Making* describes a Stakhanovite brick-layer's methods. He was assisted by two women ; one placed the bricks on the wall ready to the man's hand, the other shovelled mortar on to the spot where the brick was to rest. All the man had to do was to lift the brick, move it about twelve inches and set it down in place, which he did in about a second. This worked out at some 20,000 bricks in a seven-hour day. That is why brick walls in Soviet Russia look as though someone had just shied the bricks into place. These two girls were the Stakhanovite's personal assistants, others would have brought up the supply of bricks and mortar from the ground. In 1930 Stakhano-vism had not been invented, but at several places I saw building being done on these lines, only not so perfectly organised. The girls were obviously peasants with thick bare legs and feet, and very broad in the beam. They were fully up to the work. It is a curious thing that Russian peasant women, whether working in the fields or as labourers or navvies, usually go barefooted, while the men never do. I suppose it is a relic of the old days when the peasant, if he could afford a pair of boots, bought them for himself. If his wife demanded a pair to protect her feet in winter, she had to put up with his old ones.

In Kazan I saw a patrol of policewomen, complete with rifles, march out of the police station. That did strike rather an unusual note. They were dressed in the ordinary khaki tunic of the militiamen, but below they wore dark-blue knee-length skirts and rather long laced boots. They looked very efficient. Later on I came across another policewoman as night-watch at the entrance to our hotel in Sochi. We had returned very late from an excursion because a train had been mislaid and she wanted to see our papers and know all about us before she would let us in. Apart from these incidents, I do not think I have seen any other women militia. I imagine that the experiment was not persevered with for some reason or other.

In 1937 in the works of Zaporozhstal, the big foundry at Zaporozhie on the Dnieper, I came across a woman using a power-driven grindstone to take the crust off cast steel billets ; the stone was mounted in a suspended cradle and she had to press it hard against the steel. The work looked heavy and the noise and vibration must have been very unpleasant. Women work electric cranes and do jobs not requiring great muscular effort, but I do not think they are often found doing the really heavy jobs in foundries, engineering shops, etc. They do work underground in mines however. The fundamental labour laws adopted in the early years of the Soviet régime distinctly prohibited the employment of women and under-age workers below ground. Whether that rule has been formally revoked or merely ignored I do not know. H. R. Knickerbocker visited a Donetz coal mine in 1930 and saw women working underground. He was told it was, strictly speaking, illegal, but a few women were exceptionally allowed to perform subsidiary duties. However, the Soviet press has within the past two years or so carried photographs of women miners complete with pneumatic picks. This does not prove that women are regularly employed as coal hewers, only that they may take on the job. I can vouch for the employment of women in the underground workings of the Moscow tube railway when under construction. In 1934 I was in Moscow when the construction of the tube was in progress. A shaft had been sunk in the middle of the Sverdlovsk Place from which at certain hours the workers came off shift covered with yellowish clay. Among them were always a party of girls equally dirty ; and since I was staying in the Hotel Metropol I could not help seeing them practically every day. These particular girls, however, did not strike me as belonging to the peasant class. They looked too slight and slender and, under the dirt, too refined. But it may have been because they wore workman's rig complete with trousers and heavy boots, which makes a woman look smaller and slighter than she appears in skirts. I remember being told that these were not regular women labourers, but students or would-be students of engineering who had to do a term of practical labour before starting their theoretical studies. This may have been the truth.

My own forecast is that the employment of women in heavy and taxing work, such as mining and engine-driving, will not become a permanent thing in Russia. It came about from three causes, the spiritual reaction of women to the theories of the revolution, the intense demand for labour and the low standard of living. I fully believe that when the demand for labour becomes less intense and the general standard of living is materially improved, women will neither desire nor be urged to compete with men in heavy and strenuous industrial labour. On the other hand, I should say that women will continue to play an increasingly prominent part in the professions and in business administration. I have no hesitation in saying that the Russian woman of to-day shows more intelligence and organising capacity than the average man. At various times I have had many interviews with officials, heads of industrial, commercial and

financial institutions and other people from whom I wanted
information. It is a peculiarity of Soviet Russia that one
scarcely ever has an interview with anyone alone, almost
always an assistant director or somebody with less obvious
reason is present or drifts in early in the proceedings. The
fact is, I believe, that nobody is trusted, or trusts himself,
to have a solo interview with a foreigner lest he says something he should not, or gives away confidential information.
The satellites may be there merely to give moral support or
possibly as G.P.U. agents. One never knows. As a case
in point, in 1939 our party stayed a few days at Saratov
where we visited an agricultural institute, a collective farm
and a school among other things. Every time a scrubby
individual turned up, who, although pointedly ignored by
our hosts, always shoved himself forward so he could hear
what was said. So far as we could see he never tried to
address anyone or was spoken to, but it was rather significant that at the agricultural institute one of the professors,
a venerable old gentleman of Tsarist vintage who spoke
quite good English, refused to speak anything but Russian
when this pest was around. Quite frequently a woman is
among those present at interviews, sometimes in the capacity
of an assistant director or departmental manager, to give
information in her special sphere, sometimes as secretary and
interpreter, useful to explain technical terms, though the
conversation be conducted in Russian. Almost invariably
the woman shows a much readier grasp of what one is
driving at and is much more clear and intelligible in explanations than the men. In my experience the women are as
a general rule much better educated, and mentally quicker
than the men. Of course there are well-informed and well-
educated Soviet officials also speaking foreign languages,
but almost always they are Jews who have served the Soviet
Government abroad in commercial missions, etc. The
ordinary Russian official, even in really important posts, is
often very ill-educated, not to say boorish, and covers up
his ignorance of his job with a lot of communist slogans.
That is to say, he just behaves as one would expect from
a *parvenu* worker promoted on account of his political

reliability and communist zeal.

Intourist interpreters and guides are nearly all girls, and
I think most foreigners who have had much to do with
them have a great respect for their tact, energy and organising abilities. Theirs is not by any means an easy job
because the ordinary tourist knows nothing of the difficulties
they are up against. They do not tell you the rules under
which they work, but quite obviously one is that they must
never say, or give the impression, that anything a tourist
wants to do is forbidden. Of course all sightseeing, excursions and what-not for the entertainment and instruction
of foreigners are carefully chosen and arranged and have to
be approved by the G.P.U. But the tourist must never
realise that he is being shepherded all the time, and it is
up to the guide to see to it. She must be ready at any
moment to think up a plausible excuse or reason why it is
impossible to do this or go there. Her bugbear is the
foreigner who talks a little Russian and gets around by
himself. Then she must always be a buffer between her
charges and the ridiculous red tape that infuriates people
accustomed to the elasticity of private enterprise elsewhere.
Naturally she must take every opportunity of making propaganda, but she has to be careful not to overdo it and to
refrain altogether when she has got a sceptic or someone
who knows the facts. Even if one speaks Russian and
knows the ropes, one has to have a guide, because without
her it is impossible to get into most institutions. Picture
galleries and museums are about the only things one can
visit without a *propusk* (a pass) or an accredited guide. I
remember an incident in the Pechersky Monastery at Kiev
which must have been most embarrassing to our guide.
The place contains a number of mummified saints ; some
of the most saintly have a finger projecting through the lid
of their coffins for the faithful to kiss. The guide had just
been explaining that when the original finger was worn out
the monks used to substitute an artificial one, " but," she
added, " that is not necessary now, because nobody believes in
these things any longer ". At that moment a woman leading
a small child came up, crossed herself, genuflected, kissed a

finger and lifted the child up to do the same. I looked at
the guide, but forbore to comment : she found something
to show us in another direction.   Then in 1939 our party
was taken to see a sawmill at Stalingrad, the most prominent
object at the entrance being a watch-tower complete with
searchlight and armed sentry.   The official description was
a look-out for fires, for of course sawmills are most inflam-
mable.   " Then I suppose," one of us chipped in, " the
searchlight is to see the fire at night and the armed sentry
is to shoot it out."   Quite so, concurred the guide.   Later
on we saw, owing to bad staff work, a gang of prisoners
being marched to work, which, of course, was the true
explanation of the watch-tower.

Most of *intourist* guides are hand-picked for political reliability. I was told this by one who was not a Party member.
But there are not enough Party members with the languages
and address required, so a good few are not Communists.
The best-informed are, as might be expected, the older
women with pre-revolutionary education. I met one such
in the Crimea, who could talk interestingly and with knowledge on history, architecture and botany ; but practically
all the younger ones know nothing except the extraordinary
travesties of facts and theories that are taught in Soviet
schools.   Also most of them are astonishingly ignorant of
conditions and customs in Tsarist Russia.   Neither the
intourist girls nor the secretaries in government and commercial offices seem to come from the real working class.
Judging from their manners and speech, I should say the
majority belong to professional and bourgeois families.
Some of them may well have aristocratic antecedents, but
naturally they do not say anything about it.   Now and then
one lets slip an illuminating remark, for instance that her
mother has told her about her visits to Paris and London
before the revolution, and one realises that her people must
have been wealthy and more or less in society.   A fairly
large proportion are Jewesses, particularly in the organisation known as V.O.K.S. (the Society for Cultural Relations
with Foreign Countries), which spreads the light of Soviet
art and letters among intellectual foreigners.   One meets

at its Moscow receptions the most extraordinary gatherings of intense, fervent people of all nationalities and colours, with a common adoration of the Soviet system. The fluency and accuracy with which the *intourist* and V.O.K.S. girls speak foreign languages is rather surprising, considering that few of them have ever had an opportunity of studying abroad, and that the routine teaching of languages in schools is incredibly bad. I imagine that there must be special courses of languages for those who want to specialise for work in connection with foreigners, including diplomatic and consular officers serving abroad.

CHAPTER XVII

INDUSTRIAL PROLETARIATE AND AGRICULTURAL PROLETARIATE

ONE of Lenin's platform slogans was the *smychka* between industry and agriculture. By this he meant community of interests and the assimilation of the peasants and industrial workers. Tsarist Russia had not been immune from the conflict between agriculture and industry that in some degree is a feature of all countries possessing an appreciable industrial population. In order to pay their taxes and the land indemnity annuities (payments to indemnify the former serf owners for the land they had to surrender to the peasants at the emancipation), the peasants were compelled to sell more produce than was needed to feed the urban and industrial population, and not infrequently to the detriment of their own proper nourishment. The surplus was exported and brought in the greater part of Russia's foreign revenue. Needless to say the internal prices of agricultural produce were much below world market prices. After the turn of the last century the position tended to change. Industrial output was increasing very rapidly, but the poverty of the peasants, forming over 80 per cent of the population, restricted the internal market while Russian industry could not compete in foreign markets to any extent. The land reforms of 1906 and the following years were calculated to improve the situation by concentrating the land into fewer, but larger and more economic farms. In course of time this policy should have increased agricultural production, at the same time lowering production costs ; increased the purchasing power of the farmers and the demand for agricultural machinery and implements, at the same time reducing the demand for agricultural labour, thus setting free a large quantity of additional labour for industry or for resettlement in the sparsely populated regions of Asiatic

Russia. It was, in fact, the first step towards transferring
agriculture from its obsolete, primitive and natural economy
basis to a capitalist and commercial basis. The result would
have been to replace the innumerable small uneconomic
peasant holdings by a much smaller number of much larger
and more prosperous farms, employing part of the dis-
possessed peasants as farm labourers, who would thus
become an agricultural proletariate.

The Bolsheviks by the collectivisation of farming have
completed the policy inaugurated in 1906, only instead of
large private farms they set up co-operative enterprises
under state control and direction ; and instead of com-
mercialising agriculture they industrialised it. Because
Bolshevism is primarily an industrial movement it is not
surprising that the Bolsheviks aimed at the industrialisation
of agriculture. Practically all the leaders were and are of
proletarian or urban origin. Kalinin is commonly referred
to as of peasant origin ; whether or no in his youth he
lived as a peasant I am doubtful, in any case he is only a
figurehead. To-day the Government shows rather more
understanding of agricultural processes and problems than
it formerly had, when the authorities seemed to think that
crop yields and livestock increases could be planned as
accurately as the output of industrial machines. But there
is still a pronounced tendency to treat farming as a mechanical science.

Until the forced collectivisation of farming, which began
in 1930 (in 1929 only 5 per cent of farm land was collectivised,
by the end of 1931 about 70 per cent had been collectivised),
the economic relations between agriculture and industry
retained their market character. The peasants sold their
surplus produce in order to procure the means to buy the
products of industry. Admittedly the State had a practical
monopoly of the grain trade and kept prices artificially low
with the result that the peasants turned to producing more
perishable things like fruit, vegetables and dairy produce
for which the free market ensured more remunerative prices.
The result was that the State found an increasing difficulty
in procuring the supplies of grain necessary to feed the

rapidly increasing urban and industrial population. It was not in a position to increase the price of grain, because industry was expanding entirely in those branches manufacturing capital goods ; and to pay the peasants higher prices without increasing the supply of consumers' goods would have merely caused retail prices to rise, to the dissatisfaction of the industrial workers. The only course was to compel the peasants to deliver grain to the State. The peasants' reply was to reduce production of grain and concentrate still more on the things for which a free market was still permitted. The Government retorted by closing the free markets and doing its best to hinder the peasants from selling direct to the urban consumers.

In its conflict with the millions of independent peasant farmers the Government was at a disadvantage. It could persecute and ruin them, but it could not compel them to produce food for what they considered an inadequate return. The solution was to force the peasants into collective farms where they could be more effectually disciplined and made to work under conditions approximating to factory labour.

That was one reason for collectivisation. Another of equal importance was the necessity of creating a market for the products of heavy industry. The Bolsheviks had planned an enormous expansion of the country's metallurgical and engineering industries, partly for reasons of defence. Russian industry was quite incapable of securing a footing in world markets ; the quality of its products was such that they would have been dear at any price. Small peasant farmers could not afford nor make economic use of tractors, combine harvesters and elaborate agricultural machines, but large collective farms could do so. In fact large farming units, especially in the physical and climatic conditions obtaining in the chief agricultural districts of Russia, can be really economic propositions only if fairly highly mechanised. Though the Bolsheviks try to give the impression that their agricultural machinery industry was created to serve the interests of the peasants, it would be more correct to say that the collective farms were formed to serve the interests of industry. It is by no means a foregone con-

clusion that the peasants have benefited to any great extent
through mechanisation, for, although production per unit of
human labour is very much greater than in the old peasant
farms, the cost of mechanisation is very heavy. It is impossible to draw accurate conclusions from the information
permitted to appear in Soviet statistical year-books and
the like, but my researches lead me to think that the
remuneration of the *kolhozniki* is not very much greater
than the net income of the former independent peasants.
There is no doubt whatever that it is far less than the
average industrial wage.

Possibly the remuneration of agricultural labour will
some day be raised to the level of industrial earnings. A
prerequisite is equality of productivity. At the present
time a day's work by an agricultural labourer yields much
less in value than a day's work in a factory by an industrial
worker, though the degree of skill demanded by both may
be equal. If true Communism were in force, a unit of time-
labour demanding equal skill and endurance should be
equally remunerated. But the Bolsheviks have not succeeded in surmounting the capitalist notion that agricultural
labour shall receive a smaller pecuniary reward than industrial labour. Fundamentally this is because industrial
labour is far more mechanised than farm labour. In the
seventeenth and eighteenth centuries, when serf labour was
employed in industry and all processes depended on man
power, the industrial serf was not treated any better than
the farm serf. If anything, his lot was even less enviable.
To-day the Soviet factory worker commands infinitely more
mechanical power than the *kolhoznik* and therefore earns
much more. The obstacle to equalising earnings is the
supply of consumable wealth, which if equally distributed
would cause a severe fall in the standard of living of the
industrial workers.

The principle of payment according to productivity of
man plus machine also applies within agriculture as well as
between agriculture and industry. By far the best-paid
farm workers are the tractor drivers, many of whom can
earn in a month as much as the ordinary field worker in a

year. Driving a tractor is fairly hard work, but no harder than driving a horse plough. And though the kind of skill differs, I should doubt very much whether the degree of skill required to drive a tractor is any greater than to drive a horse plough. In any case women tractor drivers are common in Russia and not unknown elsewhere, but the woman who can vie with men in horse-ploughing is very exceptional.

The tractor driver's earnings are comparable with those of a factory worker, when he is working. Of course it is seasonal work and not constant, like factory employment. If all farm work were mechanised to the same degree, all farm labourers might earn about the same wages as industrial workers, but there would be employment for only a fraction of the existing numbers. This is the theoretical ideal envisaged by the Bolsheviks, but agriculture in present circumstances cannot be so highly mechanised. Ingenious machines have been invented to perform all sorts of agricultural tasks, but there are still many processes that have so far defied invention. As a matter of fact, the mechanisation of farming is not so far advanced in the Soviet Union as might be imagined. The Bolsheviks seem to have concentrated on large, powerful and rather spectacular machines such as tractors, combine harvesters, potato-lifters and so on, while neglecting things like fruit-graders and apple-slicers (to cut apples up for drying). The fact is, I think, that such machines would not pay because of the super-abundant supply of cheap female labour ; whereas tractors and so on replace the less abundant and more expensive male labour for which also industry competes. These considerations are precisely the same as are taken into account by capitalist employers of farm labour. I have seen gangs of women hoeing *kolhoz* fields under the supervision of an able-bodied male brigadier or foreman, idly smoking under the nearest shady tree, who if he worked with a horse-drawn cultivator could do as much as all the ten or a dozen women together.

The natural economy of the Russian peasant has been largely destroyed by the Bolsheviks. In the old days the peasants produced not only all their own food, but a great deal of their farm and household requirements. They bought such things as kerosene and lamps, cotton fabrics, iron and enamel ware, tea and sugar, window glass and nails ; but according to local supplies of raw material they made their own farm carts, harness and leather goods generally, furniture, pottery, etc., and built their own cottages of logs in the forest regions or adobe in the treeless steppes. That is not to say each household made its own requirements, but every village contained handicraft workers who made these things for sale or to barter for produce among their neighbours. The Bolsheviks are trying to revive these peasant industries on a commercial basis under state control, without any outstanding success. On the other hand, they have found no great difficulty in persuading the peasants to the habit of buying the output of Soviet industry, including prepared and preserved food and even bread baked in consumer co-operative bakeries. The more prosperous the district the more the peasants buy in the village co-operative shop or in the nearest town and the less they make at home. In their desires the younger generation is approximating to the urban proletariate, demanding the same sort of clothes, factory-made cigarettes, lipstick, toilet soap and all the other evidences of " culture ". At the same time the peasant mentality and philosophy is giving place to a proletarian outlook. In course of time, unless the course of events changes, the Russian peasant will disappear and the population will consist of an industrial and an agricultural proletariate. Perhaps then Lenin's *smychka* will be realised, but I think it will be a pity. It will, for one thing, mean a drastic depopulation of the countryside ; for if agricultural labour is to enjoy the same standard of living as industrial labour, the quantity of labour per unit of land under cultivation must be greatly reduced. Soviet statistics for 1937 give the value of gross industrial output as R.95,500 million and of agricultural as R.20,130 million. The number of workers in industry and construction was about 12·5 millions, and agricultural workers, including *kolhozniki*, independent peasants and labour employed in state farms was about

40 millions. Thus the production per head of industrial workers was at the Soviet valuation worth about fifteen times as much as the production per head of agricultural labour. That is to say, in order to bring the productivity of agricultural labour into line with industrial labour the number of agricultural workers would have to be reduced to less than 3 millions.

CHAPTER XVIII

THE JEWS IN SOVIET RUSSIA

OPINIONS may differ regarding the responsibility of the Jews for the revolution. It is in any case unquestionable that the revolution owed a great deal to Jews. In a sense perhaps Karl Marx was the pioneer of the revolution, for his teachings decided the form the movement was to take. And as he was a Jew, it may be supposed that his ideology makes particular appeal to the Jewish mentality. But the idea that the revolution was essentially a Jewish conspiracy is not warranted by the facts.

Lenin was not a Jew, though among his chief collaborators were three notable Jews, Trotsky, Zinoviev and Kamenev, who played a very important part in organising the revolution. On the other hand many equally important Bolsheviks, such as Bukharin, Tomsky and Rykov, were not Jews. Among the rank and file filling executive posts there were very many Jews, possibly they were in the majority. There is nothing surprising in this, for it was the logical consequence of the persecution of the Jews in Russia.

When Russia acquired a large number of Jewish subjects, formerly included in the kingdom of Poland, it was considered in the interests of the Russians that they should remain where they were. So the Jewish Pale was established, which meant that the Jews in the new Western Provinces were not permitted to migrate eastwards and overrun Great Russia. This restriction on the movement of the Jews lasted until near the end of the Tsarist régime. Jews could emancipate themselves by going through the motions of baptism into the Orthodox Church ; they were also permitted to reside outside the Pale if they had graduated from a university, but as the universities, even within the Pale, limited the Jewish students to a small quota, this right could touch only a very small minority.

272

Practically the only sources of livelihood open to the mass of Jews were trading, handicrafts and money-lending, for they were not allowed to own land and were barred from government service. Nevertheless it is a tribute to the pertinacity and resource of the Jews that the professions in all parts of the country were full of Jews, while not a few Jews carried on business in a large way in Moscow and other large towns. Russia being what it was, many Jews succeeded by bribery in evading the restrictions and settling outside the Pale. Now and then the authorities rounded up the Jews outside the Pale to see how many were illegally living and working where they had no business to be. In 1891, 17,000 Jewish artisans were deported from Moscow back to the Pale.

In addition to being classed as inferior citizens the Jews were periodically subject to pogroms, in which the actual loss of life has been much exaggerated, but in which loss of property and possessions was serious. Whether the Jews were persecuted because of their peculiar racial traits, or whether persecution produced in them the habits and outlook that made them a byword in Eastern Europe, may be debated. The fact remains that, given the opportunity to retaliate, they showed no mercy on their Christian conationals.

An oppressed minority naturally tends to produce revolutionaries and it was only to be expected that many Jews belonging to the intelligentsia, to whom the Tsarist régime denied opportunities, should have turned their intellectual gifts to plotting the overthrow of the régime. The Jewish Bund was the purely Jewish revolutionary organisation, but many of the Jewish revolutionaries belonged to other organisations such as the Social Democrats and Social Revolutionaries. Though on the whole the Jews were among the more extreme of the revolutionaries, in fact they were responsible for a large proportion of the assassinations, they did not form a united section or wing of the movement; they represented just as many different policies and programmes as their non-Jewish colleagues.

The bond between the Jews and non-Jews was a common

grievance against the Government that denied them the opportunities they thought they deserved. I think that if the life-history of all the leading Bolsheviks could be studied, it would be found that in a majority of cases they became revolutionaries more from a sense of personal injury than from an altruistic desire to reform society and abolish abuses. And of all the revolutionaries the Jews had the most reason to hate the Government and to thirst for revenge, not against the Government alone, but against the whole Russian nation.

It is therefore not mere chance that the most bloodthirsty of the early Bolsheviks, responsible for the wanton murders of aristocrats, policemen and the Imperial family, were mainly Jews. It is not a mere chance that the most ruthless of the heads of the G.P.U., the man probably responsible for more misery and suffering than any other single Bolshevik, was Yagoda, a Jew. But if the Jews were more cruel and ruthless than the non-Jews, it cannot be said that they discriminated in favour of their own race. In fact it is quite possible that in comparison to their numbers the Jews suffered even more than the Russians because so large a proportion belonged to the *petit bourgeois* class of small traders, shopkeepers, money-lenders and vodka-sellers who incurred the special animosity of the Bolsheviks. The fact that there is no evidence at all to show that the course of the revolution was ever influenced in favour of the Jews at the expense of other sections of the community, seems, I think, to rule out the idea that the revolution was a Jewish movement originating in and organised for a Jewish vengeance.

Had the Jews combined to turn the revolution to their own advantage, their numbers and influence ought to have given them success. Perhaps they were afraid to seize the opportunity lest it lead ultimately to fresh retribution ; possibly their revolutionary ideology was stronger than racial ties and consideration of material gain ; and equally possibly they proved incapable of combining for a common cause of such magnitude and scope. But my own conclusion is that the Jewish Bolsheviks never consciously thought of themselves as different from their non-Jewish colleagues,

and the reason, I think, was their repudiation of Judaism.
The bond between Jews is Judaism rather than a common
racial origin (in any case the Jews, particularly in Eastern
Europe, must be of very mixed ancestry), and when they
renounce their faith they dissolve this bond. Judaism was
persecuted by the Bolsheviks equally with Christianity and,
somewhat surprisingly, with more success. For, while one
constantly sees references in the Soviet press to the failure
of the anti-God movement to kill Christianity, one seldom,
if ever, comes across any references to synagogues continuing to function, or to the practice, even surreptitiously, of
Jewish rites.

Another point worth noting is the large number of Jews
who were liquidated in the Great Purge. Between August
1936 and the end of 1937 practically all the remaining Old
Bolsheviks and Lenin's closest collaborators were wiped out ;
they included Zinoviev, Kamenev, Radek (sentenced to ten
years' imprisonment), Pyatakov, Sokolnikov (ten years' imprisonment), Serebriakov, Grinko, Rosengoltz, Yagoda, all
Jews and all in their time high up in the Bolshevik hierarchy,
as well as numerous smaller fry. It seems unlikely that such
a holocaust of Jews could have taken place had the Jews
really exerted great influence in the Party and been conscious
of a common ancestral tie.

At the present time only two undoubted Jews occupy
really important positions in the Party and Government,
namely Lazar Kaganovich and Mekhlis, the People's Commissar of State Control. The elimination of Jews from the
highest posts in the Government and Party is sometimes
attributed to anti-semitic tendencies in the innermost circles.
The dismissal of Litvinov from the Commissariat of Foreign
Affairs certainly might have been influenced by a desire on
Stalin's part to remove a possible obstacle to better relations
with Hitler. But I have failed to find any real evidence of
a deliberate policy to exclude Jews from the most important
government and Party posts. The explanation may be that,
seeing that the rebels and Trotskyite opposition consisted
so largely of Jews, Stalin thought it best not to have too
many Jews in his immediate circle.

On the other hand there is no apparent reduction in the actual numbers or relative proportions of Jews in the state bureaucracy. The higher officials in the commercial and financial institutions are predominantly Jews. Indeed there is a very high ratio of Jews in all executive posts. They are less frequent in technical positions such as engineering, agriculture and the defence forces, though two or three of the generals liquidated along with Tukhachevsky were Jews. The Political Commissars were often Jews. Gamarnik, who avoided arrest by committing suicide, and his successor Mekhlis (now Commissar of State Control) in the post of Chief Political Commissar in the Red Army, were both Jews.

There is no need to seek for obscure explanations for the disproportionate number of Jews in the new bureaucratic aristocracy. If Jews succeed in rising to the top in finance and commerce in other countries, how much more likely are they to do so in a country where the native possesses far less natural organising ability and business instinct and acumen than the Western European ? And it must also be remembered that the revolution destroyed almost the whole of the middle-class business section of the population, leaving the young Bolshevik Jews a clear field. The superior commercial sense of the Jews has been practically demonstrated by the improved position of the administrative and organising bureaucracy and intellectual professions generally relative to the manual workers. As I noted in an earlier chapter, Lenin himself expressed the opinion that anyone with some knowledge of figures and ordinary intelligence should be able to run a business enterprise. He believed that the high rewards earned in capitalist countries by business managers and executives were unjustified by merit, but were the results of a class conspiracy against the manual workers : for he was obsessed by the Marxist doctrine that all value is the result of physical labour. Whether he discovered before he died that organisation and administration play a much more important part than he thought is not clear. But the Bolshevik leaders soon were forced to realise that manual labour without organisation and direction is impotent and that good organisers and administrators are far less numerous than good manual workers. With the rapid increase both in the number and size of industrial, commercial and financial organisations the demand for competent managers, organisers and brain workers increased faster than the supply ; and the same qualities that earned so many of these posts for Jews inspired them to exact favourable terms for themselves.

The old endemic anti-semitism, which periodically flared up into pogroms in the towns of Western Russia, seems to have been appeased. Now and then one comes across reports of trials of persons accused of petty persecution of an individual Jew, usually in White Russia or the Ukraine, as might be expected. But the former indiscriminate and universal aversion to Jews is no longer evident. The fairly obvious reason is that the conditions which caused the Jews to be unpopular no longer exist. To-day there are no Jewish money-lenders nor landlords to exploit the poorer citizens, nor can Jewish traders any longer bilk their wholesalers by fraudulent bankruptcy. And with the suppression of religion the Jews are no longer segregated into a separate community. The religious bar which formerly inhibited marriage between Jews and Gentiles no longer operates, and with the decline of Yiddish the last symbol of sectarianism is disappearing.

I have only once stayed a few days in a town formerly within the Jewish Pale, and that was Kiev in 1937, where it is now comparatively rare to hear Yiddish spoken in public. In the old days Yiddish was at least as frequent as Russian or Ukrainian in the meaner streets. In Kiev I ran across a Chicago Jew who had emigrated to America as a small child and still had an uncle living in the town of Vinnitsa, whither he made a day's excursion to see his relations. Knowing that he spoke no Russian, I asked him how he got on with the language problem. He explained that he spoke Yiddish to his uncle and aunt, but admitted a difficulty with his young cousins, who spoke it very imperfectly. He had found that with the breakdown of Jewish exclusiveness and the loss of their religion the younger generation of Jews now speak Russian among themselves, and when the old generation dies out Yiddish will practically become extinct in Soviet Russia.

The Soviet census of January 1939 gave the total number of Jews as 3 millions, which placed them seventh in the list of recognised races. Unfortunately the census taken two years previously was suppressed. One of the particulars to be filled in by every citizen was his religion, if any. The 1939 census omitted this question, so it is unknown how many people confessed to Judaism. As a matter of fact, it is not clear upon what grounds a citizen was registered as Jewish ; it could scarcely have been decided by language as in the case of other racial minorities, nor territorially, for the Jews are scattered over the whole Union. Presumably it was left to the individual to say whether he considered himself racially a Jew or not. And since nowadays there is no disability nor stigma attaching to Jewish origin, it may be taken that nearly all persons of undoubted Jewish parentage entered themselves as such.

Formerly the surname was an almost infallible indication of the Jew. Nowadays it is rather fashionable to change one's name, which can be done with the least formality. The example was set by the Old Bolsheviks, for Lenin, Trotsky, Zinoviev, Kamenev, Litvinov, Stalin, Molotov, Maisky and very many others are pseudonyms. But while the non-Jews affected *noms de guerre* epitomising their real or imaginary attributes — *e.g.* Stalin = man of steel, Molotov = the hammer — the Jews unblushingly appropriated respected aristocratic Russian names, among which Trotsky, Litvinov, Zinoviev and Kamenev may be classed. Another cause of later uncertainty regarding family antecedents will certainly be the custom of women to retain their maiden names after marriage, while children may take either the father's or mother's name or any utterly irrelevant one that takes their fancy. Thus in a generation or two family identities will tend to become obliterated and large numbers of Soviet citizens will be hard put to it to name their grandparents. And this will apply particularly to the Jews, who more than most are addicted to wandering, and less than most cherish sentimental ties with the ancestral town or village. For all these reasons, unless present trends are sharply reversed, the assimilation of the Jews will soon be accomplished.

From what I have said above it will, I imagine, cause no surprise when I express the opinion that the links between Soviet Jews and international Jewry are rapidly falling apart. Among American Jews whom I have met in Russia as tourists revisiting their old homes I have detected a certain sense of disappointment. I have been told of actual instances of Soviet Jews refusing to meet relations from America because they were capitalist bourgeois. Still another pointer was the negative Soviet reaction to the idea that Russia should provide an asylum for fugitive Jews from Nazi Germany. A young Jewish hostess at V.O.K.S. (the Society for promoting Cultural Relations with Foreign Countries) explained to me that they did not want a large influx of bourgeois-minded Jews, whether victims of persecution or not ; and she was definitely not prepared to say that Soviet Jews on racial grounds felt any more sympathy for German Jews than for any other victims of persecution. It is common knowledge that the Jewish Autonomous Area of Birobidjan in Eastern Siberia has not attracted Jews in large numbers, from other parts of the U.S.S.R., or still less from abroad. The chief reason is that Jews are poor colonists, preferring the amenities of urban life and intellectual activity to country life and manual labour.

Undoubtedly Jews are doing great work in Soviet Russia to-day as organisers and planners, in art and in science ; without them economic progress would probably have been less than it has been. Although many of the Jewish Bolsheviks are as genuinely disinterested and as devoted to communist ideals as any others, there is a certain class of arrogant, domineering young Party officials who, under cover of affected but spurious political activity, seek only their own advancement. These are responsible both by their overbearing manners and their mode of life for a great deal of the enmity felt by the masses for the new bureaucracy.

CHAPTER XIX

THE BUREAUCRATIC "ÉLITE"

THE Second Five-Year Plan ended with the year 1937. The
Central Executive Committee and the Council of People's
Commissars set down, among the other results to be achieved,
a doubling of real wages, an increase of two and a half times
in the consumption of the most important food products
and manufactured goods, and a reduction of 35 per cent in
retail prices. The results actually recorded compared with
the original Plan for 1937 included —

	Plan	Realisation
Number of workers and employees in National Economy	28·9 millions	27·0 millions
Wage fund	R.50·7 milliard	R.82·2 milliard
Average wage	R.1755	R.3046
Industrial Output —		
Gross value at 1926–7 prices	R.92·7 milliard	R.95·5 milliard
(a) Producers' goods	R.45·5 ,,	R.55·2 ,,
(b) Consumers' goods	R.47·2 ,,	R.40·3 ,,
Coal	152·5 million tons	128·0 million tons
Iron	16·0 ,, ,,	14·5 ,, ,,
Steel	17·0 ,, ,,	17·7 ,, ,,
Petroleum	46·8 ,, ,,	32·2 ,, ,,
Paper	1·0 ,, ,,	0·83 ,, ,,
Cotton fabrics	5100·0 ,, metres	3448·0 ,, metres
Woollen fabrics	220·0 ,, ,,	108·3 ,, ,,
Footwear	180·0 ,, pairs	182·9 ,, pairs
Sugar	2·5 ,, tons	2·4 ,, tons
Meat	1·2 ,, ,,	0·8 ,, ,,
Soap	1·0 ,, ,,	0·5 ,, ,,

The output of consumers' goods generally increased very
materially over 1933, but not quite to the extent promised ;

280

at the same time money wages increased very much more than was planned, which rendered any reduction in prices out of the question. In fact, the single prices ruling on the retail market in 1937 were considerably higher than the weighted average of ration and commercial prices in 1932. I paid a visit to the Soviet Union in the early spring of 1937 with the special aim of investigating the distributive system. I came to the conclusion that the supply of goods was much better than in 1934 and that the average standard of living had improved, but prices were a good deal higher. These I judged by the prices in both years of such things as wine, tobacco, fruit and other more or less luxuries that were not rationed in 1934. Of course the prices of staple foodstuffs and ordinary clothing in 1937 were enormously higher than the rationed prices of the same goods in 1934. What, however, impressed me more forcibly was that the rise in the standard of living was unequal. The higher income groups, generally speaking the official class and those in responsible administrative positions, had benefited far more than the rank and file of industrial labour. To put it concisely, the rich had become relatively richer and the poor relatively poorer. Persons I had met in 1934 in the State Bank and other big offices were obviously much more prosperous in 1937. Formerly they had appeared a little threadbare and shabby ; in 1937 they were not only much better dressed, but obviously had money to spare for reasonable luxuries. I think one probably got the most powerful impression of improved circumstances in the theatre audiences. In the stalls and lower tiers of boxes in the Moscow Opera House one no longer saw kerchiefed women and belted men. In fact the sartorial standard was about what one would find in any large Central European city except Berlin, Vienna and perhaps Warsaw and Budapest. Both in habit and behaviour these people were no longer industrial proletariate but respectable bourgeois. In the provinces, naturally, the proletariate was more in evidence, but it was obviously striving to emulate the official aristocracy.

I am inclined to think that 1936 and the beginning of 1937 were, for the time being, the heyday of the Soviet bureaucracy and official *élite*. A ruling class was crystallising out of the mass and would soon have made its position impregnable had not Stalin's purge shattered it. During the course of the Second Five-Year Plan the industrial manual worker had become displaced from his position as the Soviet aristocrat by the intellectual worker. And, I am convinced, this was really due to the latter's cleverness in raising his own income and standard of living proportionately much more than the mass of industrial labour. The Communists, for instance, had long before revoked their self-denying ordinance in respect to salary and took all they could get. Between 1933 and 1937 the average wage and salary increased by about 95 per cent, which barely covered the rise in the cost of living consequent on the abolition of rationing. As a matter of fact, the consumer, who bought 25 per cent of his food on the commercial market and 75 per cent against his ration card in 1932, had to pay more than twice as much in 1937 for the same quantities. I have no figures showing the increases in the average incomes of different sections of the population, but I am sure that the salaries of the middle and higher ranks of intellectual workers rose by more than 100 per cent, and in addition to this a very large number had subsidiary sources of income. Some engaged in journalism, some had part-time teaching posts in schools or universities, and many high government officials held two or more salaried positions ; while lots of technical experts earned substantial fees as consultants.

Professor Harper in *The Government of the Soviet Union* says (page 112), " The practice of large-scale self-enrichment seems very limited ". By this he obviously means that opportunities for graft and illegal appropriations are restricted, and adds that the penalties for embezzlement are an effective deterrent. That bribery and graft in the Soviet Union are incomparably less than under the old régime, everybody, I think, will admit. But I have come across so many well-authenticated instances of financial juggling, not to say downright fraud, that I would hesitate to affirm that the Soviet official is intrinsically more honest than the Tsarist official was. The difference is, firstly, under the old régime accepting bribes was not considered reprehensible unless it involved betraying a trust ; secondly, with the extermination of private enterprise and commerce the chief sources of bribery have disappeared. But when I say that the intellectual class, besides increasing its average salary since about 1933 proportionately more than the rise in the average industrial wage, has devised ways of supplementing its official salary, I have in mind perfectly legal and straight-forward expedients. Doctors may engage in private practice in their spare time, so long as it does not interfere with their official duties ; theatrical artistes, singers, dancers, etc., all of whom are on the salaried staff of some theatre, con-servatorium or similar institution, may accept engagements to appear in other theatres or to tour the provinces so long as they put in the number of performances stipulated in their contracts with their official employer. Popular artistes make much more out of fees than their official salary. Even ordinary shorthand typists can earn in their spare time by working for journalists and authors. The manual worker has few opportunities for supplementary earnings. A plumber, carpenter or electrician might possibly earn a little by doing jobs in his spare time for householders, but he would have to compete with the independent artisan or handicraft artels who exist by hiring out their services to casual employers. There are no doctors exclusively in private practice, unattached artistes, freelance journal-ists, etc.

Russians are among the least snobbish of people, but it would be vain to pretend that even under Bolshevism appearances are of no consequence. In the early days when the intellectual worker was often worse dressed than the factory worker, and was harder put to it to make both ends meet, his prestige suffered. If he showed some refine-ment in speech and manners it was looked on as affectation, or, at any rate, it brought him no increased respect. When the better-educated and more cultured classes re-emerged as an *élite*, the outward symbol being an increasing material prosperity, the workers soon slipped back into their old social relations with the middle class. I do not mean that the factory operative showed any sense of inferiority towards the administrative official nor paid him the deference of addressing him as *Barin* (the Tsarist equivalent of Sir). But a sense of social distinctions was recreated. One notices this everywhere, in the trains the official travels in sleeping car or " soft " compartments, the worker in " hard " compartments ; in the river and coastal steamers the official class travels first or second class, the workers third or steerage. The best hotel restaurants, especially the *intourist* hotels, are frequented by the more affluent bureaucracy, the workers go to their own *stolovaya* (eating-houses) and, as I have already explained, the more expensive parts of the theatres are full of the bureaucratic *élite*. As far as my experience goes there is very little social intercourse between the manual worker class and the official intellectual class. Just as in any capitalist State, the better-educated and higher-income groups are expected to demand and pay for the luxury of the best places, patronise the best shops and generally spend more on living than the ordinary working man. A member of the *élite* who elected to live as a workman would, I think, lose caste among his peers and the respect of his subordinates. It is to cater for the demand by the affluent official class for better service and amenities than those made available in public institutions that doctors are allowed to take private patients, that women are allowed to take private service as nurses, that private persons or small artels are allowed to work as high-class tailors and dressmakers.

The idea of equalitarianism has been entirely rejected by the Neobolsheviks. The experience of the First Five-Year Plan showed that few people were prepared to accept responsibility and expend their full energies unless they received, in their own estimation, adequate remuneration. The comparatively small number of genuinely sincere and zealous Communists who, disdaining material rewards, were ready to devote all their energies and capabilities to the cause in an altruistic spirit, were, generally speaking, not of outstanding ability in administrative or technical fields. They were specialists in revolution and communist ideology, but had for the most part neglected practical education. Thus making a virtue of necessity, Stalin discovered that the workman is worthy of his hire, and laid down the principle of differential remuneration. Curiously enough, however, the Bolsheviks still seem to pander to the old notion that Communism connotes human equality ; before foreigners they try to conceal the existence of class institutions. When in the Crimea in 1937 I visited a small seaside resort called Goursouf where I had spent some weeks in the summer of 1904. The hotel I then stayed at had become, according to an inscription at the entrance to the grounds, a rest home for members of the Red Army. It was only after persistent and prolonged questioning that the guard at the gate reluctantly admitted that the institution was exclusively for the use of officers. Later in the same trip I was at Zaporozhie, the site of the famous Dnieper Hydro-Electric Works. One of the places on the Schedule of Sights for Foreigners was a workers' club. It was an excellent club with rooms for reading, games, a hall for concerts and plays, and a restaurant complete with uniformed waitresses and clean linen. The menu raised suspicions because the prices were about the same as in the restaurant of the local *intourist* hotel. It turned out that the club was for engineers and technical employees and not for the manual workers at all. They said that the workers' club was really just as luxurious, but quite flatly refused to exhibit it. Everybody knows that these class distinctions exist ; they are the natural corollary of differentiation in remuneration, for what good would it be to pay a highly qualified and able man a much higher salary than the ordinary workman's wage if he cannot spend his money on his own gratification ?

The rise of a comparatively affluent and more or less cultured class necessitated the production of an increasing quantity and assortment of what the Bolsheviks call " cultural " goods, that is, articles satisfying the intellectual needs rather than the physical needs of the consumer. *Socialist Construction*, 1939, showing the increase in the sales of consumers' goods betweeen 1933 and 1938, gives the following :

INDEX OF SALES IN 1938
(1933 = 100)

Foodstuffs	329·7
Manufactured goods . . .	252·8
Of which furniture . . .	650·0
„ musical instruments .	1660·0
„ photographic goods .	540·0
„ sports goods . .	1480·0
Books and journals (copies printed) .	1440·0

It should be noted that the rise in the value of sales of
food is very largely due to the greater degree of preparation
and consequently in the price of food sold by the state retail
shops and to the increasing purchases of prepared food by
the rural population, which formerly consumed its own
products. In actual volume the consumption of manufactured goods increased more than the consumption of
food during the period ; though it should also be remembered
that part of the increase in the value of manufactured goods
was also due to price increases. However, the point I particularly wish to emphasise is that the sales of luxury and
semi-luxury goods, which certainly were not bought by the
ordinary manual worker, expanded noticeably more than
the sales of industrial goods on the whole. According to the
source already quoted, the index of sales of essential industrial goods in 1938 was :

Textiles and clothing . . .	243·3
Footwear	242·0
Household utensils . . .	266·4

During the same period production in volume of textiles
was increased to 132 per cent and of footwear to 214·3 per
cent of 1933. This indicates that the price per unit in 1938
was higher than in 1933, which again may have been due to
a general rise in the price level or to an improvement in
quality. In the case of textiles the production of the more
expensive fabrics of wool, silk and linen increased more in
proportion than cotton, as the following figures show :

INDEX OF PRODUCTION IN 1938
(1933 = 100)

Cotton	. .	. 127·8
Woollens	. .	. 132·4
Linen	. .	. 193·7
Silk	. .	. 226·5

From this we may deduce that part of the increased
value of the turnover of industrial goods was due to a
proportionately greater increase in the production of high-
quality and luxury sorts than of the qualities and assort-
ments bought by the rank and file. This was entirely borne
out by my own observations in 1937. The average price
of men's suits of the quality bought by the ordinary skilled
worker earning R.400 to R.500 a month was about R.500.
Suits made of very inferior stuff, mainly cotton, ill-fitting
and badly finished, might have been bought for R.200 to
R.300. In the big Moscow department store, which catered
for the comparatively well-off official class, suits of fairly
good woollen cloth and presentable cut sold at prices from
R.900 to R.1200 and were in great demand. In 1934 the
same quality suits were obtainable only in *Torgsin* for
foreign currency. Women's fur coats were sold at prices
between R.10,000 and R.15,000. I could quote further
instances of the supply of high-quality and luxury goods
for the satisfaction of the desires of the new *élite*, but I think
I have made it clear that of late years there has been a remarkable change-over in the Bolshevik standpoint regarding
class differentiation.

A great deal has been written about the Great Purge,
which started in August 1936 with the trial and sentence
to death of Zinoviev, Kamenev and several other Old
Bolsheviks, and came to an end in the spring of 1938 after
an unknown number of persons had been shot or committed
to prison or convict camp for terms of five to ten years.
I cannot pretend to any authoritative information on the
causes behind the purge ; but I think it very likely that,
whether or not an actual conspiracy against Stalin and his
ruling clique was discovered, a contributory reason was the

emergence of a bureaucratic aristocracy or *élite* which threatened to become an exclusive ruling class with vested interests and arbitrary privileges. Such a class might soon have got beyond the control of the ruling clique and defied the communist programme of the Party. It is important to realise that a very large proportion of the bureaucracy was Jewish. An analysis of the names of the principal victims of the purge shows this, while I can testify from my own experience that among the officials and employees in Soviet banks and trading organisations Jews are very prominent and predominate in the higher posts. Jews having far more financial and commercial acumen than the native Russian, naturally gravitate to administrative and clerical posts ; comparatively few are to be found as engineers and technical experts. Another thing, among the old pre-war revolutionary intelligentsia a large number were Jews who were driven to revolutionary activities through the oppression and persecution of their religion by the Imperial Government. Thus when the revolution decimated the ranks of the native Russian intellectual workers Jewish Communists naturally took their places, because among the whole Communist Party they were the best educated and best fitted for executive posts. I do not believe, as some people insist, that the Jews in Soviet Russia deliberately plotted and combined to revenge themselves for the wrongs they had so long suffered legally and illegally at the hands of the Russian people. But I can well understand that the Jews had no particular love for the Russians and felt no altruistic urge to sacrifice their own interests for the sake of realising the promises of the revolution. In fact, the Jews in Russia had always been segregated both physically and spiritually from the Russian people and, therefore, neither felt themselves to be Russian nor saw any reason for pride of country or for loyalty to the national idea. Naturally, when they attained positions which gave them the power to command material resources, they thought first and foremost of their own prosperity and well-being. In this they seem to have been rather short-sighted, for when it became increasingly plain that the people who had the best of everything were so largely Jews, it tended to revive the anti-semitic feelings among the Russian masses that had been quiescent since the revolution. At the end of 1936 or beginning of 1937 there seemed to be a distinct danger that a largely Jewish self-reproductive bureaucratic aristocracy would arise with little sympathy for, or sense of obligation towards, the Russian proletariate.

It may be objected that the purge disclosed no unity nor cohesion for mutual protection among the bureaucracy. Judging by the intrigues, denunciations and paying-off of old scores disclosed in reports of trials, there was no sense of solidarity at all among the ranks of Soviet officialdom, nor for that matter in the Party itself, where seemingly half the members were engaged in spying on and informing against the other half. But I do not mean to suggest that the new bureaucracy had as yet become class-conscious, though I think that the seeds of a class-conscious society were beginning to germinate. And so far as the denunciations and intrigues were concerned, this lack of loyalty to one's class or associates is a typical Russian trait, whose origin is probably to be found in the centuries of servitude under the Tatar domination.

Except for a few of the highest victims, such as Yagoda, Sokolnikov, Radek and Bukharin, to whose trials the greatest publicity was given, proceedings were not reported at all or given only cursory mention in local newspapers. The charges appear to have been partly of political heterodoxy and partly of maladministration, embezzlement and sabotage. A great many factory directors and technical managers were condemned for failing to realise planned output or planned reduction in production costs, and, of course, such failures were always found to be due to malice and not to incompetence nor unforeseen circumstances. There was never any difficulty in finding some offence to serve as an excuse for liquidating an undesirable person. The penalties were shooting, imprisonment, degradation to an inferior post and, for members of the Party, expulsion from the Party. Engineers and technical experts were often taken over by the G.P.U. and put to compulsory work in remote regions.

However, it is not so much the purge itself as its effects on the workers and industry that I want to discuss. Above all it caused a deterioration in labour discipline. This is shown by the succession of laws since the latter part of 1938 for tightening up factory discipline and preventing workers from capriciously changing their jobs. Undoubtedly a large number of factory managers were the victims of intrigue and false denunciations by ambitious young communist workers convinced that their capabilities had not received due recognition. This sort of thing naturally undermined the authority of directors and managers as a class. Then so many capable and experienced men were replaced by *vydvizhentsi* (promoted workers), who probably owed their promotion as much to their political zeal and eloquence as to their technical qualifications. When they proved incompetent they wrote to the papers complaining that the older experienced men, very probably over whose heads they had jumped or possibly whose posts they had filched, refused advice and assistance. Many students were posted direct from graduation to responsible administrative and technical positions without any practical experience in management. The official journal of heavy industry, *Industriya*, disclosed that out of 2083 high-school students graduating in the last quarter of 1937, 150 were at once made directors of factories, chief engineers, mine managers and so on ; while more than 200 were appointed heads or assistant heads of various mining enterprises. Presumably the rest were also given responsible executive jobs at once. The confidence officially expressed by government spokesmen and the newspapers, that the injection of new blood into industrial administration would result in an immediate improvement in all directions, was ill founded ; complaints were soon being voiced that the new type of Soviet manager and expert suffered from the faults of his predecessor and a few more of his own. It was simply another demonstration that proficiency in Marxism and the communist Dialectic does not compensate for lack of training in other fields. A large number of the disgraced and degraded experts had to be brought back and reinstated. But the purge had for the time being effectively broken up the incipient bureaucratic upper class, partly by bringing it into disrepute among the masses and partly by bringing about an internal disintegration.

I have not found any evidence that the purge, by disintegrating the bureaucratic ranks and impairing the prestige of the manager class, reinstated the industrial proletariate as the country's aristocracy. The workers gained no greater voice in the affairs of their employing enterprises ; and if the new directors and managers possessed less moral authority than their predecessors, this was offset by the greater severity of labour legislation.

CONCLUSION

THE SOVIET STATE

In the preceding chapters I have attempted to describe the main outlines of the economic structure of Soviet Russia and to give some idea of the conditions of life of the people. In doing this I have relied on my own observations and on facts and figures culled from official Soviet sources. But I have not been content merely to study and record the economic developments of Bolshevism ; I have constantly endeavoured to relate economic facts to the political and ideological growth of Bolshevism, to try to understand their mutual reactions and to see whither they lead.

Since politico-economic terms are often employed rather loosely, it may be as well to define the meaning of those used. By Bolshevik I mean an adherent of Stalin and a subscriber to the doctrines of Marx and Lenin ; an Old Bolshevik is a member of the original Bolshevik Party under the leadership of Lenin, in contrast with whom the present Stalinite Bolsheviks may be termed Neobolsheviks. Bolshevism is the system of government in Russia and the ideology which inspires it. Communism and Bolshevism are not entirely synonymous terms. The official designation of the Communist Party is " the All-Union Communist Party (of Bolsheviks) ", which tacitly admits the possibility of other brands of Communism, for example the Trotsky heresy. Soviet is the Russian word for council as well as counsel. It came to have a special revolutionary significance through the workers' and peasants' councils, the earliest and most primitive revolutionary governing organs. The official title of Stalin's Empire is the Union of Soviet Socialist Republics, or for short the Soviet Union. It is only foreigners who use the word Russia in a territorial sense, or Russian to denote an inhabitant of the Soviet Union. Soviet may be used as an adjective, *e.g.* the Soviet Government, the Soviet system, to denote a territorial quality, but if we want to distinguish between the form of government in the Soviet Union and anywhere else it would be more correct to speak of the Bolshevik Government. Capitalism, in the sense I adopt throughout this book, means simply an economic system based on private enterprise and the private ownership and exploitation of the means of production. Socialism has as many shades of meaning as the number of political creeds calling themselves socialist ; but I use it merely to denote the opposite of capitalism, that is, a system in which private ownership of capital and the profit motive have been abolished. Bourgeois, Bourgeoisie, is practically the same thing as middle-class or the middle-classes. But it has more political significance. In Bolshevik parlance it connotes rather a point of view than social position ; a bourgeois is one who puts self-interest before community interest and holds definite opinions about his social position. The opposite is the Proletariate, that is the masses conscious of no social distinctions, nor possessing sufficient personal property to render them apprehensive of expropriation.

The Bolshevik revolution arose out of the collapse of the autocratic régime as a result of the World War, and the ineptitude of the intermediate bourgeois socialist Government. Although the masses who supported the Bolshevik leaders were certainly actuated by economic motives, the workers desired freedom from want and the peasants wanted more land, I think it is possible to say that at bottom the revolution was not so much against capitalism *per se* as against the form of Government. It was easy to persuade the masses that when class privileges were abolished the national income could be equally distributed and everybody would have enough. No doubt the industrial workers were flattered by the prospect of social equality ; but I doubt whether this had much appeal to the peasants, among whom in their own estate social equality had always existed, and between whom and the upper and middle classes there was so great a gulf that they regarded these not as social superiors so much as inhabitants of a different world.

Comparisons between the Bolshevik and Nazi revolutions are inevitable ; and the first difference to be noted is that the Russian revolution was led by a group of leaders, mainly middle-class intellectuals, exclusively by appeal to and for the benefit of the lower toiling classes, against a concrete and visible enemy. The Nazi revolution had nothing in common with the class war in Russia ; it was more or less a spontaneous national revolt against the impersonal and mechanist tyranny of the capitalist system and was led by a party representative of all sections of society. In Russia the toiling classes had to be convinced of the genuineness and success of their revolution by the blood of aristocrats, bourgeois and policemen. The Nazis did not demand blood sacrifices, though in a way the persecution of the Jews was the result of the need of inventing a personification of capitalism on which vengeance could be taken.

Of course the equalitarianism of the first years of the Bolshevik régime was intended to apply only to a section of the population, and thus immediately violated the principle of socialist equality. The social order was merely inverted, the industrial proletariate becoming the privileged ruling class, the former privileged classes being reduced to a condition of inferiority and the peasants left much as they were. In view of the ignorance and low standard of living of the workers, the only effective appeal was the promise of economic progress and a rising standard of living. Freedom in the higher intellectual sense meant nothing because the ordinary worker did not understand it nor want it. And it seemed obvious to them that when the workers owned all the resources of the country and all the capital, they would draw dividends vastly superior to the wages earned by working for the former owners. In the first flush of enthusiasm for the Workers' and Peasants' State the principle of equal economic reward was acquiesced in, largely I think because the national income was so small that it provided only a bare subsistence for all. Economic equality, human nature remaining unchanged, can be realised only when conditions impose equal poverty or when the national wealth is so great that the general standard of living rises beyond the dreams of avarice.

294

Disinterested service to the Cause and the Community
was its own reward, therefore all Party members voluntarily
submitted to a self-denying ordinance, limiting their money
remuneration to a comparatively small sum. However, this
was mitigated by privileges which made their money income
go further than that of the unprivileged majority. The
attempt to introduce Communism in practice broke down
within a very short time, to be succeeded by the N.E.P.
phase in which a socialist order was set up permitting a
considerable amount of private enterprise in the lower strata
of the economic structure. This immediately led to a breach
in economic equality, which was counteracted by an inverse
order of social and political inequality. Those who enriched
themselves through private enterprise thereby became politically and socially inferior.

The present system began with the First Five-Year Plan,
which in retrospect is seen to have coincided with the rise of
totalitarianism. Economic equality was partially restored
with the persecution and eventually the practical extermination of private enterprise. During the First Five-Year Plan
rationing reduced the effective difference between the purchasing power of high and low money incomes. And during
the early part of the period a distinct tendency was shown
by state enterprises to equalise wages. This phenomenon
was not welcomed by Stalin, who stigmatised it as " Petit
Bourgeois Equalitarianism " because he had enunciated the
principle of payment according to performance and the value
of the individual to the community. At about the same
time political and formal social equality were reintroduced.
The Constitution of 1936 abolished all discrimination against
persons on account of their origin, giving all citizens equal
rights to employment, education and political franchise ;
which, after all, is no more than is promised by any democratic constitution.

The Bolsheviks declare that the equality of personal
rights and opportunity theoretically obtaining under a
democratic capitalist constitution is an illusion, because it
is vitiated by economic inequality. The question is rather
whether these equalities have any more substance under

the Bolshevik régime. To begin with, it is worth noting that the Soviet Constitution does not give an unconditional guarantee of employment. It says " the right to work is ensured by the socialist organisation of national economy, the steady growth of the productive forces of Soviet Society, the preclusion of the possibility of economic crises, and the abolition of unemployment ". As we saw in Chapter XIII, the right to more than elementary education depends on ability to pass examinations or to pay for it. Equality of material rewards is not absolute, but relative to the ability of the worker, which is equitable supposing that a satisfactory evaluation of ability exists. The Bolshevik criticism of capitalist wage determination is that wages are a matter of bargaining, which drawn to a logical conclusion means that the highest wages are paid by expanding industries whose demand for labour is the most intense. But the same principle applies in the Soviet Union. The difference is that in capitalist States industries arise and expand because they produce something that the population wants and for which it is willing to pay a relatively high price, whereas in Soviet Russia it is the Government that decides what industries shall expand. This decision does not always agree, in fact probably more often than not actually disagrees, with the popular verdict.

The Marxian hypothesis, that capitalism means the progressive impoverishment of the workers, is still an article of faith among the Bolsheviks, who would refuse to believe that any capitalist employer ever pays more than the lowest wages at which he can hire the labour he needs. But it remains to be proved that Soviet industries pay higher wages than are necessary, or that the Soviet worker enjoys a higher personal income in relation to his output than the capitalist worker. The Bolshevik argument is that the whole national production of wealth is devoted to the benefit of the whole people, though only a part is distributed to the individuals composing the community. This assumes that the part of the national income appropriated by the Government for the defence and administration of the country, the development of industry and communications

and the exploitation of natural resources, is expended for
the equal benefit of all members of the community. In a
democratic capitalist country public expenditure is, so say
the Bolsheviks, mainly for the benefit of the upper, ruling
and wealthy classes. Public expenditure on maintaining
law and order chiefly benefits the wealthy and privileged
section, because they have more to lose and would lose it
were protection withdrawn. Public expenditure on social
services, education, health and recreation, they either deny
or disparage as sops thrown to the lower classes to keep
them more or less contented. Through some queer train
of reasoning they will have it that public expenditure in a
capitalist State for the benefit of the toiling masses is
pauperisation ; under Bolshevism it is not. I have met
young Bolsheviks in Russia who are absolutely convinced
that in England the parliamentary franchise belongs only to
persons with certain property qualifications and that there
is no free education nor free medical treatment apart from
what is provided by charity.

The failure of Bolshevism to provide a new order un-
questionably superior on its own merits to capitalism is
shown by the need constantly to pour out false propaganda
about the poverty and oppression of the workers in other
countries. This has sometimes resulted in somewhat embarrassing situations when foreign trade-union delegations
have visited Russia. Either, said the Soviet workmen, these
people are bourgeois masquerading as workers, or the stories
we have been told about the conditions of the working classes
abroad are not true. If these are genuine examples of the
working classes they are much too well dressed, well fed
and contented to fit the description. The Soviet workers
usually conclude that such visitors are really members of
the higher trade-union bureaucracy, which they are always
being told is hand-in-glove with the capitalists. This they
can perfectly understand, because they know that their own
trade-union bureaucrats are relatively prosperous and work
for the State. Since the principal function of Soviet Trade
Unions is to increase productive efficiency in the interests of
the State as the employer of their members, it is quite natural

for the Soviet workers to attribute the same function to capitalist Trade Unions in relation to capitalist employers.

The notion that Bolshevism has succeeded in creating the classless community is, of course, nonsense. The bureaucratic and Party *élite* is as much the governing class as the Nazi *élite* and maintains its position by precisely the same methods of suppression of personal liberty and all social units, such as cultural and sporting societies, students' fraternities, professional guilds and church congregations. No society nor association of any sort or for any purpose may exist except under Party tutelage. Even the Tsarist régime in its most reactionary periods never went to the same lengths to prevent the free association of individuals for the prosecution of common interests. The Soviet bureaucracy is rapidly becoming an exclusive and self-reproducing *élite*. One reason, probably among a number of reasons not yet fully understood, for the Great Purge of 1936–7 was the growing power of the bureaucracy. Hitler's purge of the Nazi Party in 1934 and Stalin's purge of the Bolshevik Party two years later were both new instances of the old law, that a dictator must always take the initiative in removing possible rivals and any section of his followers which begins to show the smallest symptoms of independent thought. At the same time the dictator, possibly in violation of his own principles, must permit his followers to arrogate to themselves social and economic privileges. Self-interest therefore attaches the bureaucracy to the person of the dictator and to the maintenance of the *status quo*. And because the dictator finds it expedient to permit the rise of a privileged bureaucracy, the administration of the country falls into the hands of self-seeking and mercenary men who gradually squeeze out the genuinely disinterested and honest to whose sacrifices and devotion the new régime owes its inception.

The fundamental weakness of the Bolshevik régime lies, I think, in its purely materialistic doctrine of economic progress. Naziism succeeded in Germany partly because socialism and communism had proved themselves incapable of furnishing an alternative to capitalism that satisfied the longings of the people. In the first place the ordinary human being does not view himself exclusively against an economic background, he has other values than the mere satisfaction of material desires. Naziism offered the Germans a society based on other than mere economic values. The element of mysticism in the Nazi creed perhaps appealed to the German intellect and sentiment more than it would to the British or the Russian, who are much less gifted with the power of self-deception. But I have always felt that the Marxists take an unjustifiably sordid view of human nature. So the Bolshevik promise of an increase in the standard of living of the ordinary man, superior to anything that can be expected from capitalism, did not create fanatical enthusiasm. In any case the expected improvement in living conditions was not realised, neither have the Russians shown much enthusiasm for the mission of freeing the proletariate of the rest of the world. It is perhaps not without significance that the missionary zeal of Bolshevism, as expressed in its foreign propaganda under cover of the *Comintern*, has steadily declined proportionately with the unconcealable failure to realise its economic promises in Russia itself.

Both Bolshevism and Naziism must always be militant against democracy and capitalism. It is essential to their continued existence to have an enemy to fight against, and if the enemy refuses to accept the challenge, he must be goaded and insulted until he shows signs of irritation, which will then be twisted into proof of his aggressive intentions. Bolshevism started out to bring about an international class war ; Naziism on the contrary is a national movement which started out to oppose Bolshevism. Both crusades soon became exhausted because they lacked the inspiration which arouses a crusade. The proletariate of the world refuses to unite, partly because national sentiment still transcends class consciousness, and partly because the proletariate of the world does not see why a successful revolution in a backward country like Russia should qualify the Russians to run class revolutions everywhere else. In reality the excesses in Russia and the arrogance of the Bolsheviks outside Russia went a long way towards discrediting the idea of the class war and disuniting the revolutionary forces that the Bolsheviks aspired to direct. So the Bolshevik leaders had to try to make the Russians believe that the rôles were reversed and that capitalism, instead of being threatened by the class war, was entertaining aggressive designs against Bolshevism in its own lair. The Nazis, too, switched from Communism to international finance and Jewish plutocracy as the enemy.

Rearmament without a potential enemy, real or imagined, makes nonsense. Germany's rearmament was all along intended for aggression ; but the Bolsheviks have always insisted that their object was simply and solely defence. So far their actions have not much belied their protestations. But in both countries the elimination of unemployment has been greatly assisted by rearmament, which at the same time was an obstacle to a rise in the general standard of living. It is rather a remarkable commentary on the two systems, that while in Germany the standard of living of the workers has not been substantially lowered, though it has been prevented from rising, in Russia the cost of rearmament has disproportionately fallen on the manual workers. In Germany limitation of dividends, high taxation on large incomes and a great increase in the prices of luxury goods very materially reduced the purchasing power of the wealthier groups, while wages were not cut (though working hours have, of course, been lengthened) and the prices of the ordinary essentials of life were stabilised, at least until the outbreak of the war, at a fairly constant level. In Russia, still at peace, retail prices of ordinary consumers' goods have tended to increase more than prices of luxuries, while since 1935 the rate of income tax payable by low wage groups (R.150-R.400 a month) has risen relatively more than on medium wages (R.500-R.700). But the Bolsheviks had expropriated and destroyed the well-to-do upper and middle classes at the outset, thus destroying those sections of the population that could be heavily taxed for the benefit of the poor and the needs of the State. Consequently the working classes have to bear the full burden. The Nazis did not destroy the German well-to-do classes, but left them as the State's milch cow. In the long run, if Naziism continues, the upper and middle classes in Germany will be just as effectively, but less painfully, obliterated ; for they are steadily being impoverished, and, through the Hitler Youth movement, labour camps and so on, are being socially approximated to the masses.

As I have already noted, the main plank in the original Bolshevik platform was economic progress ; to which end the exploitation of man by man was to be abolished by nationalising all the natural resources and productive forces of the country and exploiting them for the equal benefit of the community. But instead of natural wealth and capital becoming the servants of the community, humanity has become the slaves. Nowhere in the contemporary world is labour so unfree as in Russia and Germany ; the Russian worker to-day is scarcely more free than the factory serf in the eighteenth century, nor is the *kolhoznik* much freer than his agricultural serf grandfather. It is true that the freedom of the worker in a capitalist democracy is more formal than real, because economic necessity not only compels him to work, but restricts his choice of employment ; in Bolshevik Russia, however, he may not change his employment at his own free choice ; at the same time he may be compulsorily transferred from one place to another and made to work at whatever task authority may decide. The Law of Labour Reserves (see Chapter VII) even restricts his free choice of a career, by conscripting him in his early youth for training in some branch of industry. This law was made necessary by the abolition of unemployment, causing the disappearance of a floating reserve of labour from which industry could draw its needs. The Government therefore found itself forced to conscript and train immature labour and ration it out among the different branches of industry.

Further, in order to provide the capital needed for the continual expansion of industry the State manages and restricts consumption. Formal rationing was done away with in 1935, but other means just as effective are used to restrict demand to the supply of consumers' goods the Government sees fit to provide. And in all the speeches of Party and government spokesmen and in newspaper articles dealing with industrial progress and achievements the same note is struck, that increased industrial output is an end in itself. Scarcely the most perfunctory reference is made to the ultimate benefits that will accrue to the people, though this was the principal theme in the propaganda that ushered in the First Five-Year Plan. To-day the emphasis is on Power ; the Soviet Union must mould its own destiny, transforming itself into the leading industrial State of the world, that is to say the strongest in the military sense.

Since to toil for a living is the unescapable lot of mankind, the question of how best to organise labour lies at the root of all economic reform. The Bolsheviks went further than any other reformers in trying to create a new attitude towards work. In their scheme work was no longer a hardship and to be avoided, but a welcome duty. They tried to replace the economic motive by two abstract principles, the altruistic impulse to increase the well-being of the community and, formerly, the moral gratification of furthering the " cause ". Latterly this has been partly replaced by the inspiration of nationalism. It is plain to see that the growth of the nationalist concept has been accompanied by a steadily increasing regimentation of labour. More and more legislation restricting the workers' freedom is explained as necessary in the interests of the State. The " withering away of the State " as predicted by Marx has proved an illusion.

Peter I was sincerely convinced that his reforms and wars were in the interest of the State. He was the first Tsar conscientiously to base his actions on the idea of service and so broke with the old concept of the Tsar's private-proprietorial rights. The State, however, was the creation of his own imagination. His reforms met with the approval of a few, but created profound misgivings, not to say discontent, among the majority of his subjects. On balance history assesses his reforms as beneficial, though too often they were introduced tumultuously and left with ragged ends. He tried to compel the scions of nobility to acquire education to become self-supporting and useful members of society. He had them sent abroad, where for the most part they succeeded only in acquiring a talent for extravagance. Because his reforms were in advance of contemporary public opinion, which they often violated by unnecessary violence, the permanent results were disappointing. All the same, Russia never slipped back into her pre-Petrine Asiatic mediaevalism and lethargy. She remained a European Power to be reckoned with.

Among the chief changes wrought by Peter were the breaches in class distinctions and privileges, for he demanded service from the humblest serf to the noblest patrician ; and the industrialisation of the country, and a great extension of education, not as an end in itself but because he needed an educated bureaucracy to administer his new state departments, manage his new industries and command his army and navy. Because so few of his own subjects possessed either the natural or acquired qualifications, he hired many foreigners. It is impossible to overlook the similarity between the events of Peter's reign and the course of Soviet history. Possibly the most intriguing comparison is between the new bureaucratic *élite* bequeathed to Russia by Peter and the growth of a Soviet bureaucratic *élite*.

Though Peter enormously increased the productivity of the country and the power of the State, his reforms did not enrich the population. Kluchevsky in his history wrote, " Peter's generation never toiled for its own benefit, but always for the benefit of the State, and, whilst performing more and better labour than preceding generations had ever done, issued from the task even poorer than they ". On the other hand, " Peter bequeathed to subsequent generations not a kopek of state indebtedness. . . . Indeed, the fact that he made himself the creditor rather than the debtor of the future was what, more than all else, constituted his superiority to his successors." Bolshevism has refulfilled this description almost to the letter and encountered the same difficulties as Peter in connection with its human apparatus. I have already in a previous chapter mentioned the maxims of decent behaviour displayed in workers' restaurants and other places. Peter also could not stand the manners of the Schliachetstvo (approximately the class of gentry from whom the bureaucracy, army officers and civil service were recruited) and recommended rules of conduct such as to refrain from picking the teeth with a knife, scratching the head ; if compelled to spit, not to spit in the middle of a group.

But Peter failed to awake in the ruling class the idea of " service " to the fatherland. To quote Kluchevsky again, " even those of them who stood nearest to the throne were virtually, as yet, only Peter's court and personal underlings, and little, if at all, fitted to act also as his agents in his reforms ". We may speculate how far this observation is applicable to the men who stand nearest to Stalin to-day.

In the natural course of events Peter was succeeded by " a mere phantom of authority ", in fact by Catherine I, his second, and in the opinion of many his bigamous wife, whose succession, according to Kluchevsky, " at once led to those people ceasing to feel responsible to anyone but themselves, and proceeding, instead, to take stock of one another, and of their mutual relations, and of their several positions in the country which now they had independently to administer ". Their experience of administration under Peter had at least taught them how to use the country to their own personal profit. For one thing, they deprived the serfs of their last shred of individual rights and reduced them to the position of human chattels. Economically the country lapsed into stagnation, the main reason being that under Peter's rule both industry and commerce had been largely under state supervision and artificially stimulated by Peter's need of munitions and all sorts of equipment˙for military and civil needs. The succeeding administration had learned how to collect taxes, but was not interested in promoting the ability of the taxpayer to earn the where-withal to pay. And, one may guess, the personal impoverishment of the population through the transfer of wealth to the State had reduced the purchasing power of the public at the same time that government demands for the products of industry declined.

Let us see whether the history of the Petrine epoch contains any further hints for the future of Soviet Russia.

The ideas and principles of Bolshevism are better understood by the Russian people than were the aspirations and reforms of Peter, in whose time but a small section of the population had any education at all, and because the notion of national prestige was completely foreign to the mass of serfs. The *kolhozniki* and industrial workers to-day are able to appreciate the gains conferred by the revolution, and since it was a revolution from below and not imposed from above, they will the more unitedly and effectively resist all attempts to deprive them of their advantages. But it does not follow that they will succeed. A point that is worth attention is that both régimes broke down class distinctions and privileges. Peter, of course, did not dream of instituting social equality, but his cancellation of the old order of aristocratic precedence and imposition of equal liability to service effected scarcely a smaller breach with the past than the Bolshevik revolution. And both régimes substituted for the former ruling class a new bureaucracy drawn from all ranks and including a considerable sprinkling of foreigners. The question that cannot be decided at present is whether the Soviet bureaucratic ruling class will prove more loyal to its ideals, more united and less self-seeking than that bequeathed by Peter, when the hand of the present dictator relinquishes control. The majority of Peter's lieutenants proved to be careerists when the test came. The difficulty of judging the higher ranks of the Bolshevik bureaucracy is the seclusion in which they lead their private lives. It is common knowledge that many, if not most, of the Nazi leaders have enriched themselves ; their houses, estates, entertainments, fashionably adorned wives, and the ceremonies attending their public appearances are well advertised and not immune from pungent criticism. There is nothing of the sort among the Bolshevik leaders, partly perhaps because public ostentation is not a Russian vice, but still more due to the ideological principles of Bolshevism whose repute would be irremediably damaged by its leaders' extravagance and luxurious living. Also Stalin, being devoid of social humour and content with the substance of power without the gilding, affects the simple life and, no doubt, instructs his colleagues that display is definitely displeasing. Which does not mean that he approves of slovenliness in appearance or vulgarity in address. It is also difficult under the Bolshevik order to accumulate wealth in great amount. It is impossible to invest in shares or property. The only opportunities are state war bonds and the savings bank. It is possible that some highly placed Bolsheviks have deposited capital abroad, but so far as I am aware, not the faintest whisper of it has ever been heard. All the same, there is no reason to think that all the leaders live ascetically. It would be found that most of them possess comfortable homes and domestic servants and are not immune to the attractions of luxury. In fact, compared with the ordinary citizen their standard of living is no worse than that of cabinet ministers and high government officials in most other countries.

Capitalism is not the only system under which the toiling masses are exploited according to the Marxist theory of surplus value. Totalitarian rulers must continually persuade their people that the difference between their production and consumption is eventually returned to them in the increasing power and embellishments of the State of which they are corporate members. It occurs to the people only when the State has become the appanage of the bureaucratic apparatus that their enforced savings are not being devoted and will never be devoted to their personal comfort and enrichment. By the time they realise that the only section of the community to gain solid material advantages from the new order is the new bureaucratic and Party aristocracy, it is too late to do anything about it. For the ruling class has dug itself in and secured its outposts by broadening its base, attaching to itself by self-interest a sufficient number of adherents from the exploited working classes. The Stakhanovites are a case in point. The only precaution the new rulers must in all circumstances take is to provide employment for all. It does not matter so much about remuneration so long as it does not fall below the subsistence level, for it is always possible to explain that the State needs more investment capital.

The Bolsheviks are fortunate in possessing an enormous

territory full of undeveloped natural resources. The field for investment is illimitable, so they are spared the problem of finding ways to employ the population ; unlike the Nazis, whose solution was rearmament and *Autobahnen* of doubtful economic utility. Every new enterprise needs administrative and technical managers, accountants and statisticians requiring higher technical education ; so the annual intake into the universities and technical high schools increases by leaps and bounds (the number of students in high educational institutions increased from 160,000 in 1928 to more than 600,000 in 1938), and so does the bureaucratic class whose interests are bound up with the stability of the State. The intellectual organising and administrative classes as distinct from the industrial and manual labouring classes now forms at least 15 per cent of the total population. This is a much higher proportion than the upper and middle classes under the Tsarist régime, which at most accounted for less than 10 per cent.

The steady growth of the bureaucratic *élite* affords correspondingly more opportunities for the ordinary citizen to rise above the rank and file. This gives colour to the Bolsheviks' boast of equality of opportunity, because in the circumstances it is inevitable that a very considerable proportion of responsible officials have risen from proletarian or peasant origin. The army, too, offers an attractive career to the industrial worker or peasant, for in spite of theoretical social equality a definite social status adheres to a commission as much in the Red Army as in any other. It is perhaps worth noting that as the difference between the uniforms of officers and men in the democratic armies tends to be minimised, the opposite tendency obtains in the Red Army. At first the only distinction was the officer's rank badge. In 1935 the Continental system of rank titles was adopted instead of the former functional designations, company commander, battalion commander and so on, after which officers' uniforms became definitely better in material and cut than those of the men, while the higher ranks blossomed out into velvet collars and gold lace.

So Stalin's boast that the Soviet Union is now a classless State is without foundation. In relation to himself as to the autocratic Tsars all men are equal, for he can promote or degrade at his pleasure. Some of Stalin's utterances indicate that he regards his subjects as graded into categories, which was precisely the old Tsarist concept. Each category has its own place and function in the State and none forms a definitely superior and ruling class. But though a dictator may be convinced that no particular group or category shares his power or has more influence than another in the formation of policy, the fact remains that the group which organises and executes policy has power over those who merely work and obey.

The Russians have never been sticklers for the legitimacy of succession of their rulers. Of the thirteen successors of Peter I, only five were heirs apparent at the decease of their predecessors ; of the remaining eight, seven owed their succession to palace or army intrigues. There is no legitimate successor to Stalin, and if the Russians run true to form, the influential sections should endeavour to appoint a successor who will permit the ruling minority to emancipate itself from obligatory service to the State. It is as yet impossible to forecast the influence of the new religion on the actions of the leaders, but there seems no reason to suppose that the Neobolshevik aristocracy will find their principles incompatible with their material selfish interests. And with the emancipation of the ruling class a progressive curtailment of the rights of the masses may be looked for. It is possible that this process has already begun, at least the freedom and rights of the industrial workers and peasants have been materially restricted by government measures enacted since the outbreak of the present war ; which at the same time may quite conceivably have increased the independence and influence of the bureaucracy, for no dictator in a time of threatening crisis can afford to carry out a purge of his lieutenants. Stalin's assumption of the post of President of the Council of People's Commissars and his more frequent direct and personal intervention in diplomatic negotiations may be explained in various ways, but as good an explanation as any is that he fears completely to trust his subordinates.

POSTSCRIPT

THOUGH the Soviet régime has lasted nearly a quarter of a century, it has not yet reached a final and complete form. The Constitution dates only from 1936, since when not a few new fundamental laws have been passed modifying the structure of the Government and affecting the relations between the Government and the people. The present war will influence the future development of the Soviet system in ways which as yet cannot be clearly seen, but whose trend can probably be foretold.

The Bolshevik revolution was, in a sense, a revolution from below ; but this view must be modified by the theory, translated into practice by Lenin, that a revolution is not the spontaneous movement of the proletariate, but must be organised and led by a small body of intellectual and professional revolutionaries who use and are supported by the masses. Only since the Constitution of 1936 has the Party allowed the people to have even the semblance of participation in the government of the country. In spite of the creation of a parliament, in the form of the Supreme Soviet, the decisions of the Party leaders on questions of major policy still remain dominant and unchallenged.

The war has narrowed the gap between the leaders and the masses. They have become dependent on each other to an extent undreamed of in peace and, it may be supposed, have acquired a great measure of respect for each other. The Party no longer dominates the situation ; its supremacy has been in various ways surrendered to the Army, which, though a very high proportion of the higher ranks are Party members, does not tolerate political interference in its conduct of the war. Two of the most exalted and influential Party heads, Marshals Voroshilov and Budenny, were removed from their commands in the field because their military skill did not correspond to their Party standing.

It is, of course, possible that the Party and bureaucratic

aristocracy will endeavour to maintain its ascendancy and privileges after the war, but it is unlikely that the people, having acquired a new self-respect and confidence, will suffer themselves to be again reduced to their former subordinate position. Having been initiated by their leaders into the forms of democracy, they will see to it that they secure the substance. The G.P.U., which through the exigencies of the war has had to modify its political inquisitorial activities and devote itself to hunting down spies and fifth columnists, will not be permitted to revive its old arbitrary powers. In fact it may well disappear.

Every major war in which Russia has been engaged since the beginning of the nineteenth century has had more or less serious repercussions on the internal political situation, always tending towards a restriction of the autocratic power and towards a more liberal form of government. The present war (defeat excluded) is not likely to result in any convulsion comparable to the events following the Russo-Japanese war and the war of 1914–18, but unless history is reversed some liberalising of the Soviet form of government may be expected.

INDEX

311

Index

Management —
  circulation of staffs, 129
  collegiate, 131-135
  difficulties of, 100, 101, 239, 240
  factory directors, responsibilities of, 117, 118
  foremen, status of, 119
  responsible single heads, 60
  single or collegiate management, 35
  staffs, inflation of, 122
  workers' committees of, 34
Market —
  " black ", the, 70
  labour, 65, 137, 235
Medical Services —
  hospitals : cottage, 205 ; accommodation in, 204
  private practitioners, 205
Money —
  attempt to discredit, 33
  distribution, a means of, 233
  purchasing medium, not a constant, 53
  restoration of, 37
  Soviet money, nature of, 243-245, 247
Mutual Guarantee, abrogated, 23

Nationalism, recent growth of, 10
Naziism, Bolshevism compared with, 293, 298-300
New Economic Policy —
  close of, 43
  introduction of, 36, 37

Obrok, 19
Oudarnik (shock-worker) —
  how to become, 46
  privileges of, 50, 51

Passports, reintroduced, 61
Peter I —
  concept of the State, 302
  industrial policy of, 17
  " Westerniser ", the, 14
Planning —
  advantages of, 230, 231
  case for and against, 237-240
  distribution, of, 232
  methods of, 227-229
  prices : and profits under, 229 ; function of, under, 241, 242
  production, of, 231
  reasons for, 227

Planning — contd.
  wage incomes, of, 234
Political Commissars, in the Red Army, 8
Population, increase of urban, 62
Prices —
  food, of, in 1927-8 and 1939, 187
  planning, under, 126, 229, 231, 241, 242
  rationing : after, 73 ; under, 69
  " scissors " crisis, the, 40
Private Enterprise —
  labour, as employer of, 38
  NEP, under, 37
Professions, improved status of, 66
Public Health, lack of statistical information, 206

Rationing —
  classes benefited, 49
  discrimination in, 50
  end of, 73
  proportion of rations to total consumption, 181
  reintroduction of, 48
Red Army, social status of, 307
Religion, historical parallels, 7
Revolutionary Societies, 27
Rouble, the —
  inflation of, 33
  purchasing power of, 75, 170
Russian character, the —
  industry, in, 21
  politics, in, 2
  tolerance of, 5

Salaries, of intellectual workers, 171, 172
Sanatoria, in the Crimea, 209
Savings (see also State Loan) —
  compulsion of, 236
  volume of, 217
Serfdom —
  origin of, 19
  reasons for, 94
Serfs —
  emancipation of, 21
  employment in industry of, 17
  obrok, on, 20
Shakhty Trial, the, 55
Shops, commercial, 69
Social Classes —
  distinctions between, 284
  Tsarist Russia, in, 28

313

314

Index

THE END

Printed in Great Britain by R. & R. CLARK, LIMITED, *Edinburgh.*